UNDERSTANDING SCHOOLING THROUGH THE EYES OF STUDENTS

Linda Holste
Dressage Champion

UNDERSTANDING SCHOOLING THROUGH THE EYES OF STUDENTS

Joseph F. Murphy

CORWIN
A SAGE Publishing Company

CORWIN
A SAGE Publishing Company

FOR INFORMATION:

Corwin

A SAGE Company

2455 Teller Road

Thousand Oaks, California 91320

(800) 233-9376

www.corwin.com

SAGE Publications Ltd.

1 Oliver's Yard

55 City Road

London EC1Y 1SP

United Kingdom

SAGE Publications India Pvt. Ltd.

B 1/I 1 Mohan Cooperative Industrial Area

Mathura Road, New Delhi 110 044

India

SAGE Publications Asia-Pacific Pte. Ltd.

3 Church Street

#10-04 Samsung Hub

Singapore 049483

Acquisitions Editor: Arnis Burvikovs
Associate Editor: Desirée A. Bartlett
Editorial Assistant: Andrew Olson
Production Editor: Kelly DeRosa
Copy Editor: Cate Huisman
Typesetter: C&M Digitals (P) Ltd.
Proofreader: Laura Webb
Indexer: Judy Hunt
Cover Designer: Candice Harman
Marketing Manager: Anna Mesick

Copyright © 2016 by Corwin

All rights reserved. When forms and sample documents are included, their use is authorized only by educators, local school sites, and/or noncommercial or nonprofit entities that have purchased the book. Except for that usage, no part of this book may be reproduced or utilized in any form or by any means, electronic or mechanical, including photocopying, recording, or by any information storage and retrieval system, without permission in writing from the publisher.

All trademarks depicted within this book, including trademarks appearing as part of a screenshot, figure, or other image, are included solely for the purpose of illustration and are the property of their respective holders. The use of the trademarks in no way indicates any relationship with, or endorsement by, the holders of said trademarks.

Printed in the United States of America

Library of Congress Cataloging-in-Publication Data

Names: Murphy, Joseph, 1949- author.

Title: Understanding schooling through the eyes of students / Joseph F. Murphy.

Description: Thousand Oaks, California : Corwin, a SAGE Company, 2016. | Includes bibliographical references and index.

Identifiers: LCCN 2015048522 | ISBN 9781506310039 (pbk. : alk. paper)

Subjects: LCSH: Teacher-student relationships. | Educational psychology. | Learning, Psychology of. | Students—Attitudes. | Effective teaching.

Classification: LCC LB1033 .M78 2016 | DDC 371.102/3—dc23
LC record available at http://lccn.loc.gov/2015048522

This book is printed on acid-free paper.

SFI Certified Sourcing
www.sfiprogram.org
SFI-00453

16 17 18 19 20 10 9 8 7 6 5 4 3 2 1

DISCLAIMER: This book may direct you to access third-party content via Web links, QR codes, or other scannable technologies, which are provided for your reference by the author(s). Corwin makes no guarantee that such third-party content will be available for your use and encourages you to review the terms and conditions of such third-party content. Corwin takes no responsibility and assumes no liability for your use of any third-party content, nor does Corwin approve, sponsor, endorse, verify, or certify such third-party content.

CONTENTS

Preface	vii
About the Author	ix
PART ONE Seeing Student Eyes	1
Poem Drowned But Not Dead #1	2
1. The Centrality of Student–Teacher Relationships	5
2. Understanding Student Eyes	23
PART TWO Student Views of Culture	51
Poem A Good School #1	52
3. Care	53
4. Support, Safety, and Membership	73
PART THREE Student Views of the Academic Program	115
Poem A Good School #2	116
5. Engaged Teaching	119
6. Constructed Learning	135
PART FOUR Evidence on Student Views	163
Poem High School #1	164
7. Students Have It Right	165
References	223
Index	249

PREFACE

The goal of this book is to help educators "see" schooling through the eyes of students. Because we know that relationships between educators and children are essential for this "seeing" to occur, we embed this powerful idea in trusting relationships. We also focus on "seeing" schooling through the eyes of students on the two dimensions that explain academic and social learning—academic press and supportive culture.

Why student eyes? The first point in this book is that students' perspectives are often unseen in schools. They are often unseen because we do not seek them out. When we do listen to students, we often do not hear them, or so they tell us. We are too often focused on using student perspectives to reinforce what we have already decided.

Our second point is that when we inadequately see classrooms and schools through the eyes of youngsters, we miss opportunities to do our job more effectively, to improve our skills and knowledge in enhancing meaningful academic challenge, and to create caring and supportive learning environments. Worse, foregone chances often morph into costs. We not only fail to move forward, we foster conditions and states such as reduced sense of social integration, lack of motivation, and disengagement that run counter to our goals and hopes for young people. We are often only marginally successful in fostering the trust necessary for students to allow us to lead and help carry them to learning.

Our third point is that when we do fight harder to see the world through the eyes of our students, good things are likely to materialize: the understanding and wisdom that help us be more effective as educators and that provide meaning and joy to work that is often arduous and sometimes frustrating.

From here, the rest of the book falls into place. We undertake a journey to see schooling through the eyes of students. We begin by peering into how students see the culture of schooling. We collect and array their insights about the four cultural norms that define great schools—care, support, safety, and membership—and the essential elements that in turn compose each of the norms. We then explore how youngsters see teaching and learning in schools, using the essential elements of "engaged teaching" and "constructed learning" to collect and array these insights.

The summative message in these chapters is that we can do better. The fog of boredom and disengagement is prevalent in schools. There are avenues open to change this condition. But many of those pathways do not address fundamental insights that students tell us mark their lives in schools. This book explores these insights in the two core domains of schooling, the academic program and the culture of schools.

In the final chapter we spend considerable time exploring the relationship between what we see through the eyes of students and the work of scholars exploring the dimensions of effective educational practices. The critical conclusion here is that what students tell us is important to them is nearly isomorphic with what researchers tell us is effective in promoting academic and social learning.

Although by design we focus on what is absent, the goal of the book is not to underscore deficits, to blame ourselves once again, and to reengage in the ritual of self-flagellation. Rather, the intent is to help us remember and hold central the core idea that we and our young charges are engaged in a mutual enterprise, which in turn is forged in trusting personal relationships. Therefore, students need to be active players in the endeavor, not simply recipients of what we have to offer. If they are to take on this role, we must not only help them see the world of schooling through the perspectives and values of educators, but we must also become more adept at seeing the world through their eyes. It is my intent that this volume will carry us in this direction, revealing important strategies and markers along the journey.

ABOUT THE AUTHOR

Joseph F. Murphy is the Frank W. Mayborn Chair and associate dean at Peabody College of Education at Vanderbilt University. He also chaired the teams that revised those standards (2008) and created Professional Standards for Educational Leaders (PSEL) (2015). He has also been a faculty member at the University of Illinois and The Ohio State University, where he was the William Ray Flesher Professor of Education.

In the public schools, he has served as an administrator at the school, district, and state levels, including an appointment as the executive assistant to the chief deputy superintendent of public instruction in California. His most recent appointment was as the founding president of the Ohio Principals Leadership Academy. At the university level, he has served as department chair and associate dean.

He is past vice president of the American Educational Research Association and was the founding chair of the Interstate School Leaders Licensure Consortium (ISLLC). He is coeditor of *AERA Handbook of Research on Educational Administration* (1999) and editor of the National Society for the Study of Education (NSSE) yearbook, *The Educational Leadership Challenge* (2002).

His work is in the area of school improvement, with special emphasis on leadership and policy. He has authored or coauthored 23 books in this area and edited another 12. He has also written 120 articles and 65 book chapters for the academic community, and 85 articles for colleagues in practice.

Drowned But Not Dead #1

Straddling two worlds

Borrowing another self

Buying decaying hope

A geography of cross-hatched expectations

Well marked spaces

Uncleansed air

Engaging with the keepers

Foraging for crumbs of care

Accepting meaninglessness

Finding invisibility

Timid acquiescence

Learned self-doubt

Challenging marginalization

Stoking imaginary fires of power

Withdrawing from the field

Honoring the false gods of victory

The answer is, perhaps, an obvious but often overlooked one: to find new directions for improving schools we must take as our starting point the classroom itself and explore teaching and learning through the eyes of those most clearly involved. (Flutter & Rudduck, 2004, p. 2)

It is important for teachers to come to know the world of school from the perspective of students. (Weinstein, 1983, p. 302)

I think we do need to strive to look through students' eyes, thereby building bridges between their understandings and the concepts and skills most likely to advance their opportunities. But the only way we can truly begin to look through students' eyes is to reject the notion that our own view of the world is always right. (Ellwood, 1993, p. 77)

ONE

THE CENTRALITY OF STUDENT–TEACHER RELATIONSHIPS

> How students feel about and do in schools is, in large part, determined by their relationships with teachers. (Johnson, 2009, p. 101)

Our narratives about student perspectives attend to three core ideas: the importance of understanding schooling through the eyes of students, the hallmark place of teacher–student relationships in discerning what students see, and the venues in which those relationships occur, the school culture and the academic program. The critical point is that we do not see nor do we present student viewpoints in a decontextualized fashion. We have a good deal of knowledge from students about how they see culture and academic program in schools, and we unpack student views in these two core domains in Parts 2 and 3. We devote Chapter 2 to an analysis of seeing schooling through the eyes of students, what it means to use such language, how such efforts can unfold, and what can be uncovered from careful attention to the needs, interests, and perspectives of students. In this chapter, we pull out the two ingrained pieces of our narrative for discussion: (1) the integrated success pathway of culture (support) and academic program (press) and (2) the hallmark role of student–teacher relationships in determining how students come to see and describe classrooms and schools.

THE RELATIONAL VENUE: CULTURE AND ACADEMIC PROGRAM

> These results suggest that classrooms must be intellectually challenging to encourage growth in achievement and understanding as well as cohesive and satisfying to encourage student interest and motivation. (Moos & Moos, 1978, p. 263)

In chapters 3 through 6 (parts 2 and 3 of the book), we employ the overarching framework of supportive culture and academic press to peer into student perspectives of education, to understand how they see schooling. We establish the importance of that framework here. We begin with the knowledge that what is "related to sustained increases in learning is the combination of academic press and social support for learning" (Appleton, Christensen, & Furlong, 2008, p. 381), the importance of "the teacher's role in creating supportive affective and instructional contexts" (Davis, 2003, p. 212). Or, at a slightly higher level of expression: "The constitution of a classroom as a functioning social entity is dependent upon both the social and instructional activities of the teacher" (Mergendoller & Packer, 1985, p. 592).

> Thus, the emergent picture of the classroom where students report a great deal of content learning combines an affective concern with students as people with an emphasis on students working hard. (Trickett & Moos, 1974, p. 8)

We also commence our journey in seeing what students convey about schooling with the knowledge that these two powerful foundations of learning are highly integrated (Bandura, 1993); "affect and

Chapter One: The Centrality of Student–Teacher Relationships 7

intellect [are] interconnected and inseparable" (Goldstein, 1999, p. 654), that is, there is a "seamless union of the cognitive factors and the affective volitional factors of intellectual life (Goldstein, 1999, p. 648)—a "merging of caring and the notion of the construction of knowledge" (Goldstein, 1999, p. 649).

> Teachers function as attachment figures, as physical caregivers, as socialization agents, as mediators of peer contacts, and as teachers. From a systems perspective, to cleave these functions into those that are purely academic and those that are nonacademic is to create an artificial distinction that neglects important aspects of classroom life. (Pianta, 1999, p. 83)

"If schools are to be made more effective, we must understand both their academic and socialization functions" (Hamilton, 1983, p. 332) and realize that the "integration of cognitive and affective aspects of the learner [are] necessary to effective growth and development" (Hayes, Ryan, & Zseller, 1994, p. 16). Or, as Davis (2003, p. 221) reminds us, "It is the balance between the socialization and the academic institutional functions of schools that is the issue." The important messages here are clear. Both domains require attention in an integrated fashion. We also need to seriously question "whether any interaction or classroom task can be considered solely 'academic' as well as the implication of choosing to label something as 'personal' rather than 'academic'" (Davis, 2003, p. 226). Finally, we will see throughout the book, but often in indirect ways, that it is attention to both culture and program in an ongoing rolling fashion that produces the largest impact. Attending to press or culture alone is not a recipe for success (Becker & Luthar, 2002).

We have penned this three-part storyline elsewhere as follows (Murphy, 2013, p. 27): "(1) Academic press and supportive culture are the two critical components of school improvement; (2) they are most powerful in tandem; and (3) they work best when they wrap around each other like strands of a rope." Schooling marked by both a robust instructional program and a rich culture of support is essential (Thompson & O'Quinn, 2001; Becker & Luthar, 2002). So too are the harmonies between the two (Shannon & Bylsma, 2002).

8   **Part One:** Seeing Student Eyes

Relational Dynamics

> Students typically evaluated a given school year in terms of their experiences with the teacher. (Quiroz, 2001, p. 337)
>
> Teacher–child interactions suggest teacher relationships make a unique contribution to children's social and cognitive development. (Davis, 2003, p. 208)

Seeing and responding to schooling through the eyes of students requires focused attention to relationships in classrooms and schools (Bandura, 1993; Furrer & Skinner, 2003). Relationships are the cardinal dimension of education, what Cruddas (2001, p. 66) refers to as "the heart of education": "Education is fundamentally interpersonal in nature" (Davis, 2001, p. 431). As we will illustrate in chapters 3 through 6, it is these connections that bring life to the cultural and academic dynamics of schooling. That is, these personal linkages promote the development of care (Chapter 3) and support, safety, and membership (Chapter 4) and nurture the growth of engaged teaching (Chapter 5) and constructed work (Chapter 6).

Relationships with teachers, according to Pianta (1999, p. 21), "are an essential part of classroom experiences for all children and potential resources for improving developmental outcomes." "The social interactions of the classroom become a critical element in classroom learning" (Arnot, McIntyre, Pedder, & Reay, 2004, p. 51); these "bonds are central to the learning process" (Zanger, 1991, p. 183). Indeed, "student participation, engagement, and eventual success are powered by connections and relationships (Cooper, Ponder, Merritt, & Matthews, 2005, p. 14). These relationships "either facilitate or impede motivation and learning" (Davis, 2003, p. 212). In fact, because "the teacher's mode of interacting or relating to his or her students may be seen by young adolescents as more important than the subject matter being presented" (Veaco & Brandon, 1986, p. 221), a number of analysts conclude that respectful relationships between children and teachers must be crafted before real involvement with academic content can occur. These reviewers also conclude that these relationships "appear to be necessary antecedents of attitudes toward oneself" (Harper, 1989, p. 124) and

Chapter One: The Centrality of Student–Teacher Relationships

"toward school, education, and the wider community" (Ogbu, 1974, p. 133). On this point, Hartup (1989, p. 120) reminds us that "a child's effectiveness in dealing with the social world emerges largely from experiences in close relationships" and that a good amount of this capital is garnered in relationships with teachers.

Researchers inform us that

> experience in two major kinds of relationships seems to be necessary to the child's development. First, children must form *vertical* attachments, that is, attachments to individuals who have greater knowledge and social power than they do. Second, children must also form close relationships that are *horizontal*, that is, relationships with individuals who have the same amount of social power as themselves." (Hartup, 1989, p. 120)

In Chapter 7, we underscore these horizontal connections. Through most of the book, however, the spotlight is on the vertical linkages. We employ various terms to capture these teacher–student relationships (e.g., "person-centered interactions" [Veaco & Brandon, 1986, p. 227]). Scholars who study these relationships often portray a continuum of connections with "positive feelings at one end of the continuum and alienation at the other" (Crosnoe, Johnson, & Elder, 2004 p. 61). Lynch and Cicchetti (cited in Pianta, 1999, p. 81) capture "five patterns of relatedness between children and teachers: optimal, adequate, deprived, disengaged, and confused." Other reviewers illuminate some of the elements of student–teacher relationships. They help us see that connections are "negotiated, context specific, dynamic, changing, and culturally bound" (Davis, 2003, pp. 222, 225).

The development of the student/teacher relationship is a dynamic process influenced by the beliefs, values, and skills of each member of the dyad. From this perspective, students are viewed as active participants in the development of the student/teacher relationship; bringing to the relationship beliefs and skills that may influence the likelihood of developing a positive relationship with their primary teacher. (Davis, 2001, p. 447)

"Relationship dimensions measure the nature and intensity of personal interactions in the setting" (Moos, 1979, p. 248). Connections here represent "an unspoken but powerfully motivating compact that depends on mutual recognition, involvement, enjoyment, communication, and respect" (Moos, 1979, p. 91).

Conditions that enable or hinder the development of relationships between children and teachers are laced through the literature. "Since teacher support, involving trust and personal concern for students, tends to evolve slowly" (Moos, 1979, p. 147), time for teachers and students to get to know each other is most valuable (Connell & Wellborn, 1991; Poplin & Weeres, 1994). Relatedly, we see physical proximity as an important enabler (McMillan, 1996; Ogbu, 1974). So too is "psychological proximity seeking, the degree to which children desire to be psychologically closer to [an] adult" (Pianta, 1999, p. 92). Out of concern for the objective of the relationship, support for the "growth of the other person" surfaces (Veaco & Brandon, 1986, p. 227). The goods such as "interpersonal skills" and "self concept beliefs" (Davis, 2003, p. 211) that participants bring to the linkages are valuable relationship enablers (Harter, Waters, & Whitesell, 1997). Organizational conditions, "environmental characteristics" (Davis, 2003, p. 211), and "environmental stimuli in schools" (Birch & Ladd, 1998, p. 943) can also work to assist or hinder relationships. Particularly relevant here is the "embedded context" (Connell & Wellborn, 1991, p. 72), or the historical debris piled high in education that views children as untrustworthy and in need of control rather than empowering relationships (Cook-Sather, 2002; Farrell, 1990; Ogbu, 1974). Especially disheartening here, scholars document, is "the bureaucratization of the adult-child relationship" (Larkin, 1979, p. 199). "Responsiveness to children's needs" (Davis, 2003, p. 211) is an enabler as well, a reality that introduces the importance of teachers' motivations and beliefs.

Colleagues who study the world of teacher–student connections help us peer into some of the relational dynamics here as well. As we examine in more detail below, an obvious but essential point is "that students do not enter their classrooms as 'tabula rasa.' Instead they bring expectations, attitudes, and behaviors that will impact the quality of relationships that they develop with teachers" (Davis, 2003, p. 214). We also know that "teachers respond differently to students in the same classroom based upon characteristics that they bring to the educational setting" (Harter et al., 1997, p. 165). A third dynamic attends to the reciprocity of relationships (Noddings, 1988; Oldfather, Thomas, Eckert, Garcia, Grannis, Kilgore, & Tjioe, 1999). This means that the traditional focus on "view[ing] teacher–child relationships as unilateral" (Silverstein & Krate, 1975), from teacher to student, is not justified. "Students are sophisticated in assessing teachers' attitudes and behavior... [they] calculate whether to invest in a cooperative teacher–student relationship on the basis of whether they think it will pay off" (Muller, Katz, & Dance, 1999, p. 314). What this means is that "we need to analyze how teachers and students each decide to invest in, not invest in, or disengage from the relationship" (Muller et al., 1999, p. 301). We need to get better at "connect[ing] with students' own understandings of adult–child relationships" (Davis, 2003, p. 219), "to take into account the child's behavior and personality as contributing to interaction" (Silverstein & Krate, 1975, p. 219).

Relational Influence

> Aspects of youth identity are shaped *in relation* to schools and teachers. (Weis, 1990, p. 116)

To begin with, reviewers help us see that these student–teacher relationships are the means by which trust develops in schools (Bryk, Sebring, Allensworth, Luppescu, & Easton, 2010). They also uncover trust as the bridging variable between relationships and valued outcomes (Murphy & Torre, 2014). And this carries us into a delineation of categories and a description of the evidence about the outcomes of these relationships, as seen at least partially through the eyes of students. We note here as an advance organizer that the results of trusting interpersonal relationships between teachers and students create "transcendent legitimization" (Larkin, 1979, p. 152) and the allegiance of students to the work of the school.

At the general level, we know that connections with teachers play a special and valuable role in students' lives (Kennedy, 2011), that "student-teacher relationships matter for the development of children" (Adams, 2010, p. 258). "The nature and quality of relationships between students and teachers acts as a framework that guide[s] actions and thought" (Davis, 2003, p. 219) and "that experience in well-functioning relationships is associated with good functioning in the child" (Hartup, 1989, p. 125). We learn of "the importance of relationship processes in many aspects of classroom performance" (Pianta, 1999, p. 71). "Personalized relationships, according to students, significantly influenced the student experiences across schools" (Rodriguez, 2008, p. 764). Perhaps most powerfully, these relationships "subtly define the child's present being and mode of becoming, as well as constructing an image of what the child will become" (Wilcox 1982, p. 293). On this latter front, there is growing evidence that not only are student–teacher relationships at the center of productive climate but they provide significant power for academic press (Darling-Hammond, Ancess, & Ort, 2002; Rodriguez, 2008); they provide the basis "from which specific instructional activities derive their meaning" (Moos & David, 1981, p. 59). Through their influence on press and support, we know then "that the quality of teacher–student relationships influences children's social and cognitive development" (Davis, 2003, p. 210). They provide the resources or social capital (Adams & Forsyth, 2009) to support "intellectual, social, and emotional development" (Davis, 2003, p. 207). "Personality development is optimized through the maintenance of relatedness" (Ryan, Stiller, & Lynch, 1994, p. 229).

Sense of Attachment

Productive linkages between children and teachers create "students' sense of belonging" and attachment at the school (Battistich, Solomon, Watson, & Schaps, 1997; Crosnoe, 2011; Voelkl, 1987). Scholars routinely "point to the importance of the interpersonal experiences between teachers and students in facilitating adaptation within the domain of education" (Ryan et al., 1994, p. 246). Productive interpersonal relationships lead to identification with the school, what Eckert (1989) labels as a merging of the personal and institutional. Scholars describe this state in a variety of ways: membership (Eckert, 1989; Gonzalez & Padilla, 1997), belonging (Battistich et al., 1995; Fredricks, Blumenfeld, & Paris, 2004), integration (Scanlan & Lopez, 2012), affiliation (Newmann, 1981; O'Connor, 1997), attachment (Alexander, Entwisle, & Horsey,1997; Conchas, 2001), inclusion (Ma, 203; Voelkl, 1997), connection (Feldman & Matjasko, 2005; Roth & Brooks-Gunn, 2003), fitting in (Crosnoe, 2011), and acceptance (Goodenow & Grady, 1993).

Chapter One: The Centrality of Student–Teacher Relationships 13

Underlying these various markers for identification is a sense of being part of the school, of being valued by the institution and by peers, of "feeling oneself to be an important part of the life and activity of the class" (Goodenow & Grady, 1993, p. 25) and school—"of feel[ing] personally accepted, respected, included, and supported in the school" (Ma, 2003, p. 340). It is about affinity (Conchas, 2001).

Weak or unhealthy relationships, on the other hand, are an invitation to weak student identification with and/or possible disaffiliation with the school, "an absence of highly developed feelings of valuing and belonging" (Voelkl, 1997, p. 296). Students in such schools are often portrayed as "just passing through" (Eckert, 1989, p. 65). Rather than being bonded to the school, they are independent actors, ones who often feel a sense of disconnection and alienation toward teachers and peers (Antrop-Gonzalez, 2006; Newmann 1981). They display what Farrell (1990, p. 112) calls "absenting behavior," a "culture that is dominated by the private as opposed to the institutional" (Eckert, 1989, p. 172). Separation and exclusion are elements of disidentification. So also are estrangement, detachment, and isolation (Newmann, 1989)—"emotional and physical withdrawal" (Voelkl, 1997, p. 294).

Identification (or disidentification) impacts commitment to the school and a sense of obligation to those at the school (Gamoran, 1996). Positive identification helps build a sense of legitimacy around the school and a valuing of the institution (Fredricks et al., 2004; Goodenow & Grady, 1993). According to Voelkl (1997, p. 296), the idea of valuing schooling

> include[s] the recognition of the value of the school as both a social institution and a tool for facilitating personal advancement. That is, the youngster regards school as a central institution in society and feels that what is learned in class is important in its own right and that school is instrumental in obtaining his or her personal life objectives . . . the belief that schoolwork is both interesting and important.

Valuing also leads to a "commitment to and identification with the goals of the institution" (Eckert, 1989, p. 103); its values and purposes (Ancess, 2003; Baker, Terry, Bridger, & Winsor, 1997; Marsh & Kleitman, 1992); its norms and practices (Battistich et al., 1995; Battistich & Hom, 1997; Voelkl, 1997); "the means it prescribes for members to pursue goals" (Newmann, Wehlage, &

Lamburn, 1992, p. 20), that is, its structures, policies, and practices (Hallinan & Kubitschek, 1999); and its sanctioned outcomes (Marsh & Kleitman, 2002, Voelkl, 1997). In schools with healthy student–teacher connections, children become invested in the life of the classroom (Freiberg, Huzinec, & Templeton, 2009) and school (Marsh & Kleitman, 2002).

Psychological States

Researchers also document strong linkages between healthy teacher–student relationships and the psychological health of students (Feldman & Matjasko, 2005; Ma, 2003) and conclude that the relationship is reciprocal in nature (Ma, 2003). These scholars remind us that the work here is two-pronged, the creation of pathways to positive psychosocial characteristics (e.g., self-concept) and the development of fortifications to protect against negative life events and sources of stress (Wright, 1982) that could undermine mental health (Jackson & Warren, 2000). Relations with teachers "can serve as a buffer to risk—a resource for development" (Pianta, 1999, p. 20), especially during periods of school transition (Akos, 2002; Smetana & Bitz, 1996) and especially for students placed at risk (Eccles, Wigfield, Midgley, Reuman, Iver, & Feldlaufer, 1993; Murphy, 2010). Indeed, as Pianta (1999, p. 20) reminds us, "It is through these relationships that the social behavior, self-control, and achievement motivation of children with serious problems can be improved."

We know that the major quest for youngsters is for personal identity (Csikszentmihalyi & Larson, 1986; Farrell, 1990), what Crosnoe (2011) calls identity work and Feldman and Matjasko (2005) talk about as learning to understand oneself. Analysts also document that identity and self-esteem are tightly yoked. Each student's self-concept is crafted in good measure by the relationships forged with teachers and peers (Battistich & Hom, 1997; Guest & Schneider, 2003; Marsh & Kleitman, 2002). That is, students "come to an understanding of their own social worth by seeing how they are treated by others" (Crosnoe, 2011, p. 139). "The quality of a person's functioning in terms of autonomy, confidence, and self reliance can be related directly to an experiential set one has regarding significant others" (Ryan et al., 1994, p. 227). Supportive interpersonal relationships help nourish the formation of healthy self-concept and stronger self-esteem (Demaray & Malecki, 2002a; Pounder, 1999), thus positively shaping the nature of students' developmental pathways (Feldman & Matjasko, 2005) and, consequently, prosocial attitudes and actions (Battistich et al., 1997; Rothman & Cosden, 1995). Unhealthy relationships for students, on the other hand, can lead to reduced self-esteem, nonproductive developmental pathways, and counterproductive attitudes and behaviors (Crosnoe, 2011). These behaviors and attitudes, in turn, are related to engagement and school success (Finn & Rock, 1997; Mulford & Silins, 2003; Rumberger, 2011)—for better or worse.

Positive student–teacher relationships are associated with student sense of expectancy and self-efficacy (Battistich et al., 1995; Goodenow & Grady, 1993; Scanlan & Lopez, 2012), concepts that are "among the most robust predictors of academic achievement" (Scanlan & Lopez, 2012, p. 607). Personalized relations also promote a sense of control and autonomy (Ancess, 2003; Goodenow & Grady, 1993). Strong relations "ignite agency" (Rodriguez, 2008, p. 774) as well (Felner, Brand, DuBois, Adan, Mulhall, & Evans, 1995; Fredricks et al., 2004), providing students with what Csikszentmihalyi and Larson (1984) depict as internalized standards of performance. Personalization strengthens students' internal locus of control (Marsh & Kleitman, 1992). That is, as Osterman (2000, p. 329) in her seminal review reminds us,

> autonomy develops most effectively in situations where children and teenagers feel a sense of relatedness and closeness rather than disaffiliation from significant adults." Autonomy is not about isolation and private space" but, instead, refers to the individual's sense of agency or self-determination in a social context." (Osterman, 2000, p. 329)

Related dynamics of a healthy self also grow in positive student–teacher relationships. We know, for example, that self-confidence is often augmented in schools characterized by authentic membership and support (Croninger & Lee, 2001; Farrell, 1990; Goodenow & Grady, 1993). Personalized relationships are also welded tightly to feelings of competence (Laffey, 1982; Osterman, 2000; Silins & Mulford, 2010) and resilience (Gonzalez & Padilla, 1997; Crosnoe, 2011).

Dispositions Toward Learning

A thick line of research has established that caring teacher–student relations influence students' orientation toward school and learning and promote the development of positive educational values and attitudes (Battistich et al., 1995; Sweetland & Hoy, 2000; Osterman, 2000) and subsequent achievement-related behaviors (Adams & Forsyth, 2009; Goodenow & Grady, 1993). Students in healthy relationships are more likely than peers in communities of low care and support to find value in school (Adams & Forsyth, 2009) and have "a positive orientation toward school" (Osterman, 2000, p. 331). These youngsters often have a greater interest in school and like school and classes more than students in communities assessed as low in relational power (Birch & Ladd, 1997; Gonzalez & Padilla, 1997; Osterman, 2000). They identify with their schools more and invest more in their learning (Ancess, 2003; Marsh & Kleitman, 2002; Wentzel & Looney, 2007). Relationships also exert a strong shaping force on "prosocial attitudes, beliefs, and behaviors, including concern and respect for peers and teachers, conflict resolution, acceptance of out groups, [and] intrinsic prosocial motivation and behavior" (Osterman, 2000, p. 334). The obverse of the research-themed storyline above is true as well. Impersonal connections with teachers and perceived lack of care produce negative orientations toward school (Larkin, 1979; Ogbu, 1974; Osterman, 2000). They nurture values and attitudes that often lead to counterproductive coping strategies (Crosnoe, 2011; Eckert, 1989; Farrell, 1990), ones that undercut meaningful engagement and social and academic learning (Demaray & Malecki, 2002b; Hattie, 2009; Ma, 2003).

Motivation is the most examined learning disposition in the literature on student community. Here scholars routinely find that meaningful student–teacher connections are highly associated with student motivation to work and to succeed in school (Barnett & McCormick, 2004; Bryk et al., 2010; Opdenakker, Maulana, & Brock, 2012). According to Battistich and associates (1995, 1997), personalized relationships motivate students to adopt and honor school classroom norms and values and enhance the desire to acquire competence. Motivation is important, in turn, because it impacts engagement and social and cognitive outcomes (Battistich et al., 1995; Hattie, 2009; Opdenakker et al., 2012).

Studies have also shown that sense of support and belonging forged in relationships with teachers is correlated with student commitment to the school and the work they do there (Ancess, 2003; Baker et al., 1997; Battistich et al., 1995). Self-confidence is impacted by these linkages (Ancess, 2000; Wilson & Corbett, 2001). With strong relations in place, students become more invested in their academic achievement (Ancess, 2000); demonstrate a greater appetite for learning (Felner, Seitsinger, Brand, Burns, & Bolton, 2007; Munoz, Ross, & McDonald, 2007), that is, "greater interest in challenging instructional activities" (Johnson & Asera, 1999, p. 100); and exhibit more "academically oriented forms of agency" (Conchas, 2001, p. 501). Relations grow the important disposition of future orientation (O'Connor, 1997). In particular, educational aspirations are shaped by strong and healthy student–teacher relationships (Laffey, 1982; Marsh & Kleitman, 2002).

Relations nourish possibility and hope (Eckert, 1989; Farrell, 1990; Rodriguez, 2008). Students ensconced in strong relationships are likely to develop a robust sense of industry and a robust work ethic, a commitment to and feeling of accomplishment in undertaking schoolwork, and a commitment to learn the adaptive skills (Demaray & Malecki, 2002b) and master "the habits of work necessary for school success" (Ancess, 2003, p. 21). In particular, students in such relationships demonstrate greater self-directedness (Birch & Ladd, 1997; Farrell, 1990) and exercise more leadership (Demaray & Malecki, 2002b). They are willing to take risks in the service of learning (Goodenow & Grady, 1993), exercise meaningful "pursuit in the demands and struggle for quality performance" (Ancess, 2003, p. 41), and assume responsibility for their work (Ancess, 2003; Birch & Ladd, 1997; Silins & Mulford, 2010). Students in positively anchored teacher–student relationships learn to take and display pride in their efforts and their accomplishments (Marsh & Kleitman, 2002).

RELATIONAL CONTEXTUAL ISSUES

The literature is rich with descriptions of the importance of the contexts surrounding teacher–student relationships (Eccles et al., 1993; Pintrich, 2003; Trickett & Todd, 1972), or more specifically "person-environmental interactions" (Hamilton, 1983, p. 314). The essential messages here are (1) "In assessing children's teacher–child relationships, it is important to consider the context in which these relationships exist" (Birch & Ladd, 1997, p. 64) and (2) that "interactions and relationships with teachers may have different meanings for students" (Davis, 2001, p. 450) depending on a host of conditions that rest both outside and inside the school (Hamilton, 1983; Roeser, Eccles, & Sameroff, 2000), such as "different types of minority status and cultural frame of reference, differing conceptions of authority and help seeking, or worldviews oriented toward social interdependence" (Davis, 2001, p. 450). "The nexus of gender, race-ethnicity, and social class may create unique spaces" (Crosnoe et al., 2004, p. 77) that "underlie social-emotional functioning" (Roeser et al., 2000, p. 465) and that both shape and help establish the meaning and values of relationships between teachers and students (Maehr & Fyans, 1989). More directly, Ferreira and Bosworth (2000, p. 118) tell us that "context plays an important role in how caring is experienced." In short, the "educational contexts of schooling" (Davis, 2003, p. 212) and community matter a good deal for student–teacher relationships (Boekaerts, 1993; Maehr & Midgley, 1996). This, of course, "requires considering how cultural and socioeconomic variables (e.g., ethnic minority status) . . . may contribute to differing student perceptions of school climate" (Kuperminc, Leadbeater, Emmons, & Blatt, 1997, p. 77). Because behavior in a relationship "may be responsive to the characteristics of specific settings the task is to determine the extent of this specificity, taking into account both student characteristics and the demands of varied settings" (Trickett & Todd, 1972, p. 31). Alternatively, "the principle of interdependence calls attention to the context in which a behavior is embedded as a basis for understanding or changing it" (Trickett & Todd, 1972, p. 29). "The role of contexts cannot be ignored" (Appleton et al., 2008, p. 380).

Turning first to the larger "context beyond schooling," we discover a variety of factors that shape and define interpersonal relationships between students and teachers, almost all of which fall into the larger category of "demographic variables" (Hayes et al., 1994, p. 6). The most discussed are race, ethnicity, cultural status, and economic status. The issue of matching or discrepant racial identity is routinely cited as an influence on teacher–student relationships in schools (Davis, 2003; Hayes et al., 1994). "On an individual level, matching may provide common ground, while mismatches may hamper the ability of students and teachers to connect" (Crosnoe et al., 2004, p. 63). Because "the development of social ties to institutional agents is [so] crucial to the social development and empowerment of ethnic minority children" (Stanton-Salazar, 1997, p. 15), that is, "that affective bonds with teachers have a greater academic impact on the categories of socially and economically disadvantaged youth" (Crosnoe et al., 2004, p. 32), these mismatches and their deleterious effects receive considerable scrutiny in the research (Goodenow & Grady, 1993; Silverstein & Krate, 1975; Wentzel, 2002). In a similar fashion, there is evidence that "because individuals have strong racial in-group preferences for interaction" (Crosnoe et al., 2004, p. 63), it has been shown that "the racial-ethnic composition of the student body can affect levels of teacher-bonding in schools" (p. 63).

Investigators also establish "that gender is an important correlate of teacher bonding and that male and female students of different racial-ethnic groups may experience different levels of and reactivity to, such bonding" (Crosnoe et al., 2004, p. 62). We know, for example, that in general there are significant "gender differences in the quality of children's teacher-child relationships . . . [with] teachers reporting having significantly more closeness in their relationships with girls and significantly more conflictual relationships with boys" (Birch & Ladd, 1997, p. 68). Whatever the causes, these "gender differences may be particularly salient when considering the role of classroom context on relationship quality and consequences" (Davis, 2003, p. 224). Certainly worthy of note here is the knowledge "that relationships with teachers play a leading role in explaining the school troubles experienced by sexual minority adolescents" (Russell, Seif, & Truong, 2001, p. 124). And it is important to point out here (and for other external conditions as well) that "the interplay of gender with demographic variables" (Kuperminc et al., 1997, p. 78) requires attention.

Other conditions largely external to the school also influence the development and meaningfulness of teacher–student relationships. Economic status fits here (Graham, Taylor, & Hudley, 1998; Pianta, 1999). So too do the special needs of children (Kennedy, 2011)— "students with learning problems" (Wenz-Gross & Siperstein, 1998, p. 98), low-achieving students (Anderman, 2003; Eccles et al., 1993), other students placed at risk (Rak & Patterson, 1996), and other "low status children and youth" (Stanton-Salazar, 1997, p. 6). We find here also the notion of the needs, experiences, and interests that students bring to school and thus to relationships with teachers (Maehr & Fyans, 1989; Roeser et al., 2000), along with an acknowledgment that "there is too little emphasis on the fact that children and adolescents bring very powerful socialization histories from outside the classroom to their own school experience" (Harter et al., 1997, p. 158). Finally, family and community conditions are routinely seen as important in shaping connections between young persons and their teachers (Ryan et al., 1994; Smetana & Bitz, 1996). For example, investigators have shown "that there are considerable individual differences among children in the same classrooms in terms of how they experienced their teachers, suggesting the possibility that children may have prepotent schemata for such perceptions perhaps shaped by the home environment" (Ryan et al., 1994, p. 231). Pianta (1999, p. 70) more specifically reports that "child-mother relationships influence relationships with teachers." In particular, as we introduced above, analysts routinely reveal how family markers such as working class background (Arnot et al., 2004; Farrell, 1990) and minority status (Ogbu, 1974) shape relationships. And Pianta (1999, p. 66) brings us back to the general power of family context when he informs us that a teacher's style of relating to children that washes over all class members "may trigger a different response" in a child "depending on this child's history of relationships with parents."

When we turn the lens on "school" context, we discover another series of conditions allowing "successful interpersonal relationships [to] develop between students and teachers"—or not (Veaco & Brandon, 1986, p. 228). For example, Davis, (2003, p. 209) has established that "the quality of students' relationships with teachers may reflect the interpersonal culture of classrooms and schools, as well as their opportunities to invest in alternative relationships." We also know that the discipline or subject matter may influence student–teacher relationships (Hoge, Smit, & Hanson, 1990; McNeal, 1998). On a personal level, teacher feelings toward children matter, and it is well established that "teachers do seem to vary in their inclination and/or capacity to communicate favorable feelings" (Davidson & Lang, 1960, p. 114). The relationships the teachers have with some students influence those with others, particularly "students' perceptions of how much the teacher 'likes' the other students in the class" (Davis, 2003, p. 219). In a similar manner, the nature of peer interactions in classrooms helps shape the viability and nature of teacher–student interactions (Davis, 2003).

Student age and level of schooling receive considerable attention in the chronicle of teacher–student relationships. A variable of central interest is the transitions youngsters make as they age (Akos, 2002; Graham et al., 1998), transitions that are fraught with "unique challenges" (Birch & Ladd, 1998, p. 944), a "variety of worries" (Akos, 2002, p. 344) and "stressors" (Akos, 2002, p. 340) that influence the formation and maintenance of productive relationships between teachers and students. In general, analysts have discovered these transitions to be "particularly trying" (Patterson, Beltyukova, Berman, & Francis, 2007, p. 126). They conclude that "school transitions have been associated with increases in emotional, academic, and behavioral difficulties, especially between elementary to middle school or junior high,

Chapter One: The Centrality of Student–Teacher Relationships 21

and again to high school" (Lehr, Sinclair, & Christenson, 2004, p. 298): "Young adolescents experience rapid changes in their physical, emotional, and interpersonal development" (Kuperminc et al., 1977, p. 76) during these times. "Children value school subjects less as they increase in age [and] . . . developing task value is assumed to parallel cognitive decrements in achievement expectations and self-perceived competence" (Graham et al., 1998, p. 619). "Student perceptions of the quality of school life and feelings of belonging also plummet" (Booker, 2006, p. 2) as do "student motivation and attitudes toward school" (Akos, 2002, p. 340). "Specifically, researchers have documented declines in children's perceived competence, perceived autonomy, perceptions of classroom learning context, and their endorsement of adaptive learning goals" (Davis, 2003, p. 216).

Equally critical is that the "organizational characteristics of schools undergo significant changes in these transition periods" (Smetana & Bitz, 1996, p. 1167). In many subjects, students are faced with "changing classroom environments" (Feldlaufer, Midgley, & Eccles, 1988, p. 150), changes that often come under strong criticism from scholars (Eccles et al., 1993). "Contextual transitions commonly include additional and unfamiliar students and school staff, and multiple sets of behavioral and classroom rules and expectations" (Akos, 2002, p. 339). These two sets of changes, or "two major transitions" (Eccles et al., 1993, p. 556) for the students in the organizations they attend, bring with them "increased academic demands and social challenges" (Wenz-Gross & Siperstein, 1998, p. 91) and "changes in their academic motivation and performance" (Davis, 2003, p. 216). These changes, in turn, have meaningful implications for student–teacher relationships (Nolen & Nicholls, 1993). We know, for example, that at these periods, relationships with teachers become "particularly important" (Midgley, Feldlaufer, & Eccles, 1989, p. 989) for students. We also know, however, that the opportunity to form connections becomes less visible to students. We learn also that there are "documented declines" (Murdock & Miller, 2003, p. 384) in teacher–student relationships during and after these transition periods (Davis, 2003; Eccles et al., 1993), what Oelsner, Lippold, and Greenberg (2001, p. 466) refer to as "declines in bonding." Overall, then, the picture that develops is one of less positive teacher–student relationships (Feldlaufer et al., 1988) as students age and move through school transitions (Goodlad, 1984; Sizer, 1984).

Other analysts push us even more deeply into understanding about "a broad set of social contexts" (Connell & Wellborn, 1991,

p. 721) and student–teacher relationships (Pianta, 1999; Willms, 2000). Rodriguez (2000, p. 768), for example, surfaces the issue of "the differences between school codes and street codes" in personal connections. More concretely, Maehr and Midgley (1996) raise the issue of the multiplicity of cultures and the fact that the prevailing culture is often established by the dominant group, reinforcing the cautions of academics and practitioners about the role of student backgrounds in the student–teacher storyline (Csikszentmihalyi & Larson, 1984; Weis, 1990). "The variation among subgroups presents a possibly very important piece of information on the character of the school" (Maehr & Midgley, 1996, p. 80) and the texture and robustness of teacher–student relations.

In a similar fashion, this understanding helps us remember that we need to "focus on the overall configuration of the developmental needs early adolescents have and the social supports and opportunities adults and institutions provide" (Roeser et al., 2000, p. 465). It is more than teachers. It is "also across the broader cast of adults charged with helping them become full members of society" (Roeser et al., 2000, p. 465). Bronfenbrenner (1979, p. 18) brings this message home forcefully when he reminds us "that environmental events and conditions outside any immediate setting containing the person have a profound influence on behavior and development within that setting." So too do Crosnoe and team (2004, p. 63), who confirm that "whom individuals know, how well they know them, and how close they are to them is dependent, in part, on the larger institutions in which lives are lived." Important also must be the "recognition that teachers are themselves embedded in social context above and beyond that of the classroom . . . , social contexts [that] facilitate or inhibit teachers' own needs [for] relatedness" (Connell & Wellborn, 1991, p. 71) and the linkages they form with students.

The summative message is that the study and practice of teacher–student relationships is "an interpersonal phenomenon [and] therefore, benefits from understanding the intersection of the interpersonal and the institutional" (Crosnoe et al., 2004, p. 63) of persons and contexts. Explanations for student–teacher relationships begin with "the proposition that development never takes place in a vacuum; it is always embedded and expressed through behavior in a particular environmental context" (Bronfenbrenner, 1979, p. 27). Further, these relationships "are to be found in interactions between characteristics of people and their environments (Bronfenbrenner, 1979, p. x).

TWO

UNDERSTANDING STUDENT EYES

> Educators can find numerous studies and expert opinions about character education, but they are seldom given the opportunity to view character education through the eyes of students. (Romanowski, 2003, p. 4)
>
> If I am going to be a successful teacher, I've got to try to look through students' eyes. I've got to understand something about how they see their futures, themselves, and the world around them. (Ellwood, 1993, p. 66)
>
> It is critical that we create sacred spaces for students to have a voice on the people, places, and practices that enrich their schooling experience. (Howard, 2001, p. 147)

The goal of this volume is to show how schooling looks through the eyes of students. In this chapter, we examine why the student perspective is valuable. We begin with a definition of student eyes. We discuss the lack of attention provided to this idea across time in education. We then report on an uptick in the importance of the student perspective in the 21st century. We analyze the reasons that help explain why student viewpoints are being vitalized in efforts to strengthen education. In the second section, we describe the avenues that are being pursued to acknowledge and recognize student voices.

In the last part of the chapter, we turn our attention to the benefits that materialize from drawing upon the perspectives of students. We want to make clear at this point that the "what" of the eyes approach is not the focus of this initial discussion. Content occupies our attention in the remaining chapters of the volume.

Before we undertake these assignments, we begin with "the call" for action from key figures at the forefront of work on understanding students' perspectives, analysts such as Fielding, Flutter, Rudduck, Quaglia, Mitra, Soohoo, Cook-Sather, Corbett, Wilson, and others whose insights anchor this chapter. Cook-Sather (2002, p. 12) expresses the call as "the authorization of student perspectives," "captur[ing] the range of activities that strive to reposition students in educational research and reform" (Cook-Sather, 2006b, p. 365). Rudduck and Flutter (2004, p. 2) capture the call simply and eloquently when they remind us that improving schooling requires us to "take seriously what pupils can tell us about their experience of being a learner in school—about what gets in the way of their learning and what helps them to learn." Rudduck, Chaplain, and Wallace (1996a, p. 18) capture the call for action in similar terms: "The point . . . is that pupils' accounts of experience should be taken seriously in debates about learning." Others draw our attention to students' insights on the social environment in which learning and teaching unfold (Crosnoe, Johnson, & Elder, 2004; Eccles et al., 1993; Pianta, 1999). More succinctly, Quaglia and Corso (2014, p. 5) capture the call as follows: "It is time for student voice to lead us on a new journey."

> By looking closely at their students and raising questions about why they seem to write the way they do, by paying attention to students' reactions to tasks and assignments, by considering students' own intentions, teachers are likely to discover the picture of the classroom, as seen through students' eyes. And, as is the case with all learning, this new perspective is what ultimately might compel these teachers to revise, to see again, with new eyes. (Zamel, 1990, pp. 96–97)

Analysts tell us that "there can be no single, fixed definition or explication of the term 'student voice'" (Cook-Sather, 2006b, p. 5), nor, we would add "student eyes." The terms cover a good deal of space on the continuums from individualism to collectivism and from passive to active expression (Hadfield & Haw, 2001). In this volume, following the advice of Wilson and Corbett (1995), the concept of eyes is also powerfully linked to the interpretation and application of student insights (Cook-Sather, 2006b).

It is helpful for educators to think of voice in terms of stages. Step one is the elicitation of student perspectives. This is especially important when working with young people who have been silent (and silenced) actors in the work of schooling (Cook-Sather & Shultz, 2001). Step two is listening to voices and watching the visuals students provide (Lincoln, 1995). There is considerable evidence that adult listening and watching often occur, according to students, absent real attention. "Mere asking does not qualify as listening. Listening is . . . characterized by what happens next, . . . clear acknowledgment that students have been heard" (Quaglia & Corso, 2014, p. 3). So step three is hearing and seeing students' perspective (Cook-Sather, 2006b). "We must show that we have understood their perspective" (Quaglia & Corso, 2014, p. 3), including the "emotional tenor" (Larkin, 1979, p. 129) of their viewed narratives. Step four is adult responsiveness (Flutter & Rudduck, 2004; McIntyre, Pedder, & Rudduck, 2005), action that includes feedback to students (Rudduck & Flutter, 2004), feedback that reveals "what happens next" (Quaglia & Corso, 2014, p. 3).

We know that perspective on student eyes can assume a number of forms in schools (Bragg, 2007; Murphy & Torre, 2014) or occur in a variety of venues. We also know that student insights can run in narrow channels or be quite broad, covering many significant dimensions of the schooling experience (Flutter & Rudduck, 2004). Analysts on student perspective inform us that the concept works best in the service of improvement when the focus is on positive change, not solely critique of the past, and when perspective gathering is active and ongoing (Clark, 1999; Rudduck et al., 1996a).

While all of this sounds relatively straightforward, even simple, analysts on student perspective are quick to note that what passes for adult attention to students in many instances falls short of meaningfully addressing these elements (Bragg, 2007; Larkin, 1979). Much of what occurs is designed to allow for voice on the margins of substantive issues, to provide for the appearance of attention and/or to co-opt youngsters (Burke & Grosvenor, 2003; Fine, Torre, Burns,

& Payne, 2007). Efforts often appear to have more to do with getting students to do what educators want than to addressing student concerns and desires (Alderson, 2008; Cook-Sather & Shultz, 2001; Fine et al., 2007). Efforts even when meeting essential stages are often quite limited in terms of the percentage of children involved (Flutter & Rudduck, 2004). Thus, academics, developers, and practitioners help us understand that to see what students see, youngsters have to believe the perspective-gathering processes are meaningful and genuine (Cook-Sather, 2006b; Rudduck, 2007; Taylor-Dunlop & Norton, 1997). Or as Mitra and Gross (2009, p. 534) capture the idea, students need to see that the processes are "authentic and honest," that exchanges have "importance and value." Students need to see that they have power and influence (Cook-Sather, 2006b; Fielding, 2004b). Understanding student perspective, Cook-Sather (2006b, p. 364) argues, "calls for a cultural shift that opens spaces and minds to the presence and power of students."

Scholars also proffer some cautionary text in the narrative of student perspective. They routinely caution that context always matters when crafting methods to secure and act upon student perspectives (Eccles et al., 1993; Johnson, 2009; Trickett & Quinlan, 1979). They also remind us that there are multiple student perspectives in schools (Cook-Sather & Shultz, 2001). Along with the usual array of contextual factors (e.g., grade level, gender), scholars cogently remind us that some students have voice in school while others do not. Some from the latter group, as the poem at the beginning of Chapter 1 reveals, see little reason to change well-established ways of addressing their silencing (McIntyre et al., 2005; Silva, 2001). Equally salient, analysts remind us that "pupils differ in the confidence and articulateness with which they can express ideas" (McIntyre et al., 2005; p. 155), differences that left unaddressed could reinforce inequalities. "All pupils should be listened to and not just those who are more academically and socially confident" (Rudduck, Chaplain, & Wallace, 1996b, p. 175). Even more importantly, reviewers reveal how voice- and eyes-based reforms jump from origination points to other schools without the DNA that powered them in the originating school (Murphy, 2013). In these cases, schools are left with only the appearance of voice and sight, with meaningless structures, policies, systems, and routines (Murphy, 1991, 2013).

The most insightful of the analysts teach us that reaching out to secure student perspectives is a "strategy that carries some degree of risk for all concerned" (Flutter & Rudduck, 2004, p. 23). They peel back the myth that the work is easy. Equally important, they recommend a cautious and thoughtful approach to the work. Flutter and Rudduck continue,

> Teachers may find that pupil consultation brings to light issues which are not simple and straightforward to address. The process itself can create or deepen tensions, either between staff members or between teachers and pupils. There may be reluctance among teachers and other members of staff to introduce change or to act upon pupil data; and there can be practical difficulties of finding the time and resources required. Pupils, too, may find consultation 'uncomfortable' because they may be worried that it could affect their relationships with peers; they might feel disappointed or frustrated when their views are sidelined and some may regard consultation with deep suspicion or a degree of anxiety because they are unaccustomed to having their views really listened to by adults. (p. 23)

According to Arnot and colleagues (2004, p. 3), "It is not possible to know in advance what the consequences will be of injecting strong pupil voices into a classroom teaching system that has evolved over two centuries without listening to such voices."

Finally, analysts caution us to not lose sight of the fact that the work of seeing students' perspectives requires interpretation and "interpretative analysis inevitably bears the mark of the interpreter" (Mergendoller & Packer, 1985, p. 584). "However much we convince ourselves that we are presenting their authentic voice, we are likely to be refracting their meaning through the lens of our own interests and concerns" (Rudduck et al., 1996b, p. 175).

HISTORICAL PATTERNS OF STUDENT PERSPECTIVES

> In the traditional school model, there is little room for student voice. (Quaglia & Corso, 2014, p. 2)
>
> *(Continued)*

> (Continued)
>
> Children have no illusions about their voices being heard in school, let alone acted upon. (Burke & Grosvenor, 2003, p. 81)
>
> If the programs, practices, and policies rendered within the framework of the places called school are delivered with students' best interest in mind, we must ask why their voices and viewpoints are so blatantly omitted. (Howard, 2001, p. 132)
>
> The question of how to listen to and attend to the voices of the most informed, yet marginalized witness of schooling, young people, has to [be] the most urgent issue of our time. (Smyth, 2006, p. 279)

We turn now to the matter of testing the viability of student eyes in education. We begin with a note of caution. Almost all of the scholars working on student perspective understand and therefore "see" the importance of knowing schooling partially through student eyes. However, in the overwhelming bulk of the school improvement literature, especially on the center stage issue of academic press, there is a profound silence on the issue of student voice. The result is that almost all of our knowledge on the matter of student perspective comes from colleagues who are active in the "student voice movement."

We move initially to two essential grounding points. First, "it is not what the teacher or researcher sees that is the immediate cause of the student's behavior. It is what the student sees that counts" (Maehr & Midgley, 1996, p. 87). The consequence is clear: "We need to try to understand where young people are coming from and how such understanding can help us with the task of school improvement" (Rudduck et al., 1996b, p. 170). Or as Mergendoller and Packer (1985, p. 581) capture it, "Thorough understandings of these perceptions is necessary if appropriate interventions are to be made in school organization and classroom instruction."

Second, there is a growing belief that "students can contribute a valuable perspective on education" (Spires, Lee, Turner, & Johnson, 2008, p. 497), that students should contribute to the work of strengthening schools: "Students are the experts on their own perceptions and experiences as learners" (Oldfather, 1995, p. 131). "Many of our clientele are academically ill; however, we must cease developing strategies to rectify various illnesses without asking the patients questions" (Howard, 2001, p. 132), without consulting the children (Burke & Grosvenor, 2003; Mitra & Gross, 2009; Quaglia & Corso, 2014). "It seems illogical if the very people who are at the heart of these initiatives are not consulted about the things that might be done to help them achieve" (Rudduck et al., 1996a, p. 20). Young persons "are central to the work of teachers, and they see teacher merit and worth from a point of view unlike those of administrators, teachers, parents, or researchers" (Peterson, Wahlquist, & Bone, 2000, p. 135).

> If school is about what students know, value, and care about, we need to know who students really are. We need to listen to them, pay attention to what they show us about themselves and their views, and build classroom worlds that support and teach in light of those insights. Students' voices help us understand what they need and value as learners. (Dahl, 1995, p. 124)

"Understanding how students perceive and react to their learning environments may be more useful than the analysis of the quality by outsiders (Howard, 2001, p. 133)." In a similar manner, considerable evidence suggests that the policy world has been uninterested and inattentive to the perspectives of students (Beishuizen, Hof, Putten, Bouwmeester, & Asscher, 2001; Corbett & Wilson, 1995; Smyth, 2006). Student perspectives have generally been unheard and unseen in the everyday work of teaching and learning as well (Chaplain, 1996a; Levin, 2000; Rudduck & Flutter, 2004). The overall conclusion is starkly clear: "The people most directly concerned with the problems [and possibilities] are never consulted" (Burke & Grosvenor, 2003, p. 8). In turn, "that the widening lens of reform tends to ignore students' definitions of their roles tempers our hopefulness about the prospects for success" (Corbett &Wilson, 1995, p. 16).

While it is not our intention to explain in detail why policy, practice, development, and research have systematically silenced young people, notes on two broad causes merit attention. To begin with, schooling is nested in a larger society that has developed in ways that do not devote much attention to student perspective (Cook-Sather & Shultz, 2001). The "traditional exclusion of young people from the consultative processes, this bracketing out of their voice, is founded upon an outdated view of childhood which fails to acknowledge children's capacity to reflect on issues affecting their lives" (Rudduck et al., 1996b, p. 170), from a societal perspective that views "children as incompetent and incomplete" (Holloway &Valentine, 2004, p. 5). Children needed to be told what to do, not to be empowered to participate in the development of social institutions such as schools (Rudduck & Flutter, 2004). Children were to be seen and not heard (Lodge, 2005).

On the education front specifically, Cook-Sather (2002, p. 3) helps us see that the concept of student perspective "runs counter to US reform efforts which have been based on adults' ideas about the conceptualization and practice of education." That is, for two centuries the dominant culture of schooling has evolved in a manner to privilege adult values and voices (Bragg, 2007). Holloway and Valentine (2000, p. 8) refer to this as the evolution of an "adultist discipline." "The social organization in traditional classrooms is constituted and controlled by teachers" (Dillon, 1989, p. 254). Students have been cast in largely passive terms (Flutter & Rudduck, 2004; Weinstein, 1983), "almost entirely as objects of reform" (Levin, 2000, p. 155). In addition, recent forces on the accountability front in schools have reinforced nondemocratic foundations of schooling (Mitra & Gross, 2009), employing "conceptions of childhood that regard young people as dependent and incapable" (Flutter & Rudduck, 2004, p. 3), based on the idea of children as "recipients" (Levin, 2000, p. 156).

STUDENT PERSPECTIVES IN THE 21ST CENTURY

There is a sense in the literature that the deeply ingrained role of the passive, unheard student is beginning to change (Hadfield & Haw, 2001; Lodge, 2005); that is, the idea of seeing schools through the eyes of students is receiving increasing recognition (Cook-Sather & Shultz, 2001; Rudduck & Flutter, 2004). More specifically, the literature suggests that in the last quarter of the 20th century there were one or two upticks in the importance of student perspectives

(Mergendoller & Packer, 1985; Weinstein, 1983) but that they were short lived (Rudduck & Flutter, 2004). While there was greater attention to student perspectives in the research world, evidence that educators and policy makers shifted their understandings on this matter is more difficult to unearth. Rudduck and Flutter (2004, p. 113) capture the time well when they conclude that although the era "strengthened the legitimacy and usefulness of focusing on pupils' perspectives [and] ... laid the foundations for that work," it did not reach the status of a movement. And it is instructive to remind ourselves that while discussion of the importance of honoring students' perspective is receiving greater recognition, much of that acknowledgement comes from the "student voice movement." It is more difficult to discern deep recognition in the general literature or to find it in the actions of schools (Cook-Sather, 2006b; Flutter & Rudduck, 2004; Quaglia & Corso, 2014). It is also helpful to recall that the language in these uptick periods had strong "radical, utopian, and libertarian" roots (Bragg, 2007, p. 680). Perhaps the best comment on the current state of affairs has been provided by Rudduck (2007, p. 590): "Student voice may have a better chance of survival now than in previous incarnations."

The question at hand is the reverse of the one discussed above; that is, what can account for the increased attention to student perspectives in education over the last two decades? "Why in the present climate is pupil perspective gaining ground in schools?" (Rudduck & Flutter, 2004, p. 100). One line of explanation explores shifts in the larger social forces that envelop schools. The second focuses on the changing dynamics of schooling. And, of course, there is considerable overlap between the rationales. Collectively, explanations rest on deeper rationales than those used with the earlier upticks in the area of student voice (Weinstein, 1983).

On the larger front, "there is clear evidence that the political and social climate has begun to warm to the principle of involving children and young people" (Flutter & Rudduck, 2004, pp. 138–139). Most noticeable perhaps is a changing understanding of childhood among researchers, practitioners, and policy makers, understanding consistent with the development of a postindustrial society (Alderson, 2000; Lodge, 2005): "Children and young people, rather than being passive subjects of social structures, are coming to be recognized as being active in shaping their social identities and as competent members of society" (Burke & Grosvenor, 2003, p. 3).

> The social context in which we now place children and minors is a rapidly changing one, directed away from the view of children as chattel property and toward a view of children as both the inheritors and the inheritance of the future. In this social context, the emphasis on children as repositories of hope and change represents a powerful paradigm shift. (Lincoln, 1995, p. 888)

There is a visible line of explanation here about the growth of rights (and responsibilities) of youngsters (Cook-Sather, 2006b; Lodge, 2005; McIntyre et al., 2005). In the newer literature, we witness "a shift towards recognizing children as competent agents in their own lives" (Valentine, 1999, p. 141), "competent social actors who are no longer seen as simply subsumed" (Alderson, 2008, p. 277). There is "a cultural shift away from an adult-centric, infantilizing, and disempowering set of attitudes" (Cook-Sather, 2006b, p. 372). Energy is also being directed toward the needed rebirth of democracy and citizenship, with discernible recognition of the important role that young persons play here (Flutter & Rudduck, 2004).

> In an emerging political context, we are beginning to understand that the support of a democratic, just, and economically viable and prosperous society requires active participation and critical thinking skills far beyond what many of our students experience in school. The 'laboratory' where such skills are learned or not learned is the largest public social institution remaining in the United States: the public schools. Exercising 'voice' in public affairs or the normal duties of citizenship requires that individuals have found their voices. (Lincoln, 1995, p. 89)

With the doors of legitimizing student perspectives open—"the principle that pupils can bring something worthwhile to discussions about schooling" (Flutter & Rudduck, 2004, p. 5)—we are finding, perhaps not surprisingly, increasing evidence that youngsters have important contributions to make (Lodge, 2005; McIntyre et al., 2005; Storz, 2008), what Levin (2000, p. 158) refers to as "unique knowledge and perspectives." We are also discovering that "young people are capable of insightful and constructive analysis of their experiences in schools" (Arnot et al., 2004, p. 4). That is, the growing belief that the views of students should be seen is being reinforced by the evidence that youngsters' perspectives are valid, reliable, and beneficial (McIntyre et al., 2005; Peterson et al., 2000). They have "demonstrated the capacity to comment constructively and intelligently" (Flutter & Rudduck, 2004, p. 48). In particular, "students are good judges of teacher behaviors" (Murdock & Miller, 2003, p. 396), "educator effectiveness" (Part, 2012, p. 3), and classroom and school climate (Moos & David, 1981; Murdock & Miller, 2003; Trickett & Quinlan, 1979). We also learn "that students' views on teaching and learning [are] remarkably consistent with those of current theorists concerned with learning theory, cognitive science, and the sociology of work. This should come as no surprise when we consider that students spend more time in schools than anybody else except teachers" (Nieto, 1994, pp. 398–399). Overall then, scholars conclude that "pupils of all ages can show a remarkable capacity to discuss their learning in considered and insightful ways" (Flutter & Rudduck, 2004, p. 7); "children as young as nine or ten [can] make informed and perceptive observations about classroom teaching and learning, and [can] recommend improvements" (Riley & Docking, 2004, p. 167). There is threaded in this line of research on the value that youngsters can bring to classrooms and schools a subtheme that our failure to have seen schools through student eyes has inflicted damages on the educational system (Rudduck & Flutter, 2004; Kroeger, 2004). Kohl (1994, p. 47) makes this point nicely, concluding that without learning to see schooling through the eyes of students and their communities, "we will not be able to solve the major problems in the United States today."

Looking inward at education, we distill four reasons for the enhanced interest in seeing and understanding schooling through the eyes of children and youngsters. To start, we discern the growth of research methods that privilege uncovering embedded viewpoints (Holloway & Valentine, 2004; Mauthner, 1997), "research [that] takes the perspective that pupils' understanding of the nature and point of classroom events is important in its own right" (Nolen &

Nicholls, 1993, p. 414). Bradley, Deighton, and Selby (2004, p. 209) present this line of approach as follows:

> If traditional social scientific ways of understanding young people have broken down, we must assume that the best clues to the problems facing youth are found, not in expert knowledge, but in the experiences of the young.

Particularly relevant here is a new focus on "the assessment of social environments" (Trickett & Quinlan, 1979, p. 279), on "the ecological world of students" (Murdock & Miller, 2003, p. 387). There is a growing respect in the social science disciplines that anchor educational research "for children as competent social anchors" (Alderson, 2008, p. 277; see also Fine, 1993). There is also "a shift in the practice of researching on youth to with youth" (Fine et al., 2007, p. 808). And, of course, this is an iterative process: "Recognizing children as subjects rather than objects of research ... entails changing emphasis in research methods and topics" (Alderson, 2008, p. 278). Or as Holloway and Valentine (2004, p. 5) capture it, "Recognition that childhood is a socially constructed phenomenon has been accompanied by a challenge to 'traditional' approaches to the study of children." Particularly important here is that the mixture of honoring of student perspectives and new approaches to research has made important changes into the tradition of characterizing students in negative terms and/or as problems (Fine et al., 2007).

A second force pushing the importance of student perspectives has been the growth of consumerism, client-focus, and marketization in education (Murphy, 1996, 1999). As we have discussed elsewhere, for over a century schooling has been the business of professionals, a government-professional monopoly. The 21st century is witnessing the introduction of market forces into schooling. Much of that energy has been directed to issues of choice and voice, including increasing acknowledgment of student perspectives. Children's rights are not the only argument for student voice (Lodge, 2005). "Support also comes from people who endorse the perception of young people as consumers" (Rudduck, 2007, p. 589). The conclusion is that client and market focus pushes forward the idea of "young people as valued, knowledgeable, important informants, and customers" (Bragg, 2007, p. 665).

As schools are being recast to accommodate market as well as professional perspectives, they are also evolving from organizations scaffolded on the principles and values of hierarchy and institutionalism to community-anchored places of work, a third powerful internal dynamic expanding the legitimacy of student perspectives and the work to see schools through the eyes of young persons. A core issue here is the changing understanding of citizenship and how schools can best prepare youngsters for that role (Bragg, 2007; McIntyre et al., 2005; Rudduck, 2007). There is a movement away from the perspective of followership to that of productive participation (Poplin & Weeres, 1994), to "the importance of preparing young people to be citizens in a democratic society" (McIntyre et al., 2005, p. 160), although as Mitra and Gross (2009) remind us, there are powerful cross currents at work here as well. Another strand here underscores Flutter and Rudduck's (2004, p. 135) concept of school as a "community of participants," or a combination of the two strands of citizenship and community into what they refer to as "democratic school community" (p. 59). Central to the idea of community in this context is the reconceptualization of power (Lincoln, 1995; Murphy & Torre, 2014). We note here "an important shift in the status of student-teacher relationships from one that is tightly hierarchical to one that is more collaborative" (Rudduck, 2007, p. 587). To create schools where students are ensconced in and actively engaged in community necessitates honoring student views of the school.

Finally, we report that schools are undergoing a significant shift in learning and teaching, the core technology of the business, from behavioral models of learning and transmission models of teaching (Murphy, 2002). The point here for us has been nicely framed by Levin (2000, p. 157)—"Constructivist learning ... requires a more active student role in schooling," and by Cook-Sather and Shultz (2001, p. 6)—"Constructivist approaches to teaching require that teachers listen to students' perspectives." Scholars here "argue that teachers can improve their practice by listening closely to what students have to say about their learning" (Cook-Sather, 2006b, p. 369). In constructivist pedagogy, we find that students "should be afforded opportunities to actively shape their education" (p. 387). As was the case with consumerism and community forces, constructivism empowers students (Alvermann, Young, Weaver, Hinchman, Moore, Phelps, & Zalewski, 1996; Rudduck & Fielding, 2006), while reminding adults that "there is something amiss about building and rebuilding an entire system without consulting at any point those it is ostensibly designed to serve" (Cook-Sather, 2002, p. 3).

METHODS FOR SEEING

> Solutions will be far more complicated than it would appear at first. They will involve not only initiating new ways of seeing and acting but ending old ways. (Poplin & Weeres, 1994, p. 8)

Rules and Cautions

In this section, we examine ways that have been employed to see schooling through the eyes of students. As is our rule, we begin with an important caution: Providing legitimacy to the views of students does not negate the need for employing strategies to learn what we can from others both inside and outside the school (Eccles et al., 1993; Pianta, 1999). We also introduce a core reality: "In order to get student views heard and understood, forums for listening have to be appreciated and created anew" (Cook-Sather, 2006b, p. 384). Finally, while we address this issue in great detail in later chapters, we start with the conclusion that understanding student perspectives on a number of fronts adds value to the school (Furrer & Skinner, 2003; Peterson et al., 2000).

In addition to the cautions about the application of research methods in general, research on student perspectives in particular adds a number of concerns that school practitioners and academics need to hold in mind as they engage with this work. That is, working to see schooling through the eyes of children adds to the level of care needed to be undertaken by adults, perspectives and skill sets that teachers are likely not to possess (Lincoln, 1995). More specifically, reviewers remind us that there are documented obstacles across the full spectrum of activity (e.g., collecting data, analyzing data) in working to see schooling through the eyes of students (Reid, Landesman, Treder, & Jaccard, 1989). They offer an important lesson to guide us in the work: Those "who wish to elicit student voices could not find better pathways for engaging those voices than the material culture and the content of rituals and patterns of friendship, dress, music, and other accoutrements of student life as windows on student worlds" (Lincoln, 1995, p. 92). Another lesson has been penned by Clark (1999, p. 3):

Substantial skill is needed for an interviewer to step outside of their usual adult superiority and authority, and to engage children at their own level and style of competency. Normally, adults are aliens to a child's world. An adult interviewing a child needs to empower that child to "teach" the adult about the child's own experience. Simultaneously, adults need to adjust their grammar and vocabulary, avoid making questions seem like demands, monitor the level of shared rapport, and encourage the greatest possible free recall by the child.

Flutter and Rudduck (2004) remind us that reliance on a single form of data collection is no more appropriate for children than it is for adults, that triangulation is important here as well. They also argue for using both visual and verbal means to capture student perspectives. Others point out the special concerns that come into play when working with children (Mauthner, 1997). Age is an especially relevant variable, particularly finding strategies that work with very young students (Mauthner, 1997). Reid and colleagues (1989, p. 898) discuss the importance of creating or adopting methods that are "developmentally sensitive to children's cognitive and emotional understanding." We are reminded about the need to build interactive work in garnering student perspectives, interactive in the sense of shared activity and active engagement (Hart, 1997). Clark (1999), in turn, surfaces the issue of sensitivity to the linguistic competence of young children. Here, Flutter and Rudduck (2004, p. 51) suggest that educators find "ways of accessing pupils' perceptions that [do] not depend wholly on verbal skills." Rudduck and colleagues (1996) present the need to work through the reality that youngsters have a penchant to more fully address negative than positive experiences. And Flutter and Rudduck (2004) raise the caution of not privileging the insights of those students who are most vocal but finding methods to incorporate multiple perspectives in drawing conclusions.

On the analytic side of the work, Mergendoller and Packer (1985, p. 582) expose the danger of overlapping adult perspectives on the insights of youngsters. They remind us that "interpretive analysis is a particularly sensitive undertaking because it charges analysts with the revelation of assumptions made by others rather than the imposition of their own." We close with caution that student eyes must be real, an integrated aspect of the school culture. It is not a "cute idea" or a one-off activity (Jackson & Wolfson, 1971). It is part of the commitment to enabling students and student perspectives in the work of school improvement. On this last point, Cook-Sather (2006b, p. 385) provides a nice summative reminder:

> Because schools are set up on premises of prediction, control, and management, anything that challenges those premises is hard to accomplish within formal educational contexts. Until teachers, administrators, policy makers, and the wider public see that there is value in this particular kind of change prompted by attending to, responding to and following the lead of students, and indeed embracing the threat these actions carry, efforts that aggregate under the term "student voice" will not get very far.

Strategies

Colleagues working on methods for garnering student perspectives provide a useful portfolio of strategies. We learn of the importance of well-known procedures such as individual and group interviews, self-reports, questionnaires and surveys, and student consultation and focus groups. Also highlighted are "structured activities" (Mauthner, 1997, p. 25), including writing (e.g., free essays and autobiographies), mapping, student research, drawings, productions, participant observations, and role playing. Our objective here is to present options for educators to consider, to expand the tool box of possibilities for use in seeing schooling through the eyes of students. It is beyond our charge to provide in-depth descriptions or critiques of each strategy. We cluster tools into two groups: more traditional and alternative methods.

TRADITIONAL METHODS

Researchers and practitioners have employed a variety of widely used methods to gather information on students' perspectives. Note here that "traditional" applies to routine use in the larger research community. These approaches are not traditionally used in seeing schools through student eyes. It is also important to stress that the use of multiple approaches is wise policy. And many of the examples we present below rely on a mix of ideas covering traditional and alternative frames, a mixture of seeing, hearing, writing, and acting

Chapter Two: Understanding Student Eyes 39

(e.g., photo-elicitation interviews). Last, approaches can be borrowed or adapted or created to cover a wide spectrum of student viewpoints on both the academic and cultural domains of the school (Berndt & Perry, 1986; Howard, 2002; Thorkildsen, 1989).

Although not deeply employed historically, the use of student interviews has been the most widely reported tool in the student perspective tool box (Johnson, 2009, Nolen & Nicholls, 1993; Wilson & Corbett, 2001). Individual interviews are best used with older children, "five-to-six year olds find them awkward" (Mauthner, 1997, p. 23). Mauthner (1997, p. 24) informs us that "a useful approach when interviewing children is to ask them to describe specific daily events . . . as well as [to answer] questions about events, questions about feelings . . . and [questions about] routines are much more useful than direct questions about the child him/herself." Mauthner (1997, p. 25) also has discovered "that it is more profitable to encourage children to use their own language, and their own ways of communicating, and to ask them to clarify where necessary, rather than attempt to understand and reply using other people's words." Pianta (1999, p. 90) adds assistance here when he informs us that

> in interviewing children about relationships with teachers, a few general principles should be observed. First, children may not respond to direct questions about their own experiences but may readily respond to the same question if posed about children in general or about other children in their class. Second, once a child has responded, the interviewer should affirm the child's view and should gently probe to elicit specific examples of the experience in question. In fact, one goal of the interview should be to attempt to elicit information on relationships at the level of specific experiences.

A "dialogue approach to interviewing that recognizes that interviews with children [that] utilize a basic dialogue unit rather than a monologue and [that] engages children as active collaborators" (Reid et al., 1989, p. 898) can be very successful.

Scholars often point out the value of conducting group interviews with children (Arnot et al., 2004; Garcia, Kilgore, Rodriguez, & Thomas, 1995; Rudduck, 2007). Storz (2008, p. 252), for example, "holds that providing the opportunity for student interaction has the potential for enhancing student participation and building on the responses of other group members." Providing students with opportunities to nominate peers for interviews can be productive as well (Crothers & Levinson, 2004). Such efforts are often described as consultation, focus group work, and group discussions. Rudduck (2007, p. 590) defines consultation as follows: "Consultation is a form of student voice that is purposeful. It invites talking with students about things that matter in school or gathering their views through writing." Flutter and Rudduck (2004, p. 22) highlight another key issue when they define consultation as "a means by which young learners can be invited into a conversation . . . so that their role changes from being an 'object' of research attention to one of active participation." As reported above, large swathes of interest can be covered in group interviews (Flutter & Rudduck, 2004; Mauthner, 1997). And as we will see below, consultation and group discussions can be used as core elements in other approaches (e.g., student research) to seeing schools through the eyes of youngsters (Flutter & Rudduck, 2004).

Questionnaires can be used to see the school through the use of a resource that is gaining in acceptance. Many instruments are available, especially in the psychological and sociological literature, that permit educators to determine student states, such as self-esteem and agency, and learning dispositions, such as motivation and commitment (Akos, 2002; Casey-Cannon, Hayward, & Gowen, 2001; Dennis & Satcher, 1999; Dubow & Ullman, 1989; Ma, 2003; Moos, 1978; Trickett & Moos, 1974; Spires et al., 2008). While the beauty of the method is that questionnaires allow schools to gather large amounts of data to ensure broad student representation (Flutter & Rudduck, 2004), it is important to introduce a caution here. Questionnaires can be seen by students as an imposition, another request by adults for work without meaning (Fielding, 2004b). Questionnaires are also not the optimal method to garner students' perspectives (Pianta & Steinberg, 1992).

Alternative Strategies

Researchers are also deepening the ways that we can gather information on students' sense of school culture and work. We learn, for example, that a number of writing methods are available (Akos, 2002). Writing as a vehicle to see through the eyes of students includes activities such as free essays (Beishuizen et al., 2001), journals (Soohoo, 1993), biographical narratives and stories (Fine, 1986; Storz, 2006), personal logs (Flutter & Rudduck, 2004), and sentence completions (Harter et al., 1997), all of which lend themselves to class publications (Hart, 1997). Mauthner (1997, p. 26) reveals the

Chapter Two: Understanding Student Eyes   41

"draw-and-write technique" that can be used in conjunction with consultations. Hart (1997, p. 165) points to the power of mapping, a strategy that "provide[s] means of expressing spatially the relationships of organisms to their . . . living environments." Hart contends that "maps are a valuable means for allowing children to express their individual preferences, dislikes, and ideas" (p. 168). Bragg (2007), Flutter and Rudduck (2004), and Soohoo (1993) show how pupils' perspectives can be brought to life in drawings. Analysts also expose some of the limitations of this vehicle, such as adult predetermination, and provide safety nets to employ here such as using drawing in conjunction with student commentaries. Hart (1997, p. 162) explains that a particular type of drawing, storyboards, "offers great potential" to understanding school through the eyes of students: "This method can be a very useful way of convincing children that you take what they have to say very seriously" (p. 163). Related to this, Hart exposes the value of collages and drawing video slides to gather student perspectives.

Photography has been used in interesting ways to discern student perspectives, to hear student voices (Flutter & Rudduck, 2004; Harper, 2002; Marquez-Zenkov, 2007). According to Harper (2002), the power of images can help overcome the limitations of other data collection strategies especially when used in conjunction with interviews (Clark, 1999; Soohoo, 1993). In autodriven interviews or photo elicitation strategies, for example, "photographs of the child's experience serve as the basis for a child-directed interview" (Clark, 1999, p. 39). Photographs may be taken by an adult or the children themselves. On the upside (Clark, 1999, p. 43), we learn that photo interviews "enlarge the possibility of conventional empirical work" (Harper, 2002, p. 13). Photos have been reported to sharpen students' memory and to lead to new views of social existence (Harper, 2002).

> For the purpose of developing a more child-centered understanding, the photos and autodriven interviews made a valued contribution. In particular, the photographs captured and introduced content areas which otherwise (from an adult viewpoint) might have been poorly understood (or even overlooked). In addition, the photos served as a mediating prop aiding the interview process—substantially contributing to levels of rapport and child involvement—and as a window into emotional or abstract ideas. (Clark, 1999, p. 43)

Researchers have also explored the importance of student projects as a vehicle to promote and discover student perspectives (Cook-Sather, 2006a; Hart, 1997). While projects cover a good deal of ground, two strategies are most visible. One is illuminating student eyes through performances such as singing, acting, dancing, developing skits or plays, conducting puppet shows, and small-scale modeling (Hart, 1997). Also noted here are role-playing activities (Flutter & Rudduck, 2004) and storytelling (Mauthner, 1997). The second avenue is to unearth student perspectives through "youth research" (Fine et al., 2007, p. 826). Here children's voices emerge in their design, application, and interpretation of investigations that spotlight important dimensions of schooling (Lee, 1999; Oldfather, 1995; Soohoo, 1997). As is the case with other nontraditional methods of understanding how students see their worlds, training for roles and for the use of unfamiliar technologies and procedures requires attention (Crothers & Levinson, 2004; Flutter & Rudduck, 2004).

IMPORTANCE OF VOICE

> Somehow educators have forgotten the important connection between teachers and students. We listen to outside experts to inform us, and consequently, we overlook the treasure in our very own backyards: our students. Student perceptions are valuable to our practice because they are authentic sources; they personally experience our classrooms firsthand . . . we need to find ways to continually seek out these silent voices because they can teach us so much about learning and learners. (Soohoo, 1993, p. 390)
>
> Seen through multiethnic students' eyes and the eyes of other participants inside schools, the problems of public education in the U.S. look vastly different than those issues debated by experts, policy makers, academicians and the media. (Poplin & Weeres, 1994, p. 11)

We begin again with a caution. Our focus in this volume is on a subjective source of information, student perceptions. "Subjective measures have real and recognized limitations" (Epstein, 1981a, p. 3). We do not wish to compound sins of omission. It is important then to be clear that we are not suggesting that student perspectives hold a monopoly in decision-making processes. It is also essential to remember that it is what is done with student viewpoints that is critical (Cook-Sather, 2006b). "In developing student voice teachers need time to do things thoughtfully, courage to do things differently, but also the commitment to doing things reflectively. Such commitments are the bases of authenticity" (Rudduck, 2007, p. 604). The research literature also makes it clear that authenticity is achieved most effectively when buttressed by structures and supports (Cook-Sather, 2006b). Saying this, we also acknowledge that perceptions are reality (Murphy, 2011; Steele et al., 1971). "How things are is often less important than how people think—or perceive—things are" (Flutter & Rudduck, 2004, p. 6). The essential condition "is the student's interpretation of the situation, not 'objective' classroom characteristics" (Hoge et al., 1990, p. 188).

Thus our starting point is that understanding student perception is key to understanding schooling (Hayes et al., 1994; Quiroz, 2001; Soohoo, 1993). "Because they play a central role in the classroom, students' perspectives need to be explored" (Zamel, 1990, p. 94). As we discuss more fully below, "a thorough understanding of these perceptions is necessary if appropriate interventions are to be made in school organization and classroom instruction" (Mergendoller & Packer, 1985, p. 581). In so doing, "we are likely to discover the discrepancies between our intentions and goals and those of our students, we are likely to locate the mismatches between students' perspectives and our own" (Zamel, 1990, p. 94). And it is here that the door to change based on those understandings opens—"their insights warrant not only the attention but also the responses of adults" (Cook-Sather & Shultz, 2001, p. 1).

Our review of the research on student perceptions leads us to conclude that persons are deeply knowledgeable about themselves, classrooms, and schooling (Maehr & Midgley, 1996; Peterson et al., 2000; Storz, 2008); "that pupils are often highly perceptive about the factors that shape their work at school" (Flutter & Rudduck, 2004, p. 118). Or, more simply, "students have a lot to tell us that could make school better" (Rudduck, 2007, 591), by noting both the positive and negative aspects of classrooms and schools (Chaplain 1996a; Nieto, 1994; Part, 2012). Analysts also help us see that students provide accurate portraits of these classrooms and schools

(Rohrkemper, 1985; Steele et al., 1971), as well as "significant nonredundant information" (Wilson & Corbett, 2001, p. 109).

Walberg (1976, p. 159) goes further, arguing for the specialness of seeing schooling through the eyes of students: "The student . . . stands at a superior vantage point; what he takes in makes the difference in learning . . . he is a sophisticated judge with plenty of information to weigh. His perceptions, as partaker of classroom social transaction, are of great value." Indeed "adolescents' perceptions of caregivers' behavior tend to be more powerful predictors of independent assessments of social and emotional outcomes than reports from other informants" (Wentzel, 1997, p. 412).

"The importance of paying attention to learner perspectives and to learners' voices is that they help us understand what connections need to be made" (Dahl, 1995, p. 129). They can tell us accurately about the extent to which various reforms have taken hold in classrooms (Wilson & Corbett, 2001).

> In addition, educators have argued cogently that student perceptions of the classroom and school provide important feedback to teachers and administrators regarding student involvement in and satisfaction with the education process. (Mergendoller & Packer, 1985, p. 581)

Student perceptions "are the most proximal predictors of subsequent behavior" (Wentzel, 2002, p. 299). For example, Alderson (2008, p. 287) finds that "children are the primary source of knowledge about their own views and experiences." Weinstein (1983, p. 293) found that "interviews with students showed that students inferred from teacher behavior much beyond what researchers commonly think they are measuring." Steele, House, and Kerins (1971, p. 452) maintain that "students are in a much better position to report on the emphasis actually given to various class activities" than adults in the school. And "the best source of data on student attitudes is close at hand: the students themselves" (Sagor, 1996, p. 43). They are particularly knowledgeable about the so-called hidden curriculum, "the values . . . taught implicitly by the social system of the school classroom" (Hamilton, 1983, p. 313).

Students' knowledge is valuable because when tapped it often reveals discrepancies between what adults perceive and what youngsters perceive (Fisher & Fraser, 1983). They also often do not perceive conditions in ways intended by others (Peterson & Irving, 2008). We also learn that these discrepancies are often systematic and biased in the favor of staff (Fisher & Fraser, 1983; Riley & Docking, 2004); adults at school see things in a more positive light than their students. Dubow and Ullman (1989, p. 61) find, for example, that "adults' perceptions of a child's support may not correlate well with the child's perception of it." More specifically, teachers often assess the climate of their rooms more positively than do the students (Fisher & Fraser, 1983). Procedures to garner student perspective also have an important role in the legitimization of students and student knowledge (Rudduck et al., 1996b; Wilson & Corbett, 2001). The narrative of student voice reinforces understandings "of how important it is for students to be full participants in their own education" (Spires et al., 2008, p. 512).

Student perceptions can be powerful vehicles for pursuing school improvement (Arnot et al., 2004; Howard, 2001; Thorkildsen, 1989), for "finding out what works in the classroom" (Flutter & Rudduck, 2004, p. 14), for "build[ing] up a more realistic picture of what is happening" (p. 40) in schools, and for bringing to life the "growing recognition that students influence instruction and its outcomes as much as teachers do" (Weinstein, 1983, p. 287). Teachers need to start where students are (Lincoln, 1995). "Attending to children's voices allows us to know at a deeper level who children are as learners" (Dahl, 1995, p. 130). Seeing schools through the eyes of students "can enable teachers to understand problems better" (Mergendoller & Packer, 1985, p. 597). "These perceptions allow us to identify things that teachers and learners consider important and that make a difference to pupils' opportunities for successful learning" (Flutter & Rudduck, 2004, p. 2). Knowledge of perceptions can "be valuable to teachers seeking ways to involve pupils in the negotiations of the practices that govern their learning" (Nolen & Nicholls, 1993, p. 414). Seeing through student eyes provides insights into the struggles that they experience (Mergendoller & Packer, 1985; Rodriguez, 2008). According to Rudduck and Flutter (2004, p. 79), "Our research suggests that pupils are sharply aware of 'sticky patches' in their learning and that they are often perceptive in distinguishing the kinds of help that enable them to make progress." Students are especially skilled in helping adults understand how they view issues of school organization and school culture (Wallace, 1996a). Students' "perspectives can provide useful information about the quality of teaching and learning" (Flutter & Rudduck, 2004, p. 52), about pedagogy and subject content (Wilson & Corbett, 2001).

Drilling more deeply into the importance of seeing through student eyes, we note the reality that "students have singular and invaluable views from which both adults and students can benefit" (Cook-Sather, 2002, p. 3). Honoring student perspectives on a regular basis allows educators "to gain a better understanding of children's cultural capital (Flutter & Rudduck, 2004, p. 33). Storz (2008, p. 266) goes further, arguing that honoring students' perspectives "has the potential for providing educators the means to respond to students in a way that empowers both teachers and students. Valuing students' perspectives tells everyone that children offer a great deal of information about what is occurring in schools and what to do to improve them (Cook-Sather, 2002), knowledge that may be only poorly understood by educators (Howard, 2002) and that may be uncomfortable but that needs to be confronted (Rudduck, 2007).

> Students have a unique perspective on what happens in school and classroom and on the dynamics between their schools and their communities that inform what happens in those schools and classrooms. As long as we exclude these perspectives from our conversations about schooling and how it needs to change, our efforts at reform will be based on an incomplete picture of life in classrooms and schools and how that life could be improved. (Cook-Sather, 2002, p. 3)
>
> Recognition of this key point has profound implications for our endeavours to improve what happens in schools for, unless we look at the experiences of teaching and learning through the eyes of young learners, we, like Cervantes' Don Quixote, may be in some danger of tilting at windmills. (Flutter & Rudduck, 2004, p. 6)

Prominent analysts who have established the foundations of the work on student perspectives also describe the ways that student voice works. At the broadest level, Flutter and Rudduck (2004, p. 132) suggest that the potential here is in "changing our constructions of pupils and the pupil role [and] in initiating change in the structures of school." Rudduck and Flutter (2004, p. 29) refer to this potential as "a practical agenda for change that can help fine-tune or, more fundamentally, identify and shape improvement strategies." We label this school improvement work, work that holds that

> to manage school improvement we need to look at schools from the pupils' perspective and that means tuning in to their experiences and views and creating a new role for them as active participants in their own learning and within the school as a learning community. (Rudduck & Flutter, 2004, p. 111)

"What pupils say about teaching, learning and school is not only worth listening to but provides an important—perhaps the most important—foundation for thinking about ways of improving schools" (Rudduck et al., 1996a, p. 17). Moving down a level, Cook-Sather (2002, p. 3) helps us see that "the work of authorizing student perspectives is essential because of the various ways that it can improve current educational practice, re-inform existing conversations about educational reform, and point to the discussions and reform efforts yet to be undertaken." Mitra and Gross (2009, p. 526) push further, revealing the centrality of student perspectives in "fashioning a responsive and engaging educational experience" for youngsters. "Pupil involvement . . . offers the possibility of taking school improvement efforts beyond the quick-fix solutions . . . and returns schools' attention to pupils and their learning" (Flutter & Rudduck, 2004, p. 135).

Researchers who work in the area of student perspective—student voice and student eyes—confirm that the above gains are translated into improvements in the school climate and the instructional program (i.e., curriculum, pedagogy, and assessment) (Howard, 2002; Cook-Sather, 2006b; Corbett &Wilson, 1995), outcomes scaffolded on organizational goals, structures, and processes (Wilson & Corbett, 2001). On the school climate front, we find that attending to student perspectives "can help increase the tension and focus on pressing issues when needed . . . [and] can help calm turbulence occurring ... in school contexts that need resolution" (Mitra & Gross, 2009, p. 522). This perspective has also been linked to student sense of belonging (Johnson, 2009), to improved social relationships among students and between teachers and students (Flutter & Rudduck, 2004), and to the development of communities of learning (Flutter & Rudduck, 2004).

Turning to the instructional program, the seminal figures in the research on seeing schooling through the eyes of students concur, reminding us that students have a good deal to teach educators about teaching (Commeyras, 1995; Rudduck & Flutter, 2004), that is, "how [to] improve teaching and learning in schools" (Flutter & Rudduck, 2004, p. 132).

> Asking students what they understood about what was said, checking for individual differences in interpretation, inquiring about the cues that students used to determine teacher intent, and assessing students' perceptions of the climate of the classroom are all important strategies that teachers might use to evaluate the success of their own planned programmatic changes as well as to prevent misunderstandings in their communication with students in the classroom. (Weinstein, 1983, p. 303)

Lee (1999, p. 217), in particular, argues that honoring student perspectives can help "educators challenge their assumptions and understandings about low-performing students [and] on the effectiveness of particular strategies, programs, activities, and policies that are intended to ameliorate patterns of underachievement." Seeing through student eyes can be a useful "technique for supporting individual learners who are experiencing difficulties with their learning" (Flutter & Rudduck, 2004, p. 25).

The process works, according to Flutter and Rudduck (2004, p. 7), because awareness of student perspectives "has helped [teachers] to understand how pupils learn most effectively ... to make changes to aspects of their teaching practice." "By focusing on how our students see the world, we may see our own world with new eyes" (Arhar & Buck, 2000, p. 338). Seeing through student eyes has been shown to help teachers "increase the congruence between their intended and realized socialization goals" (Rohrkemper, 1985, p. 30). Thus we find that seeing through the eyes of students "can be a lever for educator learning" (Levin, 2000, p. 160). For example, Rudduck and Flutter (2004, pp. 151–152) tell us that "hearing what students have to say about teaching and learning can provide teachers

- a more open perception of young people's capabilities;
- the capacity to see the familiar from a different angle;
- a readiness to change thinking and practice in the light of these perceptions;
- a renewed sense of excitement in teaching;
- a practical agenda for improvement."

"It can help teachers make what they teach more accessible to students. Furthermore, it can contribute to the conceptualization of teaching, learning, and the ways we study them" (Cook-Sather, 2002, p. 3). Student perspective "can also be used to 'break new ground' by offering alternative ways of tackling some of the more pervasive problems faced by schools" (Flutter & Rudduck, 2004, p. 67).

We close this section on the value of student perspective with a less reported but no less important conclusion. That is, seeing schooling through the eyes of children can have positive effects beyond the school. Cook-Sather (2006b, p. 367), for example, pushes us to discern impacts on the world of research: "Student presence and involvement within conversations and efforts that have traditionally been the purview of adults has the potential to affect a cultural shift in educational research and reform." Oldfather (1995, p. 132) adds, "Through our research, we have seen how students' voices may contribute to the scholarly knowledge about teaching, learning, and motivation." Alderson (2008) makes a similar point about the world of policy. Levin (2000) informs us of the potential impact on parents. And Cook-Sather (2006b, p. 367) suggests "that listening to students and building teaching around themes that are relevant to and that emerge from students' own lives can be transformative both personally and politically."

Moving to the more distal objective of student performance, we find that "approaches involving pupil consultation and participation can help to create more positive pupil-teaching relationships"

(Flutter & Rudduck, 2004, p. 13) and new "definitions of what being a student means" (Corbett & Wilson, 1995, p. 12). Listening and seeing can also increase students' motivation for, interests in, commitment to, and engagement with school work (Rudduck & Flutter, 2004; Weinstein, Marshall, Sharp, & Botkin, 1987). Finally, in terms of "educational payoff," analysts reveal that the practice of seeing through student eyes can have positive effects on learning outcomes (Flutter & Rudduck, 2004; Walberg, 1976): "Our evidence suggests that a stronger focus on pupil participation can enhance progress in learning (Rudduck & Flutter, 2004, p. 16).

PART TWO

STUDENT VIEWS OF CULTURE

A Good School #1

A wagon team of adventure

each cart freighted with the mundane made magical

each driven by an expectant guide

each trailer brandishing a certificate of membership

The caravan traveling toward distant
    portals of possibility,

defenders of care on every horizon, guarding each passageway

wagons awash in the glow of hope

Uncharted landscape collectively explored

navigational challenges falling to communal labors

Distinctive tags of friendship decorating each backpack

badges of accomplishments proudly displayed,
    joyfully celebrated

THREE

CARE

> The attribute most frequently mentioned by the students about what created an optimal learning environment was their teachers' willingness to care about them and their ability to bond with them. (Howard, 2001, p. 137)
>
> Students, over and over again, raised the issue of care. What they liked best about school was when people, particularly teachers, cared about them or did special things for them. Dominating their complaints were being ignored, not being cared for and receiving negative treatment. (Poplin, 1992, p. 19)
>
> The academic objectives of schools cannot be met unless teachers provide students with a caring and supportive classroom environment. (Wentzel, 1997, p. 411)

Students have a great deal to say about the culture of their schools. Underlying their insights is the cardinal conclusion we established in Chapter 1, that is, student–teacher relationships compose the bedrock of school culture. Students explain what they see and feel at school in terms of social interactions (Ferreira & Bosworth, 2000; Gibson, Bejinez, Hidalgo, & Rolón, 2004), through relations with teachers in particular or what Oelsner, Lippold, and Greenberg

54 Part Two: Student Views of Culture

(2011, p. 464) refer to as "social bonding." In short, "the relational environment" (Birch & Ladd, 1997, p. 76), "close and affectionate relationships" (Pianta, 1999, p. 82), is the center of gravity in schools defined by supportive cultures (Rodriguez, 2008; Storz, 2008).

> The most surprising finding from her year-long interaction with more than 40 urban high school students was that students preferred to talk about teacher–student relationships—about respect, trust, and fairness—as opposed to curriculum and assessment. (Patterson et al., 2007, pp. 127–128)
>
> A curriculum of caring in a young person's development is brought about through continual involvement in progressively more complex patterns of reciprocal activity. (Kroeger, 2004, p. 52)

Over the last 20 years, a growing body of scholarship has been forming on the topic of caring in the helping professions, including education (Murphy & Torre, 2014). More essential for our purposes here, a small body of knowledge on how caring is seen by students is now available. And it is this subset of information that calls to us here.

> Another persistent theme in our work is the value students place on caring teachers both in the academic realm and beyond. There is a sense that caring is related to the quality of the student teacher relationship, the quality of teaching and learning, and the students' level of care for their own education. Joanne and Marcus both allude to the quality of caring in their remarks. When comparing their schooling experiences to others, students often talk about the central role teachers play, particularly in terms of how teachers are perceived as caring for the students. (Storz, 2007, p. 258)

Chapter Three: Care

We begin with notes that are ribboned throughout this volume. We find, for example, that there is "an assumption of care" in schools and classrooms, teachers perceive care that often eludes students (Taylor-Dunlop & Norton, 1997): "Although it would seem as though caring is a concept that all teachers use in their daily practice, the student data seem to suggest that it is not a common practice by all teachers" (Howard, 2001, p. 141). Poplin (1992, pp. 21–22) makes this point nicely in terms of student feedback to teachers.

> Teachers perceive themselves to be very caring people who went into teaching to give something to youth. Teachers were initially shocked at the degree to which students felt adults inside schools did not care for them. Teachers struggled as they read student comments, trying to articulate how their attention had been focused away from students. Teachers felt they were pressured to cover the curriculum, meet bureaucratic demands and asked to do too many activities unrelated to the students in their classrooms. There is little time left in the day to actually relate with students.

We also report regularly herein that conditions in schools, that is, organizational context, often hinder the development of care (Fielding, 2004b), a reality we see illuminated in the work of Noddings (1988, p. 221):

> If we were to explore seriously the ideas suggested by an ethic of caring for education, we might suggest changes in almost every aspect of schooling: the current hierarchical structure of management, the rigid mode of allocating time, the kind of relationships encouraged, the size of schools and classes, the goals of instruction, modes of evaluation, patterns of interaction, selection of content.

The summative message is that "caring is necessary for transforming schools into successful living and learning environments

(Hayes et al., 1994, p. 16) and teacher caring is "a key factor in students' achievement of success" (Muller et al., 1999, p. 298), including measures of engagement and learning (Birch & Ladd, 1997, Pianta, 1996; Rodriguez, 2008).

Caring is a somewhat difficult concept to corral and to partition into subcomponents (Smylie et al., in press). However, parsimonious and valuable frameworks can be forged, recognizing full well that viable alternatives merit notice. It is this approach that we take here, borrowing and recasting concepts from the array of scholars who expose teacher caring through students' eyes in terms such as knowing students, accepting students, being fair, and so forth. Our approach produces two bins. The first bin contains three states teachers need to cultivate to make caring possible, to create a seedbed for relationships to form and flourish: making themselves available, opening themselves to students, and getting to know and understand youngsters. The second bin contains a series of actions teachers need to undertake more directly to convey caring to youngsters (e.g., to show respect, to demonstrate fairness). We remind ourselves here that the ideas we discuss below are culled from the perspectives of students.

STATES FOR PASTORAL CARE FOR STUDENTS

> I think a good teacher is someone who will bond with the students. (Student, cited by Rodriguez, 2008, p. 776)
>
> They don't really know us. (Student, cited by Storz, 2008, p. 260)

Being Available

The first requirement for caring to flourish is teachers making themselves available to youngsters (Rodriguez, 2008). According to children, good teachers are accessible (Muller et al., 1999; Rudduck, 2007). From the students' perspective this means "teachers being available to talk with pupils about learning and schoolwork, not just about behavior" (Rudduck et al., 1996b, p. 173). We read regularly in the research that according to students, "teachers who cared for them made themselves available to comfort them and were concerned with helping them deal with school and personal problems" (Howard, 2001, p. 133). For some students,

> immediate and frequent contact with school adults and personalized relationships meant having access to school adults during the school day. For others, personalized relationships were significant when students were faced with serious personal challenges often having nothing to do with school. (Rodriguez, 2008, pp. 764–765)

Availability is about teachers who make "help seeking much easier" (Rodriguez, 2008, p. 766), who are "looking out" for youngsters (Rodriguez, 2008, p. 766), and who display a genuine investment in students (Rodriguez, 2008). Essential here, of course, is the issue of time and making time available for accessibility (Roeser et al., 2000) as well as the "personal characteristics" or "temperament" of teachers (Mergendoller & Packer, 1985, p. 591), and the "teachers' sense that accessibility will lead to productive exchanges" (Muller et al., 1999, p. 313).

Being available refers to bonding "done out of love and mutual inclinations" rather than duty (Noddings, 1988, p. 219), out of a sense of humanity (Lipman, 1995), and based "upon trust and rapport" (Gibson et al., 2004, p. 143). What seems to be important here is the reciprocal nature of availability, "mutual reciprocity" (Ferreira & Bosworth, 2000, p. 188). "Both the teacher and the student are deriving pleasure from the learning, from the activities, from the fruits of their shared labor, and from their relationship with each other" (Goldstein, 1999, p. 660). Students tell us about the feelings that power availability, how they see and feel "affective dimensions" (Goldstein, 1999, p. 660) of teachers being there for them (Bru, Stephens, & Torsheim, 2002; Burke & Grosvenor, 2003; Muller et al., 1999)—or not (Taylor-Dunlop & Norton, 1997). For example, in their research Mergendoller and Packer (1985, p. 592) found students who spoke about teachers not being there for them when they "maintained their distance and appeared relatively unconcerned with the details of students' lives, thoughts, and affections." Another student tells the story in this manner: "Teachers in high school don't care about us. I think that they do not like us. They never answer questions and they make you feel stupid for asking. They never offer to help you after class. After awhile, you just stop asking" (Quiroz, 2001, p. 332).

Opening Selves as Persons

The second aspect of creating the seedbed for caring to grow in schools is the willingness of teachers to "redefine the traditional boundaries between 'teachers' and 'students'" (Bragg, 2007, p. 669), to create the state in which students feel they can "relate to the teacher" (Shade, Kelly, & Oberg, 1997, p. 47). The critical point here is that teachers open themselves as persons, not solely as organizational functionaries (Adams & Forsyth, 2009; Antrop-Gonzalez, 2006; Kennedy, 2011). Teacher involvement is not limited "to that dictated by roles" (Hayes et al., 1994, p. 4). They are not seen primarily as "remote authoritative individuals" (Burke & Grosvenor, 2003, p. 80). They "lessen the social distance" between themselves and youngsters (Cabello & Terrell, 1994, p. 21). The teacher permits youngsters to see that she or he has needs, emotions, and interests not unlike the students themselves.

> Several of the students talked about how surprised they were to see a teacher who was willing to show such emotion and how that made them care more for her, because they could remember when they had lost loved ones and how it made them feel. They contended that these episodes helped them to see their teacher as a human being who had emotions just like their own. (Howard, 2001, pp. 138–139)

The teacher is "not simply a textbook source from which the student may or may not learn" (Noddings, cited in Goldstein, 1996, p. 659). Caring teachers "diminish the power line between student and teacher and humanize the teacher as person" (Rodriguez, 2008, p. 765). "Personal relationships" in addition to "functional relationships have a central place in teacher-student connections" (Fielding, 2004a, p. 209)—there is a "personal rather than a functional mode of human relation" (Fielding, 2004a, p. 210). "The self that teachers offer is a student self rather than a career self" (Farrell, 1990, p. 25). Such teachers reflect humanity (Davis, 2003) and "humanized" (Mitra & Gross, 2009, p. 528) teaching. Teachers do not see students as others. They do not "maintain self–other separation" or promote "psychological/emotional distance" (Heshusius, 1995, p. 118).

> Here teachers just approach their students more on equal footing so they're not, teachers aren't always these like big, scary authority figures that you have to like rebel against. They're, you know, they're not, you know, they're people, and they have connections with the students, and at a lot of schools they forget that. . . . [Another school] was much more of a conservative, much more based around the authority of the administration. It was just a classic high school. There were detentions. The teachers didn't have to teach. . . . The relationships were almost always on an authoritarian basis. There was no, like, sort of, it just didn't have the community that [Starlight] has. (Student, cited by Johnson, 2009, p. 111)

Contrary to conventional wisdom, teachers who care befriend students in meaningful ways (Trickett & Quinlan, 1979; Veaco & Brandon, 1986). They act with the knowledge that a personality is touching the lives of children (Trickett & Quinlan, 1979). Teachers remain vulnerable (Adams, 2010). They expose themselves to "psychological risk" (McMillan, 1996, p. 316). "They demonstrate connectedness with students and extend relationships beyond the classroom" (Lipman, 1995, p. 203).

Understanding Students

The third piece or state of cultivating the seedbed for caring is the work teachers undertake to understand students as persons (Johnson, 2009; McLaughlin, 1994; Moos & Moos, 1978). Or, as one student tells it, "I think a good teacher is one that not only wants the student to learn but looks out for them. And like understands where they're coming from" (Rodriguez, 2008, p. 225). Students consistently report that "a good teacher wants to know the students" (Fine et al., 2007, pp. 813–814) and understands their "need to be understood" (Mitra & Gross, 2009, p. 529). They "want their teachers to understand their needs" even when they have difficulty conveying those needs to their teachers (Arnot et al., 2004, p. 86). They prefer teachers who have the ability "to read [their] signals accurately [and] to respond contingently on the basis of those signals" (Pianta, 1999, p. 67). Caring teachers, according to students, demonstrate a "quiet sensitivity to the needs and problems of their students" (Arnot et al., 2004, p. 29). They take the time to "find out about students' backgrounds" (Dillon, 1989, p. 242), to learn to "see a class of individuals rather than just a class of kids" (Burke & Grosvenor, 2003, p. 871). Caring teachers are especially adept at getting to know students who bring "cultural scripts" that are not well matched to the organizational scripts of their schools (Booker, 2006; Fine, 1986; First & Carrera, 1988). They are good at demonstrating "a sensitive understanding that life may be more difficult for children who do not have the advantages of [a] more stable home" (Rak & Patterson, 1996, p. 371).

Caring teachers take the time and effort to "know about the larger pieces of children's lives in order to make sense of their perspectives—[both] within and outside the school" (Dahl, 1995, p. 129). As we have noted above and unpack in more detail below, caring teachers take the time to listen to students (Cruddas, 2001). Uncaring teachers, on the other hand, "don't know what the kids like, or something, and they just do it their way, and not take the kids into consideration, or anything" (Student, cited by Mergendoller & Packer, 1985, p. 592). As we saw with the other two pieces of the seedbed of cultivation examined above, getting to know and understand students entails a willingness to go beyond the confines of the classroom (McLaughlin, 1994; Smerdon, 2002) and to take the extra steps to overcome the student animosity and depersonalization that is not infrequent in schools (Mitra & Gross, 2009; Murphy & Torre, 2014; Rodriguez, 2008).

We close this section with two reminders of why knowing and understanding students as persons is so critical:

> In educational settings, the basis for decisions for appropriate and effective curriculum lies with the teacher's willingness to understand the students, their interests, and their individuality and to include the students' perspective in planning classroom activities. (Hayes et al., 1994, p. 4)

> By knowing students better, teachers are likely to worry more about their failures, provide more help directed toward improvement, take responsibility for disciplining everyone, and invest more fully in improving the whole school. (Davis, 2003, p. 218)

DIMENSIONS OF CARING FOR STUDENTS

> Exemplary teachers sent a common message of caring to students by emphasizing collaboration, support, respect, and pride. (Cabello & Terrell, 1994, p. 21)
>
> Goodlad found that students' perceptions of their teachers related to whether or not their teachers were concerned about them. (Veaco & Brandon, 1986, p. 222)
>
> It is not surprising that respect and fairness feature so prominently in pupil's taxonomies of the qualities of a good teacher. (Rudduck & Flutter, 2004, p. 76)

Showing Concern

In the section just completed, we examined the major states or conditions that need to be in place for caring and supportive teacher–student relations to take root and flourish. In this section, we explore the specific action dimensions that students tell us characterize caring teachers. To begin with, students talk in general about the concern for their well-being broadly defined that they feel from teachers, "a feeling of genuine concern and empathy" (Heshusius, 1995, p. 119). "These accounts may suggest that students are able to recognize teachers' desire for wanting their students to perform well academically and socially. More important, the students responses seemed to convey a belief that teachers who were not as emotionally and passionately concerned with their learning were teachers who 'don't even care about us'" (Howard, 2001, p. 138). Students provide numerous clues about how they see and define teacher concern for them. The notion of tenacity and rugged care are visible here, teachers taking interest in students (Brewster & Fager, 2000; Quiroz, 2001; Rak & Patterson, 1996), staying on and with young people to do their best work (Weinstein, 1983). We know, for example, that caring is seen by students when teachers show interest and invest in them (Galletta & Ayala, 2008; Croninger & Lee, 2001; Wilson & Corbett, 1999). This includes devoting considerable personal and professional capital into one's work with children and the development and honoring of reciprocal obligations (Antrop-Gonzalez & De Jesus, 2006).

It includes being accessible to students on both academic and personal fronts (Goddard, 2003; Hattie, 2009; Noguera, 1996), "in their education and their lives" (Patterson et al., 2007, p. 128). Investment tells students that they are acknowledged for who they are as persons and for their potential (Ma, 2003; Steele, 1992). At the deepest level, it includes a ferocious unwillingness to permit students to founder or fail (Farrell, 1990). Students see "teachers as truly interested and invested in enabling [them] to succeed" (Wilson & Corbett, 1999, p. 73). They feel that adults are willing to provide personal attention (Cooper et al., 2005; Cotton, 2000; Rodriguez, 2008).

Concern also addresses the important ideas of "the teacher's willing involvement with students" (Veaco & Brandon, 1986, p. 226), a ferocious commitment to providing needed help (Mergendoller & Packer, 1985), and "promoting a feeling of confidence or faith that things will work out" (Rak & Patterson, 1996, p. 370). "Mean teachers," on the other hand, were characterized as "uncaring and uninterested in their students" (Mergendoller & Packer, 1985, p. 595). They "made it difficult for students to work successfully by failing to provide the individual help they needed to complete assigned work" (Mergendoller & Packer, 1985, p. 595). Rather than concern, students felt the pressure of teacher apathy (Howard, 2001). They "mentioned teachers' lack of caring and failure to show concern ... as factors contributing to their poor performance" (Howard, 2001, p. 138). Heshusius (1995, p. 119) links the notion of concern, both positive and negative, to our earlier discussion of teachers' willingness to open themselves to students:

> Something akin to identification with the youngster took place. This seemed to dissolve some of the self-centered concerns and the resulting self-other separation. As a result, a more complete mode of attending was engaged in. This shift typically occurred well into the conversation when a certain comfort level had settled in and a spark of real interest in the youngster made it easier for the adult to relinquish concerns around the self.

Challenging Students

Care is also fundamentally about challenging students to meet and exceed robust expectations (Alexander & Entwisle, 1996;

Johnson & Asera, 1999; Roth & Brooks-Gunn, 2003). There is abundant evidence on this point: "Teachers who push students prove to be an important dimension to the personalized student–adult relationship" (Rodriguez, 2008, p. 772). Perhaps the essential point here is the integration of push and press with the elements of care (Murphy, 2013), a practice labeled as "hard caring" by Antrop-Gonzalez & De Jesus (2006, p. 413) and "rugged care" by Shouse (1996, p. 48). When this cocktail of push and support is in place, students are able to see challenge "as coming from a place of teacher concern about the students themselves" (Patterson et al., 2007, p. 136). Challenge also means providing students with as much responsibility as they can handle (Joselowsky, 2007) and upholding a commitment to help them succeed (Wilson & Corbett, 1999). Obstacles are acknowledged but they are not accepted as explanations for lack of performance (Rodriguez, 2008; Shouse, 1996).

Concern for students in a caring environment, students tell us, is laced with clear and high expectations (Newmann, 1981; Rodriguez 2008; Wilson & Corbett, 1999). They tell us that their teachers ask a lot of them—and provide accompanying support. There is strong academic and social press (Ancess, 2003; Johnson & Asera, 1999). They place higher order cognitive demands on students, moving beyond basic skills to higher order thinking (Battistich et al., 1995; Marks, 2000). They expect students "to be active builders of knowledge, rather than passive recipients" (Newmann et al., 1992, p. 185). In schools where caring concern is engrained in the culture, teachers provide more challenging assignments and tasks (Fredricks et al., 2004), "more complex and cognitively challenging class work" (Marks, 2000, p. 157), and greater depth of understanding (Newmann, 1981). They expect students to take intellectual risks and reward them for doing so (Cooper, 1996, 1999).

In strong communities, care is more than providing high expectations and challenge. Caring teachers take away the possibility of passive involvement. Students perceive that they are not permitted to check out or drift through class (Ancess, 2003; Huberman, Parrish, Hannan, Arellanes, & Shambaugh 2011). They are pulled into the game. No spectators are allowed. Neither are students allowed to easily accept failure. "Teachers not only believe that students [can] complete their work, they do everything possible to make that happen" (Wilson & Corbett, 1997, p. 77). In environments of concern, "teachers make it harder to fail than succeed" (Ancess,

2000, p. 74). They "stay on students" to complete their work (Wilson & Corbett, 1999, p. 80), requiring them to bring their A games to the classroom (Murphy & Torre, 2014). Students believe that teachers are there to help them succeed, not simply teach subject matter. They push and pull students to the goal line (Ancess, 2003; Darling-Hammond et al., 2002; Oakes & Guiton, 1995) and acknowledge and celebrate successes along the way. Classes are rich with extra help and teacher-guided second chances (Wilson & Corbett, 1999). Teachers are particularly adept at addressing "patterns of behaviors and performances that are unproductive and problematic" (Ancess, 2003, p. 76) for student development (Cooper, 1996).

Caring communities for students close down opportunities for students to select pathways of disengagement and disaffiliation. They also preclude the selection of failure in the face of rigorous expectations and standards (Ancess, 2000; Huberman et al., 2011; Shear et al., 2008). Efforts here pivot on the positive perspective of assets-based thinking and the concomitant elimination of deficit-based thinking (Antrop-Gonzalez & De Jesus, 2006; Hattie, 2009). Possibilities hold the high ground: "Youth are resources to be developed, not problems to be fixed" (Bloomberg, Ganey, Alba, Quintero, & Alvarez-Alcantara, 2003, p. 50). All of this "hard care" is layered over significant opportunities for students to be successful (Antrop-Gonzalez, 2006; Strahan, 2003).

Providing Autonomy

Caring is also defined in part by student-perceived choice and autonomy. Rudduck (2007, p. 603) introduces this point when he reports that "student voice challenges familiar expectations about who does what in schools [and that] many matters that have traditionally been assumed to be the responsibility of teachers could instead be discussed and negotiated with students." Thus we see that the student is an element of autonomy (Cruddas, 2001; Davis, 2003), although as we revealed in Chapter 2, "For the most part schooling is structured so that student opinions, voices, and critical thoughts remain silenced ... classrooms are organized more around control than conversation [and] more around autonomy of the teacher than autonomy of students" (Fine, 1986, p. 403). "These students suggest that the overall relational climate was driven by either overlooking or negating students' needs and devaluing their voices" (Rodriguez, 2008, p. 776).

Autonomy is seen as "the opportunity to make choices" (Flutter & Rudduck, 2004, p. 51) and to exercise "autonomous self-expression" (Roeser et al., 2000, p. 459). "Students spoke positively about those teachers who they felt encouraged initiative and self expression" (Mergendoller & Packer, 1985, p. 589), those who encouraged students to pursue avenues of exploration (Kennedy, 2011; Pianta & Steinberg, 1992)—a form of empowerment (Wallerstein & Bernstein, 1988) also described by students as independence of decision making and action (Fisher & Fraser, 1983; Mergendoller & Packer, 1985). "The principle of autonomy" (Rudduck & Flutter, 2004, p. 135) also features encouraging students to assume responsibility for learning (Rudduck & Flutter, 2004; Garmezy, 1991).

The central descriptors used to explain autonomy are control, authority, and power (McMillan, 1996). "Where power resides and how broadly it is distributed is an important variable in understanding the character and culture of a school" (Maehr & Midgley, 1996, p. 60) and the character of care (Murphy & Torre, 2014). Seeing caring through the eyes of students carries us toward ideas such as "control over your learning" (Rudduck, 2007, p. 598), the belief "that you can make a difference in how things are done" (Rudduck, 2007, p. 598), and "steadily increasing opportunities for autonomy [and] democratic competence" (McNeely, Nonnemaker, & Blum, 2002, p. 138). It is about "teachers giving up some control and handing it over to students" (Smyth, 2006, p. 282).

> In contrast, there was sometimes a sense of quiet outrage pervading students' descriptions of teachers who refused to let them sharpen pencils when necessary, work with other students, or engage in activities perceived as essential. Students saw no reason for these restrictions and occasionally expressed resentment toward teachers who constrained their activities in unjust ways. (Mergendoller & Packer, 1985, p. 589)

We close with a point laced through all the dimensions of care: Autonomy can make a difference; it "can be harvested to appropriate academic tasks with favorable results" (Mergendoller & Packer, 1985, p. 591), including enhanced motivation (Wentzel, 2002), "sense of personal mastery" (McMillan, 1996, p. 319), engagement, and academic achievement (Murphy & Torre, 2014).

Acting Fairly

Students almost always place teacher fairness near the top of the list of dimensions of caring (Muller et al., 1999); that is, it features "prominently in pupils' taxonomies of the qualities of a good teacher" (Rudduck & Flutter, 2004, p. 76). Students have particularly well-honed antennae when it comes to matters of justice, rights, and equity (Dillon, 1989; Cabello & Terrell, 1994; Slaughter-Defoe & Carlson, 1996) or what they describe as fairness (Thorkildsen, 1989; Weinstein et al., 1987). Students do a nice job of seeing the parts of the fairness mosaic and how the parts interlock and operate. At the heart of this dimension of caring are student perspectives on "distributive justice" (Weinstein, 1983, p. 301), or differential treatment of youngsters by teachers (Arnot et al., 2004; Burke & Grosvenor, 2003; Weinstein et al., 1987), and whether they see such interactions within adult–student relationships as appropriate (Willms, 2003). According to one student, the "teacher should never focus all their attention on one pupil, it should be equal for everyone" (Burke & Grosvenor, 2003, p. 88). Another youngster expounds on fairness as follows: "You need fairness; teachers shouldn't show favoritism. To make a good teacher you have to be fair by expecting the students to follow your rules and treating them fairly back" (Burke & Grosvenor, 2003, p. 84).

According to these and other students, fairness has a good deal to do with the presence or absence of teacher favoritism (Wentzel, 2002): "Fair does not show favoritism. It is always fair, does not show prejudice or favoritism" (Veaco & Brandon, 1986, p. 226). "And he treats everyone like that. He doesn't have favorites. He treats everybody equally" (Patterson et al., 2007, p. 131). There is "fairness to all pupils irrespective of their class, gender, ethnicity, or academic status" (Rudduck et al., 1996b, p. 172). In caring classes, students see "expressions of equity and uniformity of treatment" (Hayes et al., 1994, p. 10). "They tell us that teachers are interested in each and every child" (Hayes et al., p. 10). Students often see fairness illuminated in their teachers' grading practices. Fairness is also viewed in terms of teachers providing students with the tools and opportunities to be successful, not allowing them to flounder (Willms, 2003) nor providing them with a disproportionate share of negative comments (Weinstein, 1983).

As they do with many of the elements or dimensions of care, students routinely see themselves and their peers on the lower end of the fairness continuum (Arnot et al., 2004; Cruddas, 2001), especially in classes of teachers that they judged to be "mean." Researchers tell us that these student perceptions are often quite accurate (Hamilton, 1983; Zanger, 1993), that students are good judges of differential or preferential treatment in classes, often between high-and low-achieving students (Weinstein, 1983; Weinstein et al., 1987). For example, Weinstein and team (1987, p. 1087) present results that "suggest that individual children, regardless of grade, perceive more differential teacher treatment in 'class-identified' high differential treatment classrooms than in low differential treatment classrooms."

Fairness, or what one student describes as "know[ing] that you are your word" (Muller et al., 1999, p. 299), has consequences. It opens or closes the door for student commitment to school and respect for teachers (Arnot et al., 2004; Muller et al., 1999). McMillan (1996, p. 320) refers to "the principle of justice as a cohesive force" for classrooms and student–teacher relationships. Unfairness is associated with disengagement and dropping out of school (Murdock, Anderman, & Hodge, 2000), while "the perceived equality of class membership" (Walberg & Anderson, 1968, p. 417) is linked to a number of desired outcomes, including self-awareness, investment and effort, engagement, and learning (Muller et al., 1999; Walberg & Anderson, 1968; Weinstein et al., 1987).

Showing Respect

The fifth area of teacher practice in developing relational care is respect (Ancess, 2003; Antrop-Gonzalez & De Jesus, 2006; Hattie, 2009); that is, "another way that the students described caring by their teachers was through the ways teachers showed them respect" (Howard, 2001, p. 139). Students consistently define these teachers who help them succeed as educators who convey respect (Hayes et al., 1994). "Preferred teachers" (Veaco & Brandon, 1986, p. 227) or good teachers are defined by students as "treat[ing] students with respect and consideration" (Noddings, 1988, p. 223): "Studies querying students regarding their views about what makes good teachers reveal strikingly similar conclusions. Students frequently express that good teachers ... show them respect" (Kennedy, 2011, p. 8).

They help students fit (Nichols, 2006). On the other hand, students make it clear that "you can't succeed in a place where no one respects you for what you are" (Zanger, 1993, p. 175).

> The basic human right of being treated like people was something that pupils frequently found it necessary to assert. They wanted to be treated with respect, both by their teachers and by their classmates, and in their experience the social conditions of the classroom—including teacher–pupil dialogue—were such as to make this uncertain. (Arnot et al., 2004, p. 86)

And, as we touched on above, there is a generalized feeling among students, especially students placed at risk by society, "that teachers must give respect to get it" (Rodriguez, 2008, p. 767). Stepping up a level, "research in elementary and middle grades has revealed that students perceive caring from teachers as comprising both a demonstrated commitment to student learning as well as general respect" (Murdock & Miller, 2003, p. 385). They often equate respect with being treated as individuals (Cruddas, 2001; Goff & Goddard, 1999).

Students often see respect in terms of not being disrespected by their teachers. They define disrespect in terms of teachers looking down on them, treating them as if they are dumb, or displaying anger, especially in public (Mergendoller & Packer, 1985). Disrespectful teachers are "always in a power struggle with students" (Taylor-Dunlop & Norton, 1997, p. 275) and go out of their way to "denigrate or embarrass them" (Veaco & Brandon, 1986, p. 227). Relatedly, students see disrespect when teachers "underestimate or ignore their capacities" (Flutter & Rudduck, 2004, p. 27): "Teachers often abuse their authority. It is often seen as acceptable for the young to be treated with disrespect or to be humiliated. There is a very pronounced respect double standard in schools, which manifests itself in the way students are spoken to" (Burke & Grosvenor, 2003, p. 86). Arnot and team (2004, p. 48) remind us of the costs of disrespectful episodes: "Trust in school is breached by such moments." In addition, interpersonal understandings and adjustments are impossible (Goldstein, 1999).

Chapter Three: Care 69

Caring via respect is always described by youngsters as teachers taking the interest and time to listen to them (Cabello & Terrell, 1994; Hayes et al., 1994; Heshusius, 1995). Caring schools are "listening schools, [places] with lots of discussion between students and teachers" (Rudduck & Flutter, 2004, p. 12).

> Apart from noticing when students put forth their best efforts, these students indicated that teachers who cared listened to them. (Slaughter-Defoe & Carlson, 1996, p. 67)
>
> A good teacher is someone who's actually willing to teach you and listen to you. (Rodriguez, 2008, p. 776)
>
> I think that they knew that in an ideal situation, they wanted teachers that would listen to them, to be able to debate things that mattered to them, and that they couldn't envisage learning in an environment where that wasn't taken into account. And it isn't always taken into account, but the fact that they value it so highly and that they could see that other people valued it, has got to be a good starting point. We're on fertile ground here. (Bragg, 2007, p. 666)

Exemplary teachers in the Cabello and Terrell (1994, p. 21) study "communicated caring by listening to what students had to say and by supporting their contributions." Listening for students implies that student "voices are invited . . . and honored" (Oldfather, 1995, p. 135) and that teachers "listen authentically" (Arnot et al., 2004, p. 80). Teachers are easy to talk to, treat conversations in confidence (Veaco & Brandon, 1986) and relate to these conversations (Taylor-Dunlop & Norton, 1997).

> Students may not know they have a voice. Or, if they know they have one, they consciously repress it when in the presence of adults in authority. Consequently, patience in the process of letting student voices emerge is essential, as is active listening, probing, and the form of nonjudgmental 'brainstorming.' (Lincoln, 1995, p. 91)

Students feel heard, especially at "vulnerable moments" (Kennedy, 2011, p. 18). They learn to "take their voices seriously" (Johnston & Nicholls, 1995, p. 98).

The extent to which teachers honor students' ethnic, cultural, and racial backgrounds is also seen as an important element of respect (Hamilton, 1983; Shade et al., 1997; Zanger, 1993). Students see teacher behavior here on a continuum with disrespect and marginalization at one end and affirmation and respect at the other (Burke & Grosvenor, 2003; Miron & Lauria, 1998). Actions that support and confirm students' backgrounds are viewed as respectful (Gonzalez & Padilla, 1997; Noguera, 1996; Scanlan & Lopez, 2012). So too are behaviors that honor the assets that students bring to the classroom (Hattie, 2009). Unfortunately, because teachers often "do not understand the cultures of the children they teach" (First & Carrera, 1988, p. 51) they often fail "to allow students to build bridges between their own identity and society in ways that recognize their role in both cultures" (Shade et al., 1997, p. 55). There is considerable evidence that indeed "teachers fail to capitalize on the motivational forces" (Quiroz, 2001, p. 344) embedded in these identities (Mitra & Gross, 2009). Students, in turn, experience "cultural insensitivity" (First & Carrera, 1988, p. 56). They decipher such behavior as demonstrating lack of respect at best and disrespect at worst (McLean-Donaldson, 1994; Muller et al., 1999).

Not surprisingly, research confirms what students tell us, that is, respect makes a difference in the quality of schooling. "Respect and disrespect are critical to relationships and learning" (Rodriguez, 2008, p. 768). Respect helps enhance student motivation. We also know that "middle school students' perceptions that their teachers promote mutual respect ... have been shown to predict their self-reported academic self efficacy and self regulation" (Anderman, 2003, p. 9). Respect "ameliorates the general decline in belonging as students mature (Anderman, 2003, p. 9). "For many students respect precedes engagement. ... Students' voices across schools demonstrate that school culture that prioritizes respectful relationships can significantly mediate academic engagement and disengagement" (Rodriguez, 2008, p. 767–768).

Valuing Students

The final dimension of caring as seen by youngsters is being valued by teachers (Wallerstein & Bernstein, 1988; Wentzel, 1997), teachers "showing students that they are valued members of a community" (Sagor, 1996, p. 39). Valuing unfolds when teachers believe that the pupils' world is worth becoming engaged with (Rudduck et al., 1996). Caring teachers "send messages of dedication through their actions, their faces, their dress, and their persona. Children [are] able to sense that they [are] special and important to teachers" (Shade et al., 1997, p. 45). Part of valuing is the demonstration of "concern for students and families" (Lipman, 1995, p. 205). Another element is "placing value on each child . . . holding out the expectation that each child will succeed in life" (Rak & Patterson, 1996, p. 372). Students believe they are valued when "the teacher provides attention outside of school, is accessible, and is interested in the student's whole life" (Hayes et al., 1994, p. 9). Students tell us that they are valued when they are seen as individuals and as complex and whole persons (Shultz & Cook-Sather, 2001; Davis, 2003). They describe a "teacher–student relationship characterized by warmth, the absence of conflict, and open communication" (Wentzel, 2002, p. 288)—one about reaching out (Birch & Ladd, 1997; Ryan et al., 1994; Shade et al., 1997). While there is tension between individualization and fairness, students perceive that good teachers find the right balance between the two (Howard, 2001). Student opinions are valued (Zanger, 1993), teachers have faith in children (Muller et al., 1999), and students feel that they count (Mitra & Gross, 2009).

Valuing is also defined by trust (Lipman, 1995). Teachers, students tell us, demonstrate care by believing in children (Arnot et al., 2004). In the Bragg (2007, p. 669) study, for example,

> Children came up with categories they saw as being the main qualities of a good teacher and then voted for those they most agreed with. The quality that the children thought was most important was that the teachers trusted them. . . . The whole issue of trust is absolutely critical.

As was the case with respect, "trust is clearly linked to race" (Miron & Lauria, 1998, p. 204): "The problem of establishing and institutionalizing trusting relations between minority children and adolescents and school agents cannot be underestimated, since it represents a root cause for why the former disengage (psychically or physically) from the school" (Stanton-Salazar, 1997, p. 17).

FOUR

SUPPORT, SAFETY, AND MEMBERSHIP

> School environments that have high levels of such features as teacher support are associated with positive academic and social development for all students. (Smerdon, 2002, p. 289)
>
> Clearly, safe schools are essential for fostering increased student involvement. (McNeal, 1999, p. 298)

In Chapter 3, we investigated how students see and talk about care. Here we turn the lens onto student perspectives on three related dimensions of culture: support, safety, and membership.

SOCIAL SUPPORT

> The responsibility teachers have, or should have, to provide social support is very evident in the comments of the pupils. (Chaplain, 1996b, p. 123)
>
> *(Continued)*

> (Continued)
>
> Recently, a national survey of adolescents revealed that the single most common factor associated with healthy outcomes across all domains assessed was that youth reported having a relationship with an adult that they experienced as supportive to them. (Pianta, 1999, p. 66)
>
> An awareness of the most appropriate type of support and how to provide it is important to teachers concerned about helping young people. (Chaplain, 1996b, p. 116)

Support is the second of the core elements of productive culture for students (Conchas, 2001; Goodenow & Grady, 1993; Murphy & Torre, 2014). As is the case for care, students tell us that it operates on two fronts. On the one hand, support buffers students from events that can damage them and their success in school (Bloomberg et al., 2003; Demaray & Malecki, 2002a; Pianta & Steinberg, 1992). Or as Jackson and Warren (2000, p. 1452) so nicely capture the idea: "Social support is a possible immunity to the effects of life events" such as stress and sense of hopelessness: "Supportive relationships may compensate for 'risk'" (Davis, 2003, p. 217). Concomitantly, support unleashes a host of positive actions in the service of students (Demaray & Malecki, 2002b; Rak & Patterson, 1996). Through researchers, students help us see that this norm of support is most critical as youngsters mature, with students who lack a dense web of support outside the school, and for students placed in peril by society (Croninger & Lee, 2001; Heshusius, 1995; Murphy & Tobin, 2011). Support can best be thought of as the extension of help by teachers coupled with students' understanding that they can count on that assistance (Ancess, 2003; Antrop-Gonzalez & De Jesus, 2006; Louis & Marks, 1998). As we discussed in Chapter 1, students tell us that it is personalized relationships with teachers that make help seeking and the provision of assistance part of the culture (Demaray & Malecki, 2002a; Rodriguez, 2008). The starting point here is that "the teacher–child relationship may serve important support functions for children" (Birch & Ladd, 1997, p. 61). "Children who share a close relationship with the teacher may perceive the school environment as a supportive one" (p. 70). Pupils see teachers as there to "support them through difficulties" (Flutter & Rudduck, 2004, p. 27), to be available (Mergendoller & Packer, 1985). Central is teachers' "understanding that their supportive role appears to play a significant part on students' attitudes about teachers" and their school experience in general (Demaray & Malecki, 2002b, p. 314).

Support is tightly yoked to the norm of care (see Chapter 3). Indeed, the two share a good deal of conceptual and applied space (Bru et al., 2002; Roth & Brooks-Gunn, 2003). Perhaps the most appropriate way to think about the two norms is to observe that much of the ability of schools to create support is a function of caring connections between students and teachers (Rodriguez, 2008). Getting to know students and creating personal relationships are important in their own right. The maximum benefit occurs, however, when teachers use these linkages to support the academic and social development of students (Ancess, 2003; Croninger & Lee, 2001).

Looking at support through the eyes of students carries us directly to the principles undergirding this norm. That is, the forms of support and the subelements of support take on meaning to the extent that these principles ground work. One essential principle is that "the support available is oriented toward fostering empowering forms of human development" (Stanton-Salazar, 1997, p. 22), rather than student dependency on teachers, a condition that can actually prove harmful to the maturation of children (Birch & Ladd, 1997). A second principle is that support is available to all youngsters. Students who "are seen as the least socially attractive" (Chaplain, 1996b, pp. 126–127) are not excluded. Third, support should "facilitate the accumulation and active utilization of diversified social capital" (Stanton-Salazar, 1997, p 22). Fourth, while quantity per se is not a critical element of support (Cotterell, 1992), webs of relationships can be valuable (Taylor-Dunlop & Norton, 1997). Fifth, for support to act as a "true insurance system" (Stanton-Salazar, 1997, p. 20), especially for students placed at risk, it often needs to problematize the existing institutional dynamics in schools (Quiroz, 2001; Stanton-Salazar, 1997). We also learn from children that "to be effective, it is essential for support to be perceived as *available* and *appropriate* by the pupils" (Chaplain, 1996b, p. 115). Finally, support should increase closeness between students and teachers.

Students' insights allow us to distill overlapping types of support in personalized school cultures. In particular, analysts of student perspectives highlights the importance of emotional support (Crosnoe, 2011; Demaray & Malecki, 2002a), social support (Goddard, Salloum, & Berebitsky, 2009; Jackson & Warren, 2000), and academic support (Ancess, 2003; Antrop-Gonzalez & De Jesus, 2006). Our attention here is on emotional and social support. We examine academic support in Part 3 of the book. As did Sarason and colleagues (cited in Cotterell, 1992, p. 29), we see emotional and social attention as "the extent to which an individual is accepted, loved, and involved in relationships with open communication."

As with all the norms of productive culture, support can be defined by its essential elements or by core categories (Moos, 1978). It is useful to think of these ingredients as overlapping and intertwined strands in a web of assistance. The first norm is *teacher availability* (Arnot et al., 2004). As students tell us, the lynchpin is student access.

> Just acknowledge someone. Just know that they're there. When you walk by, give them a little nod or something. (Student, cited by Cook-Sather & Shultz, 2001, p. 4)
>
> She liked her new school. When asked, "What do you think of it here?" she replied, "I think it's cool because it's not a really big school, and like the teachers can really pay attention to you. So if you're having a problem, they can come to you and tell you, 'Well this is wrong,' or whatever. And when my grades are low, I can always know that I could go to a teacher and ask them and they're not always crowded with kids." She went on to say that she fit in primarily because of the teachers. "I think I fit in here because the, you know, like I said, the school is not too big, and I usually feel really comfortable when I could talk to the teachers or the aides and tell them, you know, just pop in. I just like talking to them and that's one way that I feel like I fit in." (Nichols, 2006, pp. 265–266)

Without contact, it is impossible to make supportive relationships come to life (Reitzug & Patterson, 1998; Rodriguez, 2008). For support to power up attachment and subsequent student commitment and engagement, and to enhance academic and social learning, the quality and depth of interactions between students and teachers needs to increase (Chaplain, 1996a). The time dimension here, a direct measure of students' judgments of teacher commitment, can be addressed in an assortment of ways. School expectations for student participation in teacher-facilitated academic and social activities are important. So too are teachers' intentional communication of accessibility (Ancess, 2003). Increasing the ratio of adults to students can create time for relationships to take root and flourish (Noguera, 1996). Enhancing proximity between teachers and students is helpful (Arnot et al., 2004; Opdenakker et al., 2012). Ancess (2003, p. 27) describes this as "creating regular and spontaneous opportunities for frequent contact." Students routinely describe it as being paid attention to (Taylor-Dunlop & Norton, 1997) and teachers being there as resources in times of need (Cooper et al., 2005; Cruddas, 2001): "You can always count on them" (Cooper et al., 2005, p. 18). Teacher interest surfaces routinely when we listen to student descriptions of support (Chaplain, 1996a). Students feel that they are "able to discuss intimate thoughts and feelings" in supportive relationships with teachers (Berndt & Perry, 1986, p. 641).

> The unique thing about our school is that we get attention—sometimes individual attention from teachers and stuff and sometimes the principal. The teachers sometimes say that they're open to help you . . . and I've noticed that this year from a lot of teachers. They are actually willing to help and willing to do stuff with you and stay after school. (Student, cited by Rodriguez, 2008, p. 769)

Both quality and depth of support can be increased through an emphasis on "extended, rather than limited, role relationships" (Newmann, 1981, p. 554) (e.g., as classroom teacher, advisor, and cocurricular program sponsor). Engagement in a range of activities rather than a single function is preferable (Ancess, 2003; Newmann, 1981). Social and academic domains both can be used to enrich student–teacher relationships (Fredricks et al., 2004), and multiple dimensions within each domain provide the hooks for linkages. A focus on "guidance and friendship inside and outside the classroom" (Antrop-Gonzalez, 2006, p. 289) is helpful. Before-school, during-school, and after-school times can be turned into avenues that foster relationships in the service of supportive communities for students. Both one-on-one connections (e.g., an advisor-advisee relationship) and linkages formed in groups (e.g., a coach) can be the basis of providing support (Demaray & Malecki, 2002a; Woloszyk, 1996). A focus on both formal and informal interactions opens the door to the formation of teacher–student attachments that promote student support (Ancess, 2003; Joselowsky, 2007). Finally, training for teachers about the importance of content of the principles and norms of support for students is essential (Roth, Brooks-Gunn, Murray, & Foster, 1998).

The second element of support is the *provision of assistance* in the face of student help seeking or intuited need for such help (Adams & Forsyth, 2009; Cabello & Terrell, 1994; Croninger & Lee, 2001). For example, in Miron and Lauria's report (1998, p. 203), students said they knew that teachers supported them because they were helpful: "Like I say, you know, they'll try to help you. If you['re] having problems they'll talk to you and offer you help on the side or stuff, or you can come in the morning or after school for tutoring or whatever." Teachers are seen by students as building rather than "undermining confidence by putting you (students) down" (Arnot et al., 2004, p. 46). "Teachers wouldn't be able to pick on the children" (Burke & Grosvenor, 2003, p. 113). Informal and formal counseling is often noted in the research here (Raywid, 1995). Navigational assistance is also discussed. Assistance in helping children learn to work with each other is also underscored in the research on support (Cabello & Terrell, 1994), helping students to build a shared community and a "shared class history" (p. 19). So too is the provision of assistance with school work (Antrop-Gonzalez, 2006; Croninger & Lee, 2001) and with helping pupils make transitions in life and schooling (Patterson et al., 2007). Included here is help during school transitions, for example, from elementary to middle school (Patterson et al., 2007); during enrollment in new schools, that is, family transitions; and during what students refer to as the inequities of teacher turnover in their schools (Jackson & Warren, 2000; Maguin & Loeber, 1996; Storz, 2008). Assistance in terms of extended roles for teachers beyond the classroom is seen as a form of institutional support by children. Students seem to be especially sensitive to help when they have "personal problems," "get into trouble" (Hayes et al., 1994, p. 10), and have "a history of academic failure and behavioral problems" (Kennedy, 2011, p. 19): As one student tells us, "She makes sure, if we need help, she'll help us" (Kennedy, 2011, p. 19). Another student remarks that the teacher "helps you when you feel bad, he'll talk to you" (Dillon, 1989, p. 241).

> The teachers are very helpful because, if we have a problem, they are not only our teachers but . . . are also a friend and a counselor toward us. They'll help us during class if we need help. That's the major thing. If we need help during class, they'll take time out during the class period and pull you on the side and talk to you, and not too many teachers can offer that. And if we—if the teachers can't help us, we also have the vice principal, the principal, or our counselors to talk to. And it's just—it's love, sort of, here, and it really helps a whole lot of children. It really does. (Miron & Lauria, 1998, p. 200)

Students often discuss the tenacity of these helping efforts (Cooper et al., 2005; Kroeger, 2004), including the availability of multiple chances in supportive relationships with teachers and teacher refusal to accept failure, a ferocious call to intervene to help make success a reality (Cooper et al., 2005).

Support includes *encouragement* as well (Balfanz, Herzog, & MacIver, 2007). Mastering school is difficult work for many students and "to invest time and energy in the present young people need to believe that there is a viable future" (Joselowsky, 2007, p. 272). Teachers, students show us, are in a unique and powerful position to help youngsters see the potential for success, what Crosnoe (2011, p. 186) calls a "future orientation." Teachers can help open these doors through encouragement (Newmann, 1992; Roth et al., 1998). Encouragement also includes a sense of constancy according to youngsters. Support is something that does not decline as youngsters hit rough patches in school or in their lives more generally (Rak & Patterson, 1996). Encouragement is also described by students as being pushed to do more than they have in the past (Fordham & Ogbu, 1986), what Cabello and Terrell (1994, p. 20) refer to as "teachers sending a 'can do' message," or their failing to do so.

> I don't really know why. I don't even know why I don't come, when I know I should come. It's just that we [black students] don't have that much support. We don't get—I know we know that we should do things, but it's—you know, you know something pushing you. And when you don't have that, sometimes you feel like nobody cares, so why should you care? It gets like that sometimes. (Fordham & Ogbu, 1986, p. 192)

Related to this last point, we see that teachers *providing safety nets* is another essential element of student support (Cooper et al., 2005). The idea here is to prevent students from falling through the cracks, to go missing or to be unnoticed (Allensworth & Easton, 2005). When productive student–teacher relationships occupy the high ground, teachers regularly use assistance interventions woven together to form these nets to support students. They do not blame children for requiring such assistance (Patterson et al., 2007). Teachers and students coconstruct these nets with the threads of deepening and extended relationships in classrooms and schools, and in the larger community (Johnson, 2009; Quiroz, 2001).

Finally *advocating for students* is a well-illuminated element of support (Murphy, Elliott, Goldring, & Porter, 2007; Rumberger, 2011). Here, support is defined as "personally negotiating" (O'Connor, 1997, p. 616) to ensure that students garner all the aid they require to be successful, both from the school and the larger community (Ancess, 2003; Cooper et al., 2005; Patterson et al., 2007). Collectively, support can be thought of as "responsibility for shepherding the student" (Balfanz et al., 2007, p. 232). "If students believe that others at school are rooting for them, are on their side and willing to help them if necessary, they have reason to believe that they have the resources necessary to be successful" (Goodenow & Grady, 1993, p. 68).

Students help us see advocacy as a form of "personalized intervention" (Stanton-Salazar, 1997, p. 11), as teachers going to bat for them, taking restorative stances within classrooms, the school, and the larger community (Kosciw, Greytak, Bartkiewicz, Boesen, & Palmer, 2012). They talk about teachers who "act as agents" for them (Stanton & Salazar, 1997, p. 14) and "back them up" (Furrer &

Skinner, 2003, p. 148)—who affirm them and who intervene on their behalf. Advocacy support is about "strategic mentorship" (Stanton-Salazar, 1997, p. 31). Students see advocates as mentors and mentors as those who offer the support of guidance (Cooper et al, 2005; Russell et al., 2001; Woloszyk, 1996), a combination of the "notions of emotional and 'informational support'" (Cotterell, 1992, p. 33).

For many students, such advocacy and guidance includes helping them to dismantle barriers and to build bridges between the cultures of the home and the community and the culture of the school (Fordham & Ogbu, 1986), to successfully help students cross borders (Stanton-Salazar, 1997) and "draw together [their] multiple worlds" (Gibson et al., 2004, p. 140). That is, it helps students develop the capacities "to participate effectively in multiple cultural worlds" (p. 22), work that begins with developing the skills to "decode" multiple environments (Gibson et al., 2004; Quiroz, 2001) and providing pathways of possibilities and hope (Mitra & Serriere, 2012; Raywid, 1995; Zanger, 1991). Here we see "teachers serv[ing] as cultural brokers, guiding their students across the rocky terrain of adjustment to the values and behaviors expected by the dominant culture" (Zanger, 1991, p. 8).

Through the eyes of young persons, we come to see advocacy as actions by their teachers that pull them out of unhealthy hiding places (Heshusius, 1995), remove barriers that differentiate between the more advantaged and students placed at risk, and protect children from gratuitous incivility and unnecessary harm (Dillon, 1989). Advocacy is also about providing "affirming spaces" (Kosciw et al., 2012, p. xvi) and "emotional space" (Cruddas, 2001, p. 65) where students report that they "can work things out" (p. 65), and crafting robust opportunities for students to succeed (Cabello & Terrell, 1994; Cooper et al., 2005).

In Chapter 6, we move beyond a singular focus on student perspectives to address the effects of positive school culture on children. We provide a preview of those findings as we conclude this section on support. We begin with the framing perspective that teacher support is an "important and often unnoticed variable for adolescent learning" (Johnson, 2009, p. 115). At the macro level, "the receipt of social support provides the individual with the information that he or she is cared for and valued by others" (Dubow & Ullman, 1989, p. 53). We also note that there is a powerful relationship between the social support that is the focus of this chapter and the academic support we take up in Part 3. More specifically, "the emphasis on teacher–student supportive interaction is an important moderating influence on the impact of task orientation" (Moos, 1978, p. 64). We also see here that support has an ignition quality to it that it spreads and transfers. That is, "children who perceive one setting as supportive tend to view other settings as well" (Dubow & Ullman, 1989, p. 58). In addition, we find that support is most robust when teachers "transmit support as part of an explicit and strategic agenda" (Stanton-Salazar, 1997, p. 15). Finally, as we make clear throughout Part 3, the impacts of support, both positive and negative, are especially critical for students placed at risk by society (Heshusius, 1995; Stanton-Salazar, 1997).

On the back end of the chronicle, there is an empirical linkage between teacher support and student academic performance (Cotterell, 1992; Davidson & Lang, 1960; Murdock & Miller, 2003): "School environments that have high levels of such features as teacher support are associated with positive academic and social development for all students" (Smerdon, 2002, p. 289). This final link to learning is, in turn, mediated by three intermediate conditions (i.e., belonging, self-esteem, and motivation) and one distal state (i.e., engagement). On the intermediate front, Murdock and Miller, (2003, p. 385) have reported that "middle school students who perceived more teacher support felt a stronger sense of belonging." Strongly supported students experience bonding with teachers and peers (Johnson, 2009; Slaughter-Defoe & Carlson, 1996). The message from the research is that "educators would do well to consistently recognize that teacher support and adolescents' sense of school membership are important factors associated with learning and motivation" (Johnson, 2009, p. 115). Students in supportive relationships with their teachers also experience increases in their self-esteem (Hoge et al., 1990; Furrer & Skinner, 2003; Wentzel, 1998). Teacher support is also associated with "higher levels of motivation as measured by effort and self-rated expectancies" (Murdock & Miller, 2003, p. 385). That is, because there is a "connection between support of students' relatedness needs and the motivation to learn" (Davis, 2003, p. 215). Teachers can enhance achievement-related motivation . . . by providing emotional support" (Roeser et al., 2000, p. 454). Social support is also linked to student work effort (Newmann, 1989) and students' willingness to deal and success in dealing with stress interfering with effort (Birch & Ladd, 1997;

Boekaerts, 1993; Wentz-Gross & Siperstein, 1998), including stress emerging from unhealthy conditions in families (Pianta & Steinberg, 1992). Researchers also confirm a connection between social support and student valuing of school (Davis, 2003; Midgley et al., 1989; Oelsner et al., 2011). "'Nurturing' relationships with the teacher tend to increase [:] help-seeking behavior in the classroom" (Davis, 2003, p. 216). Others indicate that such nurturing relationships also increase "feelings of interest and security on the part of students" (Trickett & Moos, 1974, p. 7), initiatives "to gain control over the learning situations" (Boekaerts, 1993, p. 153), and "pursuit of goals to behave prosocially and responsibly" (Wentzel, 1998, p. 203).

All of these intermediate effects are implicated in the positive narrative on enhanced student engagement that, in turn, powers academic and social learning (Furrer & Skinner, 2003; Willms, 2003). We know that students who are blessed with supportive teachers are less likely to miss school (Kosciw et al., 2012), to have lower rates of absenteeism (Moos & Moos, 1978). These youngsters also score higher on "measures of school participation and engagement" (Goodenow & Grady, 1993, p. 68). Finally, we know that a relationship with a supportive teacher is a major factor associated with prevention of dropouts" (Pianta & Steinberg, 1992, p. 64).

SAFETY

> The analysis of student responses suggested that teachers show caring by providing a safe and secure environment. (Hayes et al., 1994, p. 5)
>
> My ideal secondary school is a safe haven, not a prison. It shouldn't be somewhere you dread attending every morning, but somewhere you enjoy attending. I believe it should be social, as well as an educational experience. A school should always have a soul, there should never be a time when people are unhappy there, although there undoubtedly will be. At break there should always be laughter ringing through the corridors. (Student, cited by Burke & Grosvenor, 2003, p. 113)

Healthy cultures for students are defined by the norms of physical and psychological safety (Christle, Jolivette, & Nelson, 2005; Poplin, 1992), which in the effective schools research is referred to as the correlate of a safe and orderly learning environment (Cotton, 2003; Hallinger & Murphy, 1985; Robinson, Lloyd, & Rowe, 2008). We learn from studies across an assortment of disciplines that security needs are of major importance for students (Dinham, 2005; Fine et al., 2007), that "safety for young people is paramount" (Joselowsky, 2007, p. 272). We also know that meeting those needs is essential for their healthy development, academically, socially, and emotionally (Baker et al., 1997; Christle et al., 2005; Rumberger & Palardy, 2005): "Learning cannot effectively proceed where order, decency, civility, and respect for others is absent" (Maehr & Midgley, 1996, p. 73).

As was the case with the norms of care and support, positively charged and negatively charged analyses are intertwined throughout the research narrative on safety (Felner et al., 2007). The latter storyline attends to efforts to banish, or at least minimize, unsafe and damaging elements in the school culture (e.g., crumbling infrastructure) (Allensworth & Easton, 2005). The positive chronicle underscores actions schools undertake to promote warmth and protection (Felner et al., 2007). Collectively, these efforts create spaces in which it is safe and enjoyable for students to engage with the business of schooling and develop as persons (Antrop-Gonzalez & De Jesus, 2006; Creemers & Reezigt, 1996; Robinson, 2007). Schools become sanctuaries for students (Ackerman & Maslin-Ostrowski, 2002; Ancess, 2003), "places for refuge" (Johnson, 2009, p. 112), and "zones of comfort" (Eccles et al., 1993, p. 559), places where students feel reasonably safe and that they belong. "Their drawings and writings about the perfect school show their desire to have a school where everyone can be friends" (Poplin, 1992, p. 34).

It is also important to provide some testimony on the critical nature of relationships to the safety narrative (Hartup, 1989). And as we saw in action in Chapters 1 and 3 and in 4 to this point, these "vertical relationships" (p. 120) are essential for creating productive culture (Murphy & Torre, 2014). A note on context is required here as well. We know that creating "disciplined communities" (Freiberg, Stein, & Huang, 1995, p. 39) varies in difficulty depending on the age of the students (Akos, 2002; Smetana & Bitz, 1996). Students inform us that the work is complicated by the presence of youngsters who historically have been disenfranchised and marginalized in society and in schools (Kosciw et al., 2012). Analysts also find that children bring different conditions and states with them to school (e.g., confidence, motivations) that impact the bundle of management, control, and disciplinary strategies. Gender is of contextual interest (Arnot et al., 2004) as is family background/culture (Burke & Grosvenor, 2005; Moos, 1979; Shade et al., 1997). Finally, we must remind ourselves that it is wise to think of the various norms of productive culture as overlapping, sharing conceptual and applied spaces. It is also true that caring is the heart and soul of the chronicle; perceived caring by students fuels the growth of safety (Cooper et al., 2005).

Later in this section, we preview the evidence on the impact of safety on the academic and social learning of students. Here we simply provide an advance organizer on the linkage. We confirm that lack of safety undermines the academic function of the school (Finn & Rock, 1997; Freiberg et al., 2009; Wilson & Corbett, 1999). Many traditional school safety moves are also harmful to learning (Christle et al., 2005; Nichols, Ludwin, & Iadicola, 1999). On the flip side, relationship-anchored improvements in the safety of the school environment enhance academic performance (Maguin & Loeber, 1996; Smerdon & Borman, 2009).

When we examine safety through the eyes of students, a number of core components materialize. Of paramount importance is *protection from harm* (Alfaro, Letriz, Santos, Villanueva, & Freeman, 2001; Poplin, 1992), shame (McMillan, 1996) and victimization (Casey-Cannon et al., 2001; Kosciw et al., 2012)—from "breakdowns in pride, self-esteem and dignity" (McMillan, 1996, p. 322). Or alternatively, students confirm the importance of "security in relation to both the physical setting of the school and in interpersonal encounters" (Rudduck et al., 1996b, p. 175).

An assortment of studies that explore schooling through the eyes of students informs us that protection from harm is often lacking, especially in schooling serving high concentrations of students placed at risk of failure by home, community, school, and/or society (Mendez, Knoff, & Ferron, 2002). Students often describe "the threat of schools as unsafe places" (Poplin & Weeres, 1994, p. 33). Indeed, "for many children school represents a difficult territory that they have to negotiate from the bus journey at the beginning of the day to the completion of homework at the end" (Burke & Grosvenor, 2003, p. 108), a voyage with heavy costs.

> The quality of the contexts in which they are growing speaks to youth about how they are viewed and valued. For better or worse, these voices come to form part of the core of how a child feels about him/herself and/or the extent to which s/he is valued by others. If surrounded by decay, disrepair, and filth, with a constantly shifting stream of adults in charge, and no adult intervention to protect children, a child may come to see him/herself as worthy of little more or at least that adults see him/her as unworthy. (Fine et al., 2007, p. 811)

The language of children accumulates into the notion of students often being ensconced in a "problematic climate, school where they do not feel safe; where problems with theft, vandalism, drugs, rape, and possession of weapons have been reported; and where there is substantial verbal or physical conflict among students or between students and teachers" (McNeal, 1999, p. 304). In schools for too many students, "there is a strongly conveyed sense of vulnerability to self and others" (Burke & Grosvenor, 2003, p. 107):

> In reading these texts, what is strongly conveyed is a sense of vulnerability. Children feel small; the school environment is hard, especially when you fall; space is limited; toilets are unwelcoming or inaccessible; sick bays are inadequate; buildings are noisy; corridors are hectic; the school bus is a daily ordeal; bullies threaten; teachers shout and seem not to listen; belongings can be lost or stolen; bags are heavy; lockers are damaged; minority students feel victimised and marginalized. There is enormous pressure to conform; to be different is dangerous. (pp. 108–109)

Students regularly refer to comfortable and appealing spaces when they talk of schools they wish for in general and school safety in particular (Gray, Hopkins, Reynolds, Wilcox, Farrell, & Jesson, 1999; Rudduck & Flutter, 2004). They help us see that community for youngsters "often begins with physical space" (Joselowsky, 2007, p. 258). They carry us into preferred "environments that are moderately arousing, pleasant, mildly stimulating, and arranged for easy movement" (Shade et al., 1997, p. 45) and help us understand

Chapter Four: Support, Safety, and Membership   87

that the "physical environment, safety, and student feelings about themselves are inextricably linked" (Poplin & Weeres, 1994, p. 35). They comment on both what troubles them about conditions in schools, conditions that they often experience, as well as about those they would prefer. They are not shy about sharing their critiques about the problematic conditions they confront on a daily basis (Burke & Grosvenor, 2003; Rudduck & Flutter, 2004). We learn that what youngsters assess as "poorly maintained facilities can be a source of stress." "It's horrible, all the walls are shabby and the tables are falling apart." "The toilets are always dirty and there are no locks on the doors (Chaplain, 1996b, p. 119). "They cage us up and like they keep putting more gates and locks and stuff" (Fine et al., 2007, p. 816). Across all youngsters, "almost identical features and aspects . . . are noted as problematic: small, cramped spaces to work or play within, lack of privacy, [and] 'scary' school toilets" (Burke & Grosvenor, 2003, p. 110).

Students also talk freely about what they believe will strengthen the spaces in which they work: "With respect to student perceptions of schools, students want their schools to look more like the world in which they live. They want aesthetically pleasing environments that inspire and motivate them to learn and achieve" (Spires et al., 2008, p. 510). Starting with the outside environment,

> colourless, empty school yards surrounding the outside of a school are what the outside world sees first of a school and children express a concern here that this greyness reflects upon themselves and the way the school regards them. This awareness has been noted by others in research carried out under the Learning Through Landscapes initiative. The appearance of school grounds was also symbolic for children of the way the school valued them—a reflection of self. Because most children believed the grounds had been created—'put there'—for them, if the place was 'ugly' or 'boring' or 'gross,' this was read by the children as a reflection of the way the school felt about them. (Burke & Grosvenor, 2003, p. 46)

> The lack of aesthetically pleasing or even aesthetically acceptable environment hampers feelings about work and worth, and diminishes individual sense of responsibility for maintaining the physical environment. When students were asked to draw

or write about the perfect school, they constantly drew schools with beautiful landscapes, spacious classrooms and swimming pools. (Poplin & Weeres, 1994, p. 35)

Children have stated clearly here, in their words and in their designs, that they want more space but they also want the space to be filled with things: objects, mazes, ponds, swings, gardens, slides and swimming pools. Their material visions range from tree-houses and forts, pirate ships and adventure playgrounds (presumably made from scrap materials), to full-scale theme parks with motorised rides and all the fun of the fair.... [There is a felt] need for more natural features: water, wildlife and animals are commonly called for. (Burke & Grosvenor, 2003, pp. 45–46)

Students' "visions for an ideal school [are] imaginative, expressing a desire for contemporary environments with aesthetically pleasing designs, colors and amenities" (Spires et al., 2008, p. 510).

"Students complain even more bitterly... about the physical condition of schools" (Poplin & Weeres, 1994, p. 35). The aspects of the building, students often argue, "do not promote learning, but instead, enhance feelings of negativity. I hate waking up every weekday knowing this day, one day that is so valuable to me, will be spent in a grand magnolia prison" (Burke & Grosvenor, 2003, p. 25).

> I would like a room we could sit in instead of standing out in the cold freezing to death.... I would like the seats in the school to be leather, the ones you can put your feet up on and relax instead of having a sore back all of the time. I also think they should make the tables nice and soft so that we don't have to lean on them and have sore elbows. If the school did what we asked, they wouldn't have to have a discipline system and we would also respect our school. (p. 116)
>
> We need lockers because of all those books I have to cart around. To make it worse I need another bag for P.E. which is like transporting a ton of bricks swung around my poor weak shoulder. If you think for a minute, this amount of luggage for

> one person would make you sweat; it does. Which makes me reek and pong, now that is not at all good as you can imagine. So my school smells like an unattractive place and stops people coming near me. (p. 115)

On the desired side of the space ledger, students perceive advantages from "fun environments to learn in" (p. 73). They describe clean schools with safe and appealing spaces (Gibson et al., 2004; Johnson & Asera, 1999; Wilson & Corbett, 1999), welcoming spaces with a positive ambience (Christle et al., 2005; Joselowsky, 2007), places where people care about and attend to the image of the school (Dinham, Cairney, Craigie, & Wilson, 1995; Gray et al., 1999).

> I want colours, I want beauty in my surroundings, but most of all I want to be filled with inspiration by a place that I can call my home from home. The colour of a room is very important; a calming sky blue for instance will make the room seem less of a cell. No person wants the fundamental years of their life spent in ugliness and why should they? (Burke & Grosvenor, 2003, p. 25)

We close with a note on the importance of comfortable space in the safety equation:

An inviting learning community concentrates on establishing a pleasant physical and psychological environment that welcomes students. When they enter the classroom, they become part of school culture and how the student will function within this particular environment depends on their comfort level and the extent to which they believe the place satisfies their basic needs." (Shade et al., 1997, p. 42)

When students describe safe spaces for learning, they devote considerable time to *positively grounded management* systems at the classroom and school levels (Hayes et al., 1994). This element of safety is woven from a variety of concepts. It is clear that students prefer teachers who are in charge in classrooms. They recognize and value the need for teachers to "establish authority in the classroom" (Thompson, 2004, p. 96).

> Sherry: They don't just sit there. Yea, like on spring break an incident happened. We just let it go but other schools they just probably keep it up and see what really happened. We just let it slide by.
>
> James: Because they (other districts' schools) got more discipline. They take more charge than we do. Our district let's things happen. Like Onondaga, they have problems but they take more repercussions on it. They take more charge. We just sit back and let things happen where it can be prevented. (Storz, 2008, pp. 259–260)

Students generally are adverse to "noise and disorder" (Willms, 2003, p. 44) and not especially tolerant of what they assess as laxity in the management domain (Mergendoller & Packer, 1985). A firm approach to classroom management is supported by core ideas such as fairness and respect for students (Mendez et al., 2002; Newmann, Wehlage, & Lamburn, 1992; Trickett & Quinlan, 1979), on the scaffolding of the strong and healthy student–teacher relationships we laid out in Chapter 1. In positive management programs, rules for students are clear and known by youngsters. They are followed by teachers in a nonarbitrary manner (Thompson, 2004; Wentzel, 2002). Students appreciate firmness and teachers' "need to control events" (Arnot et al., 2004, p. 67) inside the bubble of care and support.

> Teachers must explain their class rules on the first day of school, to students and to parents, verbally and in writing; they must then remind students of the rules on an ongoing basis. The rules must make sense, and they should emphasize the need for students to treat each other and the teacher respectfully. However, the teacher must model the rules by treating students respectfully as well. (Thompson, 2004, p. 99)

As we saw with the concept of community, students tell us that everyone should be treated the same when it comes to safety via classroom management (Arnot et al., 2004).

> Thus, results from the present study could indicate that the greatest potential for improving student behavior through class management lies in improving adaptation of management to the variety of student needs, and ensuring that no student is favored over others. (Bru et al., 2002, p. 303)

Students characterize different teachers according to the responsibilities they were granted in the classroom. They are not especially charitable in their assessments when they see unnecessary restrictions and lack of voice. "They particularly resented teachers who talked down to them, blamed them unjustly, did not listen to their side of the story, shouted at them or punished the whole class and therefore the innocent as well as the guilty" (Riley & Docking, 2004, p. 175).

Looking in on students in action in classrooms and schools informs us about the power of prevention rather than intervention measures (Freiberg et al., 2009). "Good teachers' management strategies prevent continuous discipline problems" (Mergendoller & Packer, 1985, p. 596). They work on "establishing [a] learning environment that will prevent disruptions rather than focus on discipline interventions as a primary goal" (Freiberg et al., 1995, p. 43). Early identification and treatment lie at the heart of the prevention element. That is, early screening for potential and actual discipline problems and early intervention are highlighted in preventive climates (Cheney, Blum, & Walker, 2004; Ensminger & Slusarcick, 1992), especially efforts to damp down individual risk factors associated with disorder (St. Pierre, Mark, Kaltreider, & Aikin, 1997).

Prevention strategies that work well are identified in the research on safety. Generally speaking, integrating safety with the other norms of student community—care, support, and membership, receives high marks. Shaping peer cultures to support rather than contradict the values and ideals of community provides a strong platform to prevent disorder and unsafe conditions (Rutter Maughan, Mortimore, & Ouston, 1979). Working to understand and address causes of problems that interfere with the development of a safe climate is particularly helpful (Antrop-Gonzalez & De Jesus, 2006;

Balfanz et al., 2007; Nichols et al., 1999). Keeping longer term objectives in mind rather than addressing only immediate problems is important as well (Mendez et al., 2002). Involving parents is a wise policy (Mendez et al., 2002). Training in the area of social skills for students is a good preventative strategy (Catalano, Loeber, & McKinney, 1999; St. Pierre et al., 1997). Collaborative development of positively framed expectations for conduct with clear expectations for behavior is essential here (Fredricks et al., 2004). So too is a reliance on positive rather than negative reinforcement (Cotton, 2003; Rutter et al., 1979). Seeking external assistance for help in working on problems, real and potential, can be productive in preventing problems from mushrooming and damaging the climate of safety in a school (Cheney et al., 2004).

We see from the research literature that "an effective management system is built on an open mind and a positive attitude about students" (Thompson, 2004, p. 94). Scholarship affirms that reliance on negative and exclusionary practices to create safety is often dysfunctional for the school and harmful to students (Christle et al., 2005; Mendez et al., 2002; Nichols et al., 1999). An emphasis on punitive actions, especially ones unanchored to understanding, support, and personal and social development, has been found to be uniformly ineffective in the struggle to forge the norm of safety (Antrop-Gonzalez & De Jesus, 2006; Catalano et al., 1999; Nichols et al., 1999). On the other hand, positive, asset-based approaches to bringing safety to life are much more likely to be productive. Especially relevant here is an emphasis on positive consequences (Crosnoe, 2011) and positive feedback to students (Mendez et al., 2002; Rutter et al., 1979). Teachers exercise a firm but soft touch (Hayes et al., 1994), using discipline in the service of creating "an inviting classroom with firm, consistent, and loving control" (Shade et al., 1997, p. 50). Students tell us that in classes with good classroom management, teachers "'avoid harshness.' . . . The students indicate that the teacher does not get 'mad' and that the teacher remains calm and relaxed" (Hayes et al., 1994, p. 10). They demonstrate tolerance (Mergendoller & Packer, 1985). While expectations are clear, firm, and consistently enforced, actions center on students as persons not simply as occupants of the institution of school (Robinson, 2007). Inculcating the norm of safety, or what Bryk and colleagues (2010, p. 8) call norms of "civil conduct," occurs by using "soft power" (Adams, 2010, p. 265) and by engaging in "gentle schooling" (Reitzug & Patterson, 1998, p. 179). Rules, regulations, and system responses are about more than simply effective control (Wilson & Corbett, 1999). They encompass community and personalization properties such as identification and engagement (Adams, 2010; Baker et al., 1997; Bryk et al., 2010). Warmth is a hallmark ingredient in safety (Mendez et al., 2002). Positive expectations dominate the environmental climate (Roth & Brooks-Gunn, 2003). A protective culture is formed in large part through respectful relationships between teachers and children (Baker et al., 1997; Mendez et al., 2002; Robinson, 2007). Students are seen "as resources to be developed rather than as problems to be managed" (Roth et al., 1998, p. 427). Attention is directed to learning the values of the community not simply learning to comply with rules (Freiberg et al., 2009). The rules in play "are based upon principles and virtues (kindness, fairness) and are connected to respect for the community" (Baker et al., 1997, p. 592).

Support for adherence to community ideas is more important than consequences for inappropriate behavior. Appropriate behavior is defined in light of the full range of students' social and emotional needs (Antrop-Gonzalez, 2006; Mendez et al., 2002). Nourishing internal control is important (Baker et al., 1997). Students are viewed holistically, not only as violators of regulations. Developmentally appropriate work (Mendez et al., 2002) and individualization (Cheney et al., 2004) are visible in the concept of safety. So too is an emphasis on helping students learn to assume responsibility for their behavior (Ancess, 2003; Csikszentmihalyi & Larson, 1984; Johnson & Asera, 1999). Schools characterized by a norm of safety are adept at providing youngsters with three types of protective armor: personal, interpersonal, and group (Crosnoe, 2011). In safe schools, we discover that discipline is shifted from a platform "of control to one of cooperation" (Freiberg et al., 1995, p. 43). "Explicitness and consistency are crucial components of an effective classroom management system" (Thompson, 2004, p. 99) as well (Brewster & Fager, 2000). Rules that reflect students' needs and responsibilities are seen by youngsters as helpful.

The issue of "autonomy supportive" classrooms rests at the heart of positively grounded school management (Davis, 2003, p. 213). We have already reported that students tell us that they appreciate "emphasis on order and organization" (Moos, 1979, p. 149)—firm and fair structure and control with kindness (Veaco & Brandon, 1986), where everything is explicit, and transparency holds the high ground (Chaplain, 1996a). Youngsters also inform us, and researchers affirm, that safety via positive school management has a good deal to do with student involvement (Cabello & Terrell, 1994; Moos & Moos, 1978; Smetana & Bitz, 1996) and influence (Bru et al., 2002; Freiberg et al., 2009), "involve[ment] in the development of an environment that belongs to them" (Shade et al., 1997, p. 44). "Shared responsibility" is a common thread in effective discipline systems (Freiberg et al., 1995, p. 40), a damping down of the exercise of teacher power (Burke & Grosvenor, 2003) in favor of "youth–adult partnerships" (Mitra & Gross, 2009, p. 524) that garner "the potential of students and teachers as cooperative participants" (Freiberg et al., 2009, p. 63). Here we find "teachers and students working collaboratively to create opportunities for self discipline in the classroom and throughout the school" (p. 40). This approach is strategic for a variety of reasons associated with learning theory. It is also important because schools often "regulate many issues that students consider to be beyond legitimate institutional jurisdiction" (Smetana & Bitz, 1996, p. 1154).

A number of principles anchor teacher–student participative approaches to discipline and management. One is emphasis on "student self-discipline over external controlling factors that tend to rely on punitive responses to misbehaviors" (Freiberg et al., 2009, p. 63), that is, helping youngsters to learn to manage their own behavior. In lieu of excessive control (Fine, 1986; Moos, 1978), we find here "increased listening to and questioning of students' wants . . . teachers less likely to give directives and provide their own solutions to children's problems" (Davis, 2003, p. 213). A second principle, touched on above, is a "focus on prevention through cooperative discipline" (Freiberg, 1995, p. 41). A third is that structure works best when it is moderate and when it unfolds in a supportive environment (Moos, 1978).

Dysfunctional disciplinary systems, on the other hand, are perceived quite differently by students. Fear is often noted in possibilities and actions (Taylor-Dunlop & Norton, 1997). Students do not believe that teachers foreground their interests. Students talk of mean teachers who misuse power (Burke & Grosvenor, 2003; Mergendoller & Packer, 1985) and of teachers who "seem to be arbitrary in the way they exercise their power" (Arnot et al., 2004, p. 71). They point to the presence of "power struggles between teachers and students to gain the 'upper hand' as a result of teachers' excessive use of controlling behaviors" (Davis, 2003, p. 213). Cooperation is conspicuous by its absence. Students are especially sensitive to what they see as disrespectful teacher behaviors in maintaining classrooms, such as "dehumanizing words" and exclusion from the classroom (Shade et al., 1997, p. 50). They see, often much more clearly than their teachers, inappropriate teacher action based on "misunderstandings of students' cultural characteristics" (Howard, 2001, p. 138), actions that lead to well-documented disproportionate disciplinary responses or misguided excuses for and acceptance of poor behavior (Shade et al., 1997).

> In general, teachers of classes with high percentages of African American youth are more likely to be authoritarian and less likely to use the open classroom, student responsibility approach.... Others have found that teachers seem to spend more time on the lookout for possible misbehavior by African American students, particularly male students. And when misbehavior is identified, the educators are more likely to use more punishment, including corporal punishment and suspension. (p. 51)

Noted as especially valuable is the ability of teachers to use management in the service of instruction and instruction in the service of management (Freiberg et al., 2009; Garmezy, 1991; Shade et al., 1997). Indeed a major lesson from the research is that both the presence and the absence of the norm of safety via discipline is as much a product of "meaningful academic work" (Baker et al., 1997, p. 592) as it is of community building efforts: "To create an effective classroom management system, teachers must be preoccupied with teaching, instead of with discipline" (Thompson, 2004, p. 100). Instruction and curriculum that foster academic engagement and promote student success go a long way to creating a warm and protective climate (Catalano et al., 1999; Cheney et al., 2004; Garmezy, 1991). Good schools rely more on quality programs than control strategies in their quest for creating productive student communities (Weil & Murphy, 1982).

As is the case with support, there is evidence that safety has effects on variables of interest to schools, homes, and communities. Students see safe schools differently, that is, "perceptions of [the] learning environment are significantly more positive" (Freiberg et al., 1995, p. 54). We also know that belonging is enhanced in safe schools (Shade et al., 1997). For example, Anderman (2003, pp. 8–9) documents that "adolescents in a large, nationally representative sample were more likely to report a lack of 'connectedness' to school if they perceived their classes as poorly managed and characterized by conflictual relationships." There is also abundant evidence that safety impacts classroom instruction favorably.

> Student behaviors that disrupt the learning environment have a rippling effect, influencing the disruptive individual, classmates, the school learning environment, and the near community. The individual who is referred to the office loses learning time, and the teacher who stops the instruction to respond to disruptions takes away learning time from all students. Students who misbehave in school are at higher risk of dropping out of school, substance abuse, and other delinquent behaviors. A pattern of disruptions also engulfs school administration in non-instructional activities with hundreds of hours spent in responding to disciplinary referrals to the office. Sustained student misbehaviors inhibit instructional approaches by teachers that foster active learning through cooperative groups, learning centers or other interactive teachings. (Freiberg et al., 1995, p. 37)
>
> In addition, the relationship of student feelings of anger to low Order and Organization in the classroom suggests the negative implications of classroom disruption and lack of teacher preparedness for the class. A classroom which is 'out of control' is presumably not a pleasant experience for either teachers or students. (Trickett & Moos, 1974, p. 9)

"Development of the self" (Smetana & Bitz, 1996, p. 166) is more robust and self-concept increases in safe schools, while self-discipline can decrease in unsafe schools (Freiberg et al., 2009). Learning dispositions such as motivation, morale, interest in school, and

Chapter Four: Support, Safety, and Membership   97

learning expectations are also positively impacted (Burke & Grosvenor, 2003; Freiberg et al., 2009). Students' "perceptions of themselves as learners and contributors" are deepened (Shade et al., 1997, p. 45).

> For example, students from exemplary classrooms were more likely to spontaneously assist their peers in academic work or to provide feedback or support that was relevant to academic activities. Of course, the opportunity for engaging in this type of behavior was part of the system created by the teachers through their classroom management practices. (Cabello & Terrell, 1994, p. 22)

As we examine in considerable detail in Chapter 7, engagement in school work increases as the norm of safety is heightened (Bru et al., 2002; Freiberg et al., 2009; Willms, 2003). "Schools with safer climates will be perceived by students as more amenable to student involvement simply because they are seen as safe and pleasant places to spend time" (McNeal, 1999, p. 296). Or alternatively, "off-task orientation" (Bru et al., 2002, p. 300) is decreased. Finally, we learn that "detrimental school conditions can adversely affect students'... academic well-being" (Mitra & Gross, 2009, p. 524) and that student learning improves in places where "students perceive that the class is personally gratifying and without hostilities among members" (Walberg & Anderson, 1968, p. 418). That is, there are "linkages between classroom management interventions and academic achievement" (Freiberg et al., 1995, p. 59):

> There is accumulating evidence from recent meta-analyses of variables which influence school learning, that classroom management has one of the greatest influences on school learning. A meta-analysis of learning factors by Wang, Haertel, and Walberg (1993) identified classroom management as being first in a list of five important factors that influence school learning. Weade & Evertson (1988) and Evertson & Weade (1989) found similar connections between classroom management and student achievement using microanalyses of class lessons in language arts, reading and mathematics. (p. 39)

Membership

> It is increasingly clear that learning to high standards cannot take place if students feel no stake in the life of the school and classroom. (Joselowsky, 2007, p. 258)
>
> Sense of belonging and meaningful involvement in school counteracts the alienation voiced by many students. (Baker et al., 1997, p. 588)
>
> Until children feel a sense of belonging, they cannot use their energies to learn. (Shade et al., 1997, p. 99)

The core idea here is belonging, which we describe in concrete form as feelings of membership in the school (Battistich et al., 1995; Roth & Brooks-Gunn, 2003; Voelkl, 1997). "Membership refers to one's sense of belonging and to a sense of confidence that one has as a member as well as the aspect of acceptance from the group that facilitates belonging" (McMillan, 1996, p. 315). We find here "the image of students as participants" (Corbett & Wilson, 1995, p. 13) and a sense of "inclusiveness" (Flutter & Rudduck, 2004, p. 27). According to Nichols (2006, p. 266), students themselves define belongingness in terms of three dimensions of schooling: "(a) interpersonal relationships (whether they are supported socially by peers and/or teachers), (b) learning/academic community (whether they are doing well, are supported by teachers academically), and/or (c) school facilities or activities (whether the school has a playground or extracurricular activities such as band, sports, etc)." Smerdon (2002, p. 288) takes a slightly different angle, documenting that students view "perceived memberships as representing the combination of a sense of belonging, a sense of commitment to the academic work of schools, and a sense of commitment to the school as an institution. . . . Full membership occurs when students have *all* of these feelings." In research, practice, and development, "the terms belongingness, connectedness, and school membership are generally parallel and interchangeable" (Johnson, 2009, p. 100), each reflecting a "fundamental human need" (Nichols, 2006, p. 256). Newmann (1992, p. 183) captures the power of this norm when he reports "from the students' point of view, a basic cultural requirement for engagement is a sense of school membership—they key is school membership" (Newmann et al., 1992, p. 19). We know that a number of persons help determine whether youngsters are authentic members of their schools or mere tourists in the buildings. The literature also informs us that a number of the conditions that lead to authentic membership are under the control of the school, especially those associated with the school culture. In short, "the organization of the school creates the possibility of belonging" (Ancess, 2003, p. 128). "Schools cannot change students' sex, age, or SES, but they can alter the nature and the extent of opportunities for participation for all students" (Epstein, 1981b, p. 95). Effective schools develop and systematically use all available opportunities to bond young people to the central values of the school community (Roth & Brooks-Gunn, 2003; Rutter et al., 1979).

Studies that strive to illustrate membership through the eyes of students offer a number of general insights about this cardinal norm of school culture. We know, for example, "that students' opportunities and experiences with the schools they attend are a stronger factor for determining their perceptions of membership" than are cross-school variations (Smerdon, 2002, p. 293). "This finding suggests that although a student's sense of membership may be related to the type of school he or she attends, perceived membership is more strongly shaped by students' treatment *within* the schools they attend" (p. 299). While it is not our focus here (see Part 3), students inform us that the organization of academic work also explains their sense of membership. Student empowerment via cooperative constructed work is underscored on the academic side of the school narrative. Studies of student viewpoints and their actions show us what membership means and how it shifts across time. The consequence is a growing "importance for understanding the developmental process of school bonding" (Oelsner et al., 2011, p. 466). Concomitantly, we learn that "students' perceptions of belonging" and the role that schools play in "the development of these perceptions" is not especially well studied (p. 288).

The data that we do have on the state of membership is mixed. Research inside the area of student voice on empowerment is often disheartening, especially at the secondary level. For example, Rudduck and Flutter (2004, p. 45), two of the most influential investigators in this area, find that "the typical school environment of the middle years has relatively few opportunities for pupils to make important decisions." On the other hand, a majority of students themselves tell us that they feel somewhat connected to their schools (McNeely et al., 2002). In the Nichols (2006, p. 263) study, students who did not belong (20%) provided a variety of reasons. For some, the quality of relationships (with peers and teachers) was key. Others simply noted that the school failed to offer opportunities to be involved in activities such as band or soccer. And others felt they were not doing well in school (they were not smart or were unable to get the academic help they required). Where felt belonging is low for students, researchers determine that school organization and structure are often implicated (e.g., tracking programs, reliance on transmission models of teaching, inappropriate understandings of child development) (O'Loughlin, 1995; Rudduck & Flutter, 2004).

We know that in schools empowerment "must take place within the context of human connection" (Harter et al., 1997, p. 170). In the Nichols (2006, p. 262) study, "of the students who felt they belonged 67% said they did so because of their relationships with adults and/or peers." The importance of teacher–student partnerships in the process of school work is heavily featured in creating belonging (Cook-Sather, 2002). However, where we see teachers "dictat[ing] to students the conditions of their participation," that is, where we find "hegemonic relationship[s]," membership is difficult to grow (Corbett & Wilson, 1995, p. 15). Rather, based on their analyses of student viewpoints, Corbett and Wilson (1995, p. 15) and their associates in the student voice movement "invoke a collaborative image" between students and teachers, an image that based on their student interviews Rudduck and Flutter (2004, p. 104) suggest "takes time and patient commitment" to develop.

Because "perceived belonging represents the positive or negative responses to objective group membership" (Smerdon, 2002, p. 288), we feature two lines of analysis on the work undertaken to foster membership for students. One attends to the removal of the negatives associated with developing belonging. The other is the construction of positive rungs on the membership ladder. Again, we reemphasize the fact that there is considerable overlap among and integration of the four norms of student culture. This storyline of overlap and integration also applies to the two elements of the norm of membership.

The central law of school improvement that context matters is brightly illuminated here as well (Feldman & Matjasko, 2005; Guest

Chapter Four: Support, Safety, and Membership 101

& Schneider, 2003). "Thus, there is evidence that belonging is dynamic and changes across time and contexts" (Nichols, 2006, p. 257). Individual-level characteristics and school, family, peer, and neighborhood contexts each exert force on whether youngsters become members of a school or not (Feldman & Matjasko, 2005; Voelkl, 1997). "The school and community in which participation takes place matters" (Guest & Schneider, 2003, p. 91) a good deal in whether students are bystanders or active citizens in the school (Freiberg et al., 2009) and whether the desired outcomes of membership materialize or not (Guest & Schneider, 2003).

While it may seem obvious, it is still important to report that "differences in motives and/or abilities which may derive from genetic sources" (Willems, 1967, p. 1249) are part of the contextual mosaic. So too is the individual felt need for belonging. A variety of social context variables also interact with schooling to shape the story of student belonging. That is, "perceived school membership may also be a product of school composition and structure" (Smerdon, 2002, p. 217). One such factor that has received attention is the presence of minority and majority cultures in the school. Nichols's (2006, p. 266) analysis of student perspectives leads to the conclusion that "students who are part of the majority/normative culture of a school tend to feel that they are a stronger part of the school culture than other students, regardless of their majority/minority status outside school." An additional factor is the academic status of the school, with evidence accumulating that "students' sense of membership may be higher in high schools that enroll more academically successful students" (Smerdon, 2002, p. 297).

School structural conditions have an impact on membership. For example, Hamilton (1983, p. 322), using the analysis of Barker and Gump, reports that in

> small schools marginal students reported both pressures and attractions to participate in school activities at about the same rate as regular students, whereas in large schools marginal students reported fewer pressures and attractions. As a result, the larger schools included substantial groups of 'outsiders,' students with poor academic records and no extracurricular involvement, a group almost unknown in the small schools.

Track placement also is important when we examine student membership, with students from "general and vocational tracks experiencing lower perceptions of high school membership than their peers in academic tracks" (Smerdon, 2002, p. 297). As we discuss more fully below, on the cocurricular participation front, these students are overrepresented in vocational activities, while more academically oriented students and those with better grades are more likely to participate in extramural activities (McNeal, 1998) and experience "higher membership" in school in general (Smerdon, 2002, p. 297). We also know that youngsters "perceive higher levels of school membership where students have more authority over academic work" (p. 297). On another front, there is evidence that school size, that is, "the potential relationship between pupil/teacher ratio and participation" (McNeal, 1999, p. 295), is a relevant contextual variable, especially for "marginal students" (Hamilton, 1983, p. 322). Indeed, "there is consistent evidence that as size, that is, the number of persons of the unit increases, punctuality, attendance, identification with the group, and other indexes of participation, decrease" (Willems, 1967, p. 1258). This has been best documented in the area of cocurricular experiences, where "the basic finding is of higher levels of participation in small schools" (Hamilton, 1983, p. 322)—"twice as high in the small high schools as in the larger ones" (p. 321).

While the "effect of high school experiences on high school membership is stronger than the effects of SES" (Smerdon, 2002, p. 295), race, class, gender, ethnicity, and age are important. That is, "numerous individual attributes are relevant to student participation" (McNeal, 1999, p. 294). More critical still is the aggregation of these individual attributes into the "social milieu of the school" (p. 296). "Schools with non-problematic social milieus (e.g., those with fewer at-risk students, more students from higher socioeconomic [SES] backgrounds, more students from two-parent households) have better resources" (p. 296). Students in the schools enjoy a "participatory advantage ... after controlling for schools' various structural features" (p. 296).

SES is an interesting factor in the membership narrative. Looking again only at the cocurricular experiences of children, we find that "students of lower SES are underrepresented" (McNeal, 1998, p. 189)—or that there is a "'participation' advantage for higher-SES students at the individual level" (McNeal, 1999, p. 304). And as we touched upon earlier, "socioeconomic status ... may

[also] influence the types of activities students choose to participate in as well as the attainment of status within those activities" (Mahoney & Cairns, 1997, p. 250). Relatedly, there is solid support for the conclusion that "participation rates are consistently lower for risk students compared with their more competent counterparts" (p. 250). There is some support, however, for the notion that when broader measures of school participation are employed—that is, measures of participation beyond extracurricular participation—variations fall away, with Smerdon (2002, p. 295) concluding that overall "SES is not related to perceived school membership."

Gender is also correlated with membership. Looking again at extracurricular activities, we discover that "girls are more likely to participate in extra-curricular activities than are comparable boys for every type of activity, with the exception of athletics" (McNeal, 1998, p. 189). And looking more broadly, "studies have shown that females generally report a greater sense of belonging than males" (Nichols, 2006, p. 257). Nor is there any "evidence for loss of voice among female adolescents as a group" (Harter et al., 1997, p. 162). However, Harter and team find that sexual orientation, identity, and expression are important: "Androgynous girls and boys report more support for voice from teachers than do feminine girls and masculine boys" (p. 170).

> Our findings suggest that it is not gender, per se, but gender orientation that best predicts level of voice among girls. Second, our evidence suggests that a feminine orientation primarily represents a liability for the expression of voice in public contexts, namely in the school setting with teachers and classmates. (p. 163)

We know that there is a tendency for membership to decline across the grades; "research suggests that feelings of belongingness diminish as students age and that the correlation between academic engagement and relatedness to teachers is stronger for older students" (Johnson, 2009, p. 113). Overall, few ethnic variations in membership participation in extracurricular activities have been documented, although there are differences in types of experiences in which students engage (Mahoney & Cairns, 1997), with evidence that youngsters from minority cultures shy away from activities dominated by youngsters from majority school cultures (Gibson et al., 2004), confirming "a school composition effect on students' sense of belonging" (Nichols, 2006, p. 257). The take away message on cocurricular experiences has been nicely penned by scholars as follows: Racial and ethnic minorities appear to have likelihoods of participation that are either equal to or higher than those of their White counterparts. These findings are generally in agreement with qualitative research indicating Blacks and other minorities are more likely to identify with and be involved in schooling than are Whites of comparable social class. Finally, and consistent with our examination of the other norms, authentic membership seems to be especially important and productive for students at risk of failure (Felner et al., 2007; Fielding, 2004b; Hoge et al., 1990; Murphy, 2010; Murphy & Tobin, 2011; Smerdon, 2002). Indeed, "belonging could be *the* single most crucial factor in the motivation and engagement of certain categories of at-risk students" (Goodenow & Grady, 1993, p. 39). We examine the form and texture of membership through an analysis of its defining elements as seen through the eyes of students.

Involvement

In the balance of this section, we unpack "membership" into two elements: involvement and ownership. Involvement features opportunities provided by the school for youngsters to engage their "talents, skills, and interests" (Crosnoe, 2011, p. 238) in meaningful and challenging work (Newmann, 1981; Newmann et al., 1992) and in school activities (Marsh & Kleitman, 2002; Silins & Mulford, 2010). The critical issue here according to Joselowsky (2007, p. 273) is that schools "cease treating youth engagement as an add-on to improved learning outcomes but as central to student and school success." That is, "youth engagement must be conceptualized as a guiding principle of organizational operations" (p. 270). Indeed, Ma (2003, p. 347) argues "that students' participation in school activities may be the key to their sense of belonging in school." Students help us see that for schools as organizational operations, school involvement features a number of powerful principles, all based on the fact that "we see students cry out for a say on what they are doing inside schools and classrooms" (Poplin & Weeres, 1994, p. 40). We note before continuing, however, that due to the quite limited empirical base of work that examines involvement specifically through the eyes of students, we rely on a more general corpus of research than we have so far to forge an understanding of student involvement. We learn of the importance in the involvement equation of action in classrooms that is "genuine, school-wide, and socially inclusive" (Rudduck & Flutter, 2004, p. 125). The centrality of teachers (and peers) helping youngsters fit in is underscored as well (Nichols, 2006), assisting them to "develop a sense that they are an integral part of the school collective and have connections to others in the community" (Cooper et al., 2005, p. 7). Such assistance is especially needed for those "who feel absented, lost, or even those who purposefully resist the school environment" (Nichols, 2006, p. 267).

Participation is often described in terms of forms or general approaches to student involvement (Lodge, 2005), as well as points on a continuum (Fielding, 2004a) and as steps on a ladder (Alderson, 2008), with the top step devoted to "projects more fully initiated and developed by children" (Alderson, 2008, p. 282). Schools with well-formed student communities provide a host of "participatory opportunities" (Cooper et al., 2005, p. 17), "chances to participate in and contribute to the school's affairs" (Rudduck & Flutter, 2004, p. 20) centered on chances for youngsters to contribute to the school and take positions of responsibility (Johnson & Asera, 1999; Rutter et al., 1979). Given the cardinal place of student–adult connections in fostering community, it will surprise no one to learn that opportunities to develop meaningful relationships with teachers are critical to getting students involved in schools. So too are creating chances for youngsters to participate in class and schoolwide decisions (Ancess, 2003; Battistich et al., 1995; Epstein, 1981b, 1996) and school governance (Baker et al., 1997; Booker, 2006; Woloszyk, 1996)— "of increasing participation [of] students in planning and decision-making" (Cruddas, 2001, p. 64). Opportunities for leadership (Harris, 2009; MacBeath, 2009; Sather, 1999) and community service are often found in schools that are characterized by high levels of student involvement, both within the school (Ancess, 2003; Raywid, 1995) and in the extended community (Antrop-Gonzalez & De Jesus, 2006; Bloomberg et al., 2003; Eckert, 1989). Involvement at times has featured pupils as evaluators of their classrooms and schools (Lodge, 2005; Thomson & Gunter, 2006) and as in-house researchers (Rudduck & Flutter, 2004), including "student involvement in the assessment process, student-involved record keeping, and student-involved communication" (Stiggins & Chappuis, 2006, p. 13).

Participation in academic work is a keystone dimension of involvement. We hold our analysis of this dimension to Part 3. Here our attention is devoted to the dimension of school culture. Most studied here is student participation in extracurricular activities. While not without potential pitfalls, including nurturing "structural facets" and "informal mechanisms" (McNeal, 1999, p. 294) that promote exclusion and unhelpful boundary development (Hamilton, 1983; Mahoney & Cairns, 1997; Walberg & Anderson, 1968), often in terms of social class (McNeal, 1998); extracurricular school activities, when well designed and supervised, can serve as an important force in creating community and fostering a sense of school membership. In addition, they can provide students access to the types of social relationships with adults and with their peers that foster and guide school success. They also have the potential to bring students into close caring relationships with adults who can serve as mentors, advocates, role models, and friends. Unfortunately, the low-income and minority students who stand to gain the most from these sorts of activities are often involved the least, a fact that has obvious implications for school policy (Gibson et al., 2004, pp. 145–146). Schools that score well on involvement offer a significant range of such experiences (Leithwood, Louis, Anderson, & Wahlstrom, 2004). These schools are defined by inclusionary practices (Eckert, 1989), pulling large percentages of youngsters into extracurricular activities. Involvement here, as we discuss in detail in the last part of this section and more fully in Chapter 7, is linked to improved academic and social learning (Finn & Rock, 1997; Hattie, 2008; Rumberger, 2011).

Studies on extracurricular activities provide considerable guidance to educators for planning, developing, and putting these experiences into play for students (McNeal, 1998). Many of those guidelines are threaded throughout the analysis above (e.g., providing students with input about activities to be offered). The core question here has been provided by Marsh and Kleitman (2002, p. 465): "How should students spend their time for maximum academic, psychological, and social benefits to support future accomplishments?"

We know from the research that structured involvement activities are better than unstructured ones for promoting positive outcomes (Catalano et al., 1999; Feldman & Matjasko, 2005; Hattie, 2009).

Structured and organized activities trump leisure activities as well (Marsh & Kleitman, 2002). Experiences that lead to tangible outcomes are preferable (Roth et al., 1998). "Effective programs engage young people in a variety of ways, so that they are not just physically present, but intellectually immersed, socially connected, and emotionally centered" (Joselowsky, 2007, p. 260). Activities that nurture collaboration and cooperation and those that engender teamwork among students (Conchas, 2001) are generally preferable to those featuring competition (Cooper, 1996). Guest and Schneider (2003) also report that activities that foster identity and positive recognition are linked to valued outcomes. They also help us see that identity interacts with social context. That is, "activity-based identities are given meaning by school community value systems" (p. 90).

Experiences that lead to success for students from active involvement are desirable (Feldman & Matjasko, 2005). So also are programs in which peers from one's social network participate (Feldman & Matjasko, 2005) and ones where there is a strong match with the interests of the students (Eggert, Thompson, Herting, & Nicholas, 1995). Staff characteristics matter (Roth et al., 1998). Activities shepherded by strong and supportive teachers are more productive than those that are run by adults who are less committed to the programs (Roth et al., 1998). We know that getting parents on board can be an important asset in encouraging and maintaining involvement (Gonzalez & Padilla, 1997; Rumberger, 2011). Continuity of program participation is important. This includes the length of participation and the regularity of engagement (Feldman & Matjasko, 2005; Roth et al., 1998). A combination of activities from different domains (e.g., academic clubs, sports teams) is often preferable to a single concentration (Joselowsky, 2007; Roth et al., 1998). Except at the extreme end of the continuum, deeper participation, with active engagement, leads to the realization of valued ends (Feldman & Matjasko, 2005; Marsh & Kleitman, 2002). Experiences that cover "more of the contexts in which adolescents live" (Roth et al., 1998, p. 438) are desirable. "Multiple opportunities for multiple forms of access and interaction across various members of the school community" (Ancess, 2000, p. 605) provide the operational structure here.

Researchers also help us see that to be most beneficial, activities that promote involvement should be aligned with and integrated into the school culture and core school operations (Joselowsky, 2007; Marsh & Kleitman, 1992). "More comprehensive and sustained programs" (Roth et al., 1998, p. 440) lead to more positive outcomes. Within the context of the findings above, research allows us to say a few things about the types of activities that are most productive in fostering membership. Both academic and sports programs have been shown to produce positive outcomes (Guest & Schneider, 2003; Marsh & Kleitman, 2002), although, not surprisingly, academic activities have larger impacts on achievement (Hattie, 2009). School-related activities consistently lead to more favorable outcomes than out-of-school experiences (Marsh & Kleitman, 2002).

Ownership

The second dimension of membership is ownership, a concept defined in terms of student empowerment (Joselowsky, 2007; Silins & Mulford, 2010) or "sense of control" (Weinstein, 1983, p. 299), one that acknowledges the reality that "most students yearn to have a voice in their own schooling, to be free and to construct their own vibrant lives" (Johnston & Nicholls, 1995, p. 94). "The issue is the extent to which young people have the opportunity to critically define their own perspectives in the process of articulating their views" (Hadfield & Haw, 2001, p. 494). As Roth and Brooks-Gunn (2003, p. 175) document, ownership is marked by "an empowering atmosphere [that] encourages youth to engage in useful roles [and] practice self-determination." Students become "stakeholders" in the school. Thus, one aspect of the ownership subtheme of membership is student agency (Joselowsky, 2007), including meeting "students' expressed desire to have more decision-making opportunities" (Eccles et al., 1993, p. 566), meeting their need for "control over their lives in the [school] community" (Wallerstein & Bernstein, 1988, p. 380), and providing opportunities to commit to improvement and to influence actions at the school; thus enabling them to discover that their efforts will lead to positive effects (Jackson & Warren, 2000; Reitzug & Patterson, 1998). Quite relatedly, we discover that students talk about empowerment in terms of freedom/choice (Akos, 2002), power (Cook-Sather, 2002; Johnson, 2009), and responsibility (Bragg, 2007; Rudduck, 2007).

Students' comments reflect the concept of voice when they describe ownership as well (Arnot et al., 2004; Hadfield & Haw, 2004; Mitra & Gross, 2009). "Voice implies having power over the presentation of reality and meaning, and the ability to construct, articulate, and therefore shape one's experience as it is presented to others" (Quiroz, 2001, p. 328). Self-determination and autonomy are also core concepts embedded in empowerment: "the feelings that one has voice and choice about: taking action in the world or a sense of agency or personal causation" (Oldfather et al., 1999, p. 287), engaging children "in determining their own needs and priorities" (Wallerstein & Bernstein, 1988, p. 382), and providing choice and "helping children connect their behavior to their own personal goals and values" (Connell & Wellborn, 1991, p. 56). In the words of students, "I had real responsibilities, I helped plan the project. I made important decisions" (Morgan & Streb, 2001, p. 160).

In their preferred schools, students are allowed and encouraged to express themselves and their ideas (Battistich et al., 1997). Their voices are not silenced or devalued (Patterson et al., 2007; Rodriguez, 2008). "There is a willingness to move beyond the accumulation of passive data and a desire to hear what students have to say" (Fielding, 2004a, p. 2001). "Teachers learn to listen to students, not to speak for them" (Cook-Sather, 2006a, p. 6). Teachers "listen both openly and critically to students" (Cook-Sather, 2002, p. 10). Children "have voice in school affairs" (Newmann, 1981, p. 553): "Youth have opportunities that will shape their lives and the lives of their peers" (Mitra & Gross, 2009, p. 523). More important, in their preferred schools student views are heard (Dahl, 1995; McLaughlin & Talbert, 2001; Patterson et al., 2007) and honored (Ancess, 2003). Educators are "physically and emotionally present in social exchanges with students" (Adams & Forsyth, 2009, p. 268). Students' perspectives are received (Reitzug & Patterson, 1998). "Those who listen take what students say seriously" (Fielding, 2004a, p. 206); that is, "teachers take account of their perspectives" (Arnot et al., 2004, p. 4).

> Authenticity is about ensuring that the process of consultation and participation seems credible to students. From the student perspective, authenticity rests on three things: whether they have been involved in determining the focus of consultation; whether the interest of adults in what they have to say is real or contrived; and whether there is discussion of their suggestions and active follow-through. (Rudduck & Fielding, 2006, p. 226)

Ownership entails "an expression of trust and empowerment" (Atweh & Burton, 1995, p. 564) on the part of teachers (Arnot et al., 2004) and on the part of owners, students in this case (Battistich et al., 1997). Schools that build powerful communities for youngsters "maximize opportunities for students to contribute to school policy and management" (Newmann, 1981, p. 552) through both formal and informal mechanisms, assuring that students' points of view are taken into account in classroom and school decision-making (Ancess, 2003; Newmann, 1981) and in the "conception, execution, and evaluation of work" (Newmann et al., 1992, p. 25) and school-based activities. "Pupil consultation is a normal integral part of teachers' classroom practice" (Arnot et al., 2004, p. 6). Ownership includes "bringing the learner in as a full and active participant in enhancing and shaping their own learning" (Felner et al., 2007, p. 210), making youngsters "constructors of both their learning environment and learning experience" (Joselowsky, 2007, p. 265)—"children given an opportunity to solve problems for themselves" (Bragg, 2007, p. 668). Students with influence are "active agents in the creation of school success" (Conchas, 2001, p. 501). They own the school and their work (Ancess, 2003; Newmann et al., 1992). They are partners and producers, not simply categories or recipients (Joselowsky, 2007), tourists (Freiberg et al., 2009), or consumers (Eckert, 1989). They "take ownership of their own learning" (Levin & Datnow, 2012, p. 190). Relatedly, ownership implies common purpose, one that "builds a sense of membership that enhances engagement in work" (Newmann et al., 1992, p. 21). It entails the opportunity to engage in meaningful and challenging activities (Roth & Brooks-Gunn, 2003)—in "authentic academic work" (Marks, 2000, p. 158)—and includes influence over the ways in which students engage with those activities (Newmann, 1981; Newmann et al., 1992).

As we reported in Chapter 1 and revisit in Chapter 7, on the other hand, students routinely inform us that there is a palpable difference between preferred and actual schools. That is, the form of empowerment described above is weakly practiced in their education, a reality captured nicely by a student in the Rudduck and Flutter (2004, p. 202) study: "Our opinion is never asked for and never matters." We also saw in Chapter 1 many of the reasons for the limited empowerment of students. Particularly salient in the domain of voice is our adherence to naïve and somewhat troublesome views of childhood (Bradley et al., 2004; Rudduck & Fielding, 2006), understandings that operate from "the assumption of students' inability to participate in or direct their own learning" (Lincoln, 1995, p. 91). Also implicated in the disempowerment chronicle is our inability or unwillingness to envision and practice productive alternatives to transmission models of learning, hierarchical understandings of organization, and government-professional models of operating schools (Levin, 2000; Murphy, 2013).

The consequences of these forces have fostered five dysfunctional methods for addressing issues of empowerment generally defined and student voice more specifically. The implicit and most pervasive response is simply not to worry about the issue. Empowerment simply is not a viable aspect of the school landscape. The essence of empowerment is "presented as something to be taught rather than experienced in the daily life of the school" (Rudduck & Fielding, 2006, p. 223). As we reported in Chapter 2, "Pupils' views have, for the most part, been missing in schools" (Rudduck & Flutter, 2004, p. 112). Not surprisingly, analysts routinely find that systems, policies, practices, and structures in schools are antithetical to the growth of ownership—"on the whole they offer less responsibility and autonomy than many young people are accustomed to in their lives outside school" (p. 113). At other times, teachers assume, often incorrectly students inform us (Quiroz, 2001), that they speak for students (Cook-Sather, 2002), another pattern that closes down listening. Third, schools are fairly adept at providing opportunities for marginal participation—"tokenism, manipulation and practices not matching rhetoric when students participate in decision making" (Atweh & Burton, 1995, p. 564). Students here are offered choices that they do "not perceive as being real choices" (p. 572). Included here are "invitations (a) to express a view on matters they do not think are important, (b) [that] are framed in a language they find restrictive, alienating or patronizing, and (c) that seldom result in actions or dialogue that affects the quality of their lives" (Rudduck & Fielding, 2006, p. 227), as well as "consultation techniques which are experienced as irrelevant" (Arnot et al., 2004, p. 79), such as those of "the dreary sameness of questionnaires about matters of little real consequence" (Fielding, 2004a, p. 203) and "treating student voice as an instrument of teacher or state purpose" (Fielding, 2004b, p. 306).

There is also a more active dismissal of voice in play at times, what Patterson and colleagues (2007, p. 128) describe as the creation of an "underlying culture of silencing"—"school sponsored silencing" (Quiroz, 2001, p. 328)—where ownership is explicitly undermined and student voices are consciously muted (Patterson et al., 2007). Here, Bragg (2007, p. 668) informs us, "Young people are explicitly constrained." Fifth, and related to silencing, for various reasons schools at times privilege the voices of some students (Fine, 1986). Bragg (2007, p. 607) notes here the not unusual practice of "teachers training up outstanding but acquiescent pupils." The result can be that "the powerful are reaffirmed in their superiority and the disadvantaged confirmed in their existing lot" (Fielding, 2004b, p. 303). Historically, such privileging has acted to disempower youngsters from low-income and working-class homes, children of color, and those from minority cultures.

> So long as an undifferentiated notion of student voice is assumed or valorized, there is a significant danger that issues of race, gender and class are sidelined and in that process of presumed homogeneity the middle-class, white view of the world conveniently emerges as the norm. (Fielding, 2004b, p. 302)

Thus, while "it is easy to assert that a first step toward including perspectives on schooling is counting students among those who belong on the list of stakeholders with a voice in shaping educational policy and practices" (Cook-Sather, 2002, p. 9), given what we have presented the reader will not be surprised to learn that such empowerment does not simply materialize in schools. "It does not arise through an unstructured permissive process" (Bragg, 2007, p. 676). It begins with the acknowledgment "by teachers and administrators that students possess unique knowledge and perspectives about their schools that adults cannot fully replicate without this partnership" (Mitra & Gross, 2009, p. 523). "It requires extensive facilitation in order to provide a framework within which both teachers and students feel comfortable and that then enables new insights and developments to occur" (Bragg, 2007, p. 676). "'Voice' is not spontaneous, but rather carefully constructed, which underlines the importance of looking for different strategies through which children can 'express' themselves (Bragg, 2007, p. 677)." It is almost always "part of a broader plan to encourage consultation and participation" (Rudduck & Flutter, 2004, p. 22).

Plans to enhance ownership usually "cover a range of activities that encourage reflection, discussion, dialogue, and action on matters that primarily concern students, but also, by implication, school staff and the communities they serve" (Fielding, 2004a, p. 199). Cole (cited in Atweh & Burton, 1995, p. 565) provides a research-anchored set of factors related to "successful implementation of projects" that have great relevance here as well:

- that young people be involved by their own choice
- that there be maximum decision-making by the young people
- that students face authentic and genuine problems and be offered challenge and accountability, and that teachers avoid simplifying to make problems 'safe'
- that maturity be promoted
- that a real need as perceived by the young people be addressed, that is, that the need be authentic and genuine

What matters is that the principles and values of pupil empowerment are threaded through the daily interactions and communications of school life. We discover from the research that promoting empowerment includes ideas such as "encouraging multiple groupings and sites for student engagement" (Fielding, 2004a, p. 208) and "consulting pupils about who they will work with rather than imposing seating patterns that they may find arbitrary and unproductive" (Rudduck & Flutter, 2004, p. 94). Empowerment opens classroom problems to students' ideas and provides "students with responsibility for various aspects of the school environment" (p. 85). It also includes creating smaller forums for students "to present their ideas in a context where they will be listened to, heard, and understood" (Harter et al., 1997, p. 170). Ownership is "inversely associated with an emphasis on the teacher as sole authority in the classroom" (Battistich et al., 1997, p. 143) whereas having students take responsibility for their learning promotes ownership (Garmezy, 1991; Joselowsky, 2007). In empowered schools, youngsters are provided choice and responsibility to accomplish important work (Joselowsky, 2007; Roth et al., 1998; Rutter et al., 1979), in terms of both their own learning and development

(Gurr, Drysdale, & Mulford, 2005) and the improvement of the school (Joselowsky, 2007). Opportunities for students to lead are an especially important aspect of responsibility (Jackson & Warren, 2000; Roth & Brooks-Gunn, 2003; Sather, 1999).

Ownership includes the concepts of space and place. Students in meaningful communities have their own space, and they see school as a place for them (Eckert, 1989; McLaughlin & Talbert, 2001; Weis, 1990). Such tangibleness helps students "develop a sense that they are an integral part of the school collective" (Cooper et al., 2005, p. 9) and feelings of inclusiveness (Eckert, 1989; Newmann, 1992), and, as one student comments, have "space to deal with ourselves" (Cruddas, 2001, p. 65). "Space" also includes "venues to speak and be heard" (Cruddas, 2001, p. 66), places "where students can explore their views" (Rudduck & Fielding, 2006, p. 223).

Finally, we discover from watching and listening to youngsters that competence/accomplishment is an important element of empowerment (Baker et al., 1997; Crosnoe, 2011; Farrell, 1990). Two aspects of success are important. The first is a feeling of personal accomplishment (Baker et al., 1998; Dinham, 2005; Johnson & Asera, 1999). The second is the belief that one's efforts are worthwhile, that they make a meaningful contribution to the school community (Battistich et al., 1995; Csikszentmihalyi & Larson, 1984). Schools facilitate reaching both goals by centering on student competencies rather than student problems (Roth et al., 1998). They also accomplish these goals by creating a powerful sense of student responsibility (McMillan, 1996; Rudduck, 2007) and obligation (Willems, 1967), "a personal disposition that mediates between pressures to participate and actual participation" (Willems, 1967, p. 1257).

PART THREE

STUDENT VIEWS OF THE ACADEMIC PROGRAM

A Good School #2

A voyage of understanding
    shared by youthful teams of sage tutors

Guides carefully unfoiling coils of support
    providing cloaks of protection

Nurturing bonds of trust,
    weaving webs of community

Sharpening lenses of possibility,
    mediating hope

Part Three: Student Views of the Academic Program

> Students' descriptions of the teachers they wanted to have collectively painted a portrait of teachers who become deeply involved with student learning. (Wilson & Corbett, 3001, p. 122)
>
> Teachers set the stage and climate for learning that either facilitates or hampers cognitive engagement. (Shade, Kelly, & Oberg, 1997, p. 41)

In this part of the book, we continue our journey into the specifics of understanding schooling through the eyes of students. In Part 2, we examined student insights about learning climate. Here we focus on the academic program. Our question is the one raised by Graham (1995, p. 365): "What kinds of things can teachers learn from students about what they teach (the content) and how they teach (the process)?" What do they tell us about "how teaching this or that will enable and encourage the student to keep on learning?" (Maehr & Midgley, 1996, p. 25). There is an assortment of generic frameworks that can be used to address these queries. Davis (2003, p. 212), for example, informs us that "six dimensions of instructional context can influence the quality of students' engagement in class and with material ... tasks, autonomy, recognition, grouping, evaluation, and time. Rosenshine and Furst (in Beishuizen et al., 2001, p. 187) hold "that nine process variables attribute to a good learning result: clarity, variability, enthusiasm, task orientation, criticism, indirectness, student opportunity to learn, structuring comments, [and] varying the level of questions and cognitive activities." Fisher and Fraser (1983, p. 59), in turn, offer a framework with nine academic elements: involvement, affiliation, teacher support, task orientation, competition, order and organization, role clarity, teacher control, and innovation. We cover these and related elements below. However, we do so within a more parsimonious framework that underscores two macro-level dimensions of academic learning—"engaged teaching" (Chapter 5) and "constructed learning" (Chapter 6). We exit this introduction to Part 3 with a reminder: Our focus is on student eyes and voices in general; not every student sees the same as every other student (Wallace, 1996b; Wigfield et al., 1998).

FIVE

ENGAGED TEACHING

> It would be useful if schools were able to review the reasonableness of pupils' comments on teachers and teaching and monitor practice across lessons to check out whether, for a good deal of each day and week, approaches reflect what pupils would identify as "good practice" in helping them learn. (Rudduck & Flutter, 2004, p. 86)
>
> Students' perceptions of their teachers' academic support and expectations were the most consistent and strongest predictors of both engagement in school and school compliance. (Davis, 2003, p. 216)
>
> One of the central themes that students reiterated throughout the study was the myriad of ways in which their academic achievement improved based on their teachers' pedagogy. (Howard, 2001, p. 146)

While the focus of our attention in this section is on the behavioral aspects of engaged teaching, students provide insights as well about the more global dimensions of effective teachers. They tell us that four issues merit attention. The first is what Mergendoller and Packer (1985, p. 595) call "appealing temperament." Students describe such teachers as "enthusiastic and proactive" (Rudduck &

Flutter, 2004, p. 78). They have appealing personalities (Beishuizen et al., 2001). Second, students see good teachers as "knowledgeable and experienced" (Flutter & Rudduck, 2004, p. 47). They possess robust content knowledge and they employ it well (Hoge et al., 1990). Third, they enjoy and take great pride in their work, that is, teaching (Thompson, 2004; Wentzel, 2002), what Moos (1979, p. 188) calls "love of learning," enthusiasm and love of work (Burke & Grosvenor, 2003): "They care about learning and model the behaviors they wish to see in their students" (Davis, 2003, p. 227). Fourth, according to their young charges, good teachers take a strong interest in their students (Mergendoller & Packer, 1985; Miron & Lauria, 1998). Overall, Rudduck and Flutter (2004, p. 78) capture these general dimensions using a student voice: "They enjoy being a teacher, they enjoy teaching the subject, and they enjoy teaching us."

The above four points capture student views on "types" of teachers. For the balance of the chapter, we attend to the practices students see good teachers undertake. We remind ourselves that our interest in this section is on the pedagogical aspects of the core technology of schooling. In the following chapter, we attend to the curriculum, although by necessity there is considerable overlap between the two themes of the narrative. Our point of commencement is that students are sensitive to how teachers teach, and the "instructional style has a significant impact on who learns, what they learn, and how much they learn" (Wilson & Corbett, 2001, p. 61). We are attentive here to what students tell us about how teachers "encourage and enable [them] to define themselves as learners, thinkers, and doers" (Davis, 2003, p. 221). A second reminder is in order as well. This entire chapter is devoted to what students have to say about the academic aspects of classrooms and schools. We explored students' views on the cultural dimensions of schooling in Chapters 2 and 3. There are key linkages between chapters, however. One link is the foundational message that "teacher–student relations are the key to understanding who learns ... and how cohesive classrooms are formed and maintained" (Dillon, 1989, p. 255).

We close here with the cardinal lines of argumentation for the book: the understanding that (1) students' voices on essential issues concerning teaching and learning (Flutter & Rudduck, 2004) are often silenced in schools and (2) "students' own beliefs about effective instructional strategies need to be considered" (Wigfield et al., 1998, p. 92). That is, "authentic student voices provide the critical starting point for a progressive approach to teaching that maximizes the potential of pedagogy" (O'Loughlin, 1995, p. 110). We divide what students tell us here into three bundles: creating a sense of possibility, turning on to learning, and getting to understanding.

CREATING A SENSE OF VALUE AND POSSIBILITY

Listening to students' voices and seeing through their eyes leads to a number of salient aspects of engaged teaching. We learn, for example, the importance of creating learning goals in terms of values and practices (Kershner, 1996). At the broadest level, this is about helping students internalize the values of lifelong learning (Brewster & Fager, 2000; Cooper et al., 2005). It is also about instilling a sense of confidence that students can be successful (Rudduck & Flutter, 2004), a sense of optimism "about their potential for further growth" (Weinstein, 1983, p. 302). It is about forming an intrinsic orientation (Harter, 1996) and "intrinsic value for schoolwork" (Pintrich & De Groot, 1990, p. 37). It is about helping youngsters see "the relevance of education to future endeavors" (Lehr, Sinclair, & Christenson, 2004, p. 282).

At the midlevel, the spotlight is on purposeful work (Davis, 2003), an understanding of the importance of work undertaken, instilling meaning to what is often seen as empty routines (Newmann, Wehlage, & Lamburn, 1992; Warrington & Younger, 1996). At the micro level, students underscore the importance of "target setting" (Flutter & Rudduck, 2004, p. 122), "explicit learning expectations" (Thomson & Gunter, 2006, p. 853) for their work, or "lessons that have a clear focus" (Rudduck et al., 1996, p. 174). Students also emphasize clarity in reaching learning expectations (Quiroz, 2001): "Outlining in clear terms a set of steps for getting on to an answer" (Wilson & Corbett, 2001, p. 82).

When given the opportunity, students forcefully and eloquently illuminate the place of positivism in creating a sense of future (Flutter & Rudduck, 2004). They are prone to do this by calling out negative actions that they view as crippling. Of particular concern to youngsters are deficit-based school learning climates and negatively oriented teacher behaviors (Miron & Lauria, 1998; Nieto, 1994). As we see in the work of Weinstein (1983, p. 294), "Students are aware of differences in teacher treatment within classrooms." They speak openly and negatively of teacher expectations formed on the basis of race, class, immigrant status, and language (Hamilton, 1983; Slaughter-Defoe & Carlson, 1996), as well as school policies, practices, and routines that disempower and marginalize certain students (Hamilton, 1983). Ana, a Puerto Rican, echoes this feeling of abandonment by American teachers: "They don't try for us to learn anything. . . . They just leave us" (Zanger, 1993, p. 176). Students tell us that in many cases schools simply mirror the devaluation and negativism found in the larger society in which they live (Flutter & Rudduck, 2004; Nieto, 1994). There is a palpable sense of anger and disillusionment in their eyes that possibilities are equated with academic achievement levels (Chaplain, 1996a, 1996b).

> Students' photographs depicted that they believe that school should be a place where they are honoured for who they are and what they know, rather than dismissed or pigeonholed on the basis of their previous academic records, race, classes, abilities and genders. (Marquez-Zenkov, 2007, p. 144)

Looking through student eyes, we learn that the day in and day out work of forming a sense of possibility and future-oriented values has much to do with the concept of expectations discussed throughout this volume. The overall storyline has been wonderfully described by Weinstein (1983, p. 302):

> The research to date has also pointed out that students are enormously sensitive to the differential behaviors that teachers might display toward various groups of students. Students sense highly subtle differences in interaction patterns and are responsive as well to nonverbal messages conveyed. Through differential treatment, students can infer teachers' expectations for their academic performance. In classrooms where students were aware of the teachers' differential treatment of high and low expectations, the students' own expectations for themselves more closely matched the teachers' expectations, and the teachers' expectations for their students were powerful predictors of student performance.

When asked, many students tell us that even though "they want teachers who care about them and demand rigorous work" (Fine et al., 2007, p. 803), they feel locked out of possibilities—either because such hopes and possibilities for the future are not communicated or because teachers communicate the perspective that for many of them, such hopes and possibilities are unattainable. They feel as if "adults have given up on them" (Lee, 1999, p. 230). Not surprisingly, students and researchers consistently report that classroom policies and practices are formed on the scaffold of inadequacy (Brattesani, Weinstein, & Marshall, 1984).

The first link in the expectation-possibility chain is the well-documented process of low expectations being translated into differential treatment and minimal demands (Oakes & Guiton, 1995; Page, 1991). This is accomplished in both subtle and not so subtle ways (Saunders, Davis, Williams, & Williams, 2004; Shade et al., 1997). Indeed, "there is evidence that, consciously or unconsciously, teachers project through procedures, interactions, body language, and classroom management techniques the idea that some children are not worthy of being taught by them" (Shade et al., 1997, p. 47). More specifically, in discussing research by Hillard, Shade and colleagues (1997, pp. 46–47) note that teachers

- demand less of low-expectation than high-expectation students.
- give low-expectation students the answer and call on someone else rather than try to improve their response through clues or new questions.
- criticize low-expectation students more often than high-expectation students for failure.
- pay less attention to low-expectation students and interact with them less frequently.
- seat low-expectation students farther away from the teachers than high-expectation students.
- accept more low-quality or more incorrect responses from low expectation students.
- in administering or grading tests or assignments, give high-expectation students rather than the low-expectation students the benefit of the doubt in borderline cases.

The second link is that these transmitted expectations come to be accepted by students (Chaplain, 1996a). Through their eyes, we see students molding themselves to those expectations (Slaughter-Defoe & Carlson, 1996). Students ratchet down their own expectations and sense of efficacy (Eccles-Parson, Adler, Futterman, Goff, Kaczala, Meece, & Midgley, 1983; Thompson, 2004), putting in their time and doing just enough "to get by or pass" (Miron & Lauria, 1998, p. 1971). They develop a more negative perception of classroom climate, negative responses to the teacher, and reduced motivation. Or as Brattesani and colleagues (1984, p. 246) summarize it,

> teachers behave in ways that communicate their achievement expectations to their students, that students perceive these expectations from their teachers' behavior, and that these expectations influence students' own expectations.

The final link is rampant disengagement, often passive, sometimes aggressive, and reduced learning (Brattesani et al., 1984; Silverstein & Krate, 1975). For example, Murdock and team (2000, p. 34) found that "students' view of their 7th-grade teachers' perceptions were better predictors of their future college plans than was their own assessment of their academic abilities at that time." That is, there is abundant evidence "that teacher expectations and teacher treatments of youth are critical predictors of academic performance" (Fine et al., 2007, p. 816). Brattesani and team (1984, p. 245) provide us our conclusion here, documenting "that teachers do not merely sustain pre-existing differences in student achievement but can also increase these differences."

TURNING ON TO LEARNING

> Teachers establish the intellectual climate of the classroom by setting time limits, and selecting appropriate tasks and presentation style to meet the information processing preferences of their students. The competence with which teachers perform the selection and mediate the learning process determines whether or not students have access to the information in ways that facilitate their learning. (Shade et al., 1997, p. 42)

Over the years, a variety of analysts have shown that students prefer "teachers who 'turn them on' to learning" (Larkin, 1979, p. 171). Burke and Grosvenor (2003, p. 86) present this perspective quite nicely through the eyes of a 10-year old youngster: "I believe that school should teach in an exciting way because when children learn and have fun they take in more." More generally, "students' accounts underscore the importance of intellectually stimulating and engaging learning environments wherein students are actively connected to what is being taught" (Howard, 2001, p. 145), where there is "exciting and pleasurable work" (Cruddas, 2001, p. 66), where teachers "make the lesson interesting and link it to life outside the school" (Flutter & Rudduck, 2004, p. 78). According to children, turning on to learning also includes the ability of teachers to ensure that lessons are not a haphazard rush to the finish line (Flutter & Rudduck, 2004), that teachers take the time required for "students to grasp the material" (Wilson & Corbett, 2001, p. 82).

Students are consistent in their assessments of when schools fail to entice them into learning, that is, when their world is dominated by teacher monologues, when "lacklustre lessons" (Chaplain, 1996b, p. 122) dominate, when they "simply receive the dry, sterile subject-driven version [of schooling] presented to them" (Burke & Grosvenor, 2003, p. 58), and when their days are dominated with textbooks and blackboards (Nieto, 1994). "Irrelevant knowledge [and] pointless activities" (Arnot et al., 2004, p. 68) lead to boredom (Howard, 2001; Steinberg, 1996), often mediated by anger and resistance (Chaplain, 1996a; Wilson & Corbett, 2001).

> Of course, one reason why pupils turn to disruptive behaviour is that they are bored; their attention is not focused on learning and there is a dangerous circularity in that disengaged pupils' behaviour leads others to switch off learning because they feel that there is little point in trying to work under these conditions. (Flutter & Rudduck, 2004, p. 116)

And as students told Mergendoller and Packer (1985, p. 597), when teaching is boring "nearly all other characteristics of the [teacher] as well as the curriculum elude discernment." Relationships wither (Johnson, 2009). Students are also quite vocal about the positive dimensions of engagement for learning. They maintain, not surprisingly, (1) need for sufficient time to process material and engage with their teachers (Burke & Grosvenor, 2003; Flutter & Rudduck, 2004); (2) preference for "varied classroom activities" (Wilson & Corbett, 2001, p. 3); and (3) the importance of nonisolating, collective ways to tackle those activities (Alvermann et al., 1996; Freidenberg, 1971). Students also report that "the process of disengagement can be reversed if [they] feel that significant others in the school are able to see and acknowledge some of their strengths" (Rudduck & Flutter, 2004, p. 70).

Turning on to learning is also defined by what honoring student eyes have led us to call "responsive teaching." Responsive teaching at the broadest level is "demanding, critical, and expansive" (Fine, 1986, p. 407). The "emphasis is getting across to pupils the message that learning is for them rather than something 'done to them'" (Fine et al., 2007, p. 808). One element of responsive teaching routinely discussed by students is teachers' use of "different ways of showing and trying to get [lessons] across" (Student, cited by Arnot et al., 2004, p. 11). Lee (1999, p. 232), for example, tells us that students report that they learn the most when "teachers take the time to present concepts in multiple ways." In their studies, Wilson and Corbett (2001, p. 83) found that "students lauded teachers who employed multiple ways of understanding a problem or completing an assignment. . . . Teachers who taught a concept in alternative words to the textbook's explanation were labeled as particularly helpful."

Students described the importance of "learning-focused dialogue" (Flutter & Rudduck, 2004, p. 8). "When such a learning dialogue is in place, pupils will begin to gain a sense of competency and self worth, not through cajoling or threatening, but by recognising and responding to the evidence of their own efforts and achievements" (Doran & Cameron, cited in Flutter & Rudduck, 2004, p. 9). They also underscore the importance of pacing and organization in responsive teaching. Here, students emphasize the skills of teachers in breaking down "assignments into manageable steps" (Dillon, 1989, p. 250) and "explain[ing] material at varying paces depending on student comprehension" (Lee, 1999, p. 232). The skills of individualization and differentiating instruction are visible in students' comments (Burke & Grosvenor, 2003; Davis, 2003), which describe a "flexible pedagogy that understands the complexity of students' lives" (Smyth, 2006, p. 282) and a practice of "allowing and helping students learn at their own pace" (Rudduck & Flutter, 2004, p. 116). Indeed, students routinely and consistently report that individualization and sensitivity are critical ingredients in responsive teaching (Goldstein, 1999; Penna & Tallerico, 2005). As Wallace (1996a, p. 42) confirms, "The chorus of need that we see in the interviews is for more individualized support alongside clear and well-structured whole-class 'exposition.'" "The 'individual assistance' theme ranged between contrast poles describing inadequate and adequate instructional resources. "At one end of the continuum students described teachers who were not available to students or who refused to answer individual questions" (Mergendoller & Packer, 1985, p. 586). These "impersonal strategies can leave students feeling vulnerable and may cause them to question a teacher's fairness" (Davis, 2003, p. 213). Many students saw their "teachers as impatient with their lack of understanding because instructors often failed to take the time to provide needed individual attention" (Lee, 1999, p. 225). The question students leave us with then is this: "Are there any ways in which [we] can make space for more individual consultation about learning?" (Wallace, 1996b, p. 47). How can we promote "jointness" between teachers and students (Davis, 2003; Goodenow & Grady, 1993)?

Pupils also equate responsive teaching with "teachers asking questions [as] a way of sustaining deeper levels of active engagement" (Arnot et al., 2004, p. 18). Effective teaching, according to youngsters, features what Davis (2003, p. 220) describes as "scaffolding techniques . . . matching the demands of each task and the instrumental support to students' abilities." As we discuss in the next chapter, scaffolding concepts and materials are often linked with the construct of cultural responsiveness (Natriello, McDill, & Pallas, 1990; McQuillan, 1998). Finally, from seeing and talking with students analysts conclude that responsive teaching also has to do with the willingness of teachers to take risks (Wallace, 1996b), to provide students with autonomy and responsibility (Davis, 2003), and to reflect the seriousness with which learning should be engaged (Flutter & Rudduck, 2004).

GETTING TO UNDERSTANDING

Although all the ideas in this chapter on engaged teaching share common space, four stand out sufficiently to be collected into this section on "getting to understanding." Wallace (1996a, p. 38) sets up the narrative here as follows, underscoring "not" understanding:

More common was the experience of being 'lost' and this usually went beyond the confines of a single concept or topic and could attach to the subject as a whole—or even the curriculum as a whole. There are different reasons why pupils have such a feeling of being lost or not being able to get a grip on what is puzzling them. A common response in such a situation is to blame someone else, usually the teacher. Pupils talk about whole-class teaching with teachers who 'go too fast' or who 'don't explain things properly' and who, when pupils say they don't understand, blame them for 'not listening' or for 'being stupid.'

The first of the four concepts is students' sense that understanding depends greatly on the robustness of teacher explanations, on "teachers going to great lengths to explain assignments and concepts" (Wilson & Corbett, 2001, p. 3), and on teachers' "ability to make course context comprehensive" (Phelan, Davidson, & Cao, 1992, p. 700). "When teachers provide clear explanations this may improve students' perceptions of the meaning of schoolwork" (Bru et al., 2002, p. 290).

> Students' comments focused repeatedly on the clarity with which teachers explained new material and corrected students' confusions regarding the assignments they were expected to complete.... Students expected their instructors to be teachers in the root sense of the word: persons who *show* others how to master a subject. From the students' point of view, an instructor who abandoned students in the face of ambiguous worksheets and confusing lectures was cheating students of the high quality of instruction to which they felt entitled. Students seemed to consider the interactive processes of teaching and learning to be two parts of a bargain; they were willing to learn the assigned material as long as teachers' instructional practices facilitated their learning. When teachers did not keep up their part of the classroom contracts but continued to assess and reward student performance, mutterings of "foul" appeared in the transcripts. (Mergendoller & Packer, 1985, pp. 586–587)

Wilson and Corbett (2001, p. 64) corral all this quite eloquently. Understanding through student eyes means "the teacher explained things until the 'light bulb went on' for the whole class."

> A teacher's being willing to help meant that the teacher found a way for the student to get continued explanations of a concept, problem, or assignment until the student understood it.... The important point was that the help had to result in the students' understanding. Students praised the teacher who "makes sure that I got it," who "makes sure I understand," who "teaches me so I can do it," who "makes it easier to understand," who "makes it clear," who will "actually teach." That was the sole criterion of effectiveness. (Wilson & Corbett, 2001, p. 23)
>
> Our analysis suggests that students were in agreement about significant aspects of teaching and learning, such as having the teacher make explicit the learning expectations and explaining things clearly. (Thomson & Gunter, 2006, p. 853)

Students report that the best explanations are "clear and incorporate plenty of examples and involve concrete demonstrations of new concepts and ideas" (Arnot et al., 2004, p. 11).

> Taken as a whole, the definition statements concerning instructional facility suggested that students wanted to learn the material they were assigned and sought to complete their academic tasks competently. Students expressed disappointment and anger when they perceived teachers' instructional behaviors as impending their understanding and completion of their assigned work. Conversely, the seventh graders seemed quite appreciative when teachers helped students to learn by giving clear explanations of the material they were expected to master and by being responsive to each student's questions and problems. (Mergendoller & Packer, 1985, p. 587)

The second element of "getting to understanding" is teacher feedback (Kershner, 1996; Weinstein, 1983). Flutter and Rudduck (2004, p. 10) in their analyses of student voice conclude that "supportive assessment procedures can make a difference to pupils' engagement with learning," that is, "students acknowledged the value of providing a feedback loop to make sure [they] understood the material" (Wilson & Corbett, 2001, p. 84). A review of the research on feedback to students reveals a number of effectiveness criteria domains, such as closeness in time to work completion, specificity, "sensitivity to the needs of . . . learners" (Flutter & Rudduck, 2004, p. 10), accuracy, frequency, detail, personalization, and usability (Stanton-Salazar, 1997; Thompson, 2004). We know that feedback that underscores learning and support rather than accountability is desirable; that is, input about things that are changeable and controllable (Pintrich, 2003) is more useful. Students tell us that they prefer "honest criticism and constructive feedback that offer[s] guidance rather than empty praise and encouragement" (Peterson & Irving, 2008, p. 240). Getting students in the feedback loop by teaching them to assess their own efforts is preferable, as is the use of feedback that "does not undermine intrinsic motivation" (Wigfield et al., 1998, p. 96).

The third element of "getting to understanding" is the provision of academic care (Murphy & Torre, 2014; Murphy, 2016), or "pedagogies of care" (Johnson, 2009, p. 100), a state that leads to enhanced student motivation, engagement, and learning (Feldlaufer et al., 1988; Howard, 2002). When academic care is felt, students describe their teachers as people who create a supporting classroom (Lehr et al., 2004). Critical here for students is the sense that they have meaningful relationships with their teachers, that they are not simply cogs in the learning machine (Davis, 2003). They describe caring teachers as helpful, as making time to provide assistance (Mergendoller & Packer, 1985). They see them as active listeners, as guides who understand "that making time to talk with pupils about learning can reap tremendous rewards" (Flutter & Rudduck, 2004, p. 8). Students underscore the nonadversarial behavior of teachers who care (Murdock et al., 2000), as well as their willingness to stay with them even when it is inconvenient (Wilson & Corbett, 2001), a kind of "hang withedness." They also routinely characterize care in terms of teachers pushing them to do their best work and staying with them to ensure success (Fredricks et al., 2004; Sanders &

Harvey, 2002). Young people see the importance of teachers working hard in the caring equation (Felner et al., 2007; Roeser et al., 2000), as well as teachers taking an interest in them (Johnston & Nicholls, 1995). When pedagogical care is present, "students perceive their teachers as someone who respects their interpretations, provides opportunities for personal expression, and in general 'honor[s] their voices'" (Davis, 2003, p. 220).

Turning the lens on themselves, students define academic care as being seen and known on a personal level (Lewis, 2008; McLaughlin, 1994; Shannon & Bylsma, 2002) and as being acknowledged (Powell, Farrar, & Cohen, 1985; Wehlage, Rutter, Smith, Lesko, & Fernandez, 1989). They describe the feeling of being allowed to be vulnerable (Rudduck & Flutter, 2004). "Students applauded teachers who did more than just pass along content to them. They especially appreciated teachers who made the effort to understand and believe in them" (Wilson & Corbett, 2001, p. 86). Being valued, believed in, respected, and taken seriously as individuals are core ingredients in the idea of academic care according to students (Arnot et at., 2004; Chaplain, 1996a; Phelan et al., 1992). From students' perspectives, "Teachers who fail to acknowledge the knowledge, beliefs, and skills students bring to activities and interactions and the ways in which students resist conceptual change limit their ability to connect with their students" (Davis, 2003, p. 20).

Finally, and related to the developing narrative, we turn to the fourth factor of "getting to understanding," providing support (Bru et al., 2002; Nieto, 1994), or, closer to the language of the children, not giving up on them (Patterson et al., 2007). Although we have seen support threaded through the analysis to this point, for purposes of clarity and reinforcement, we extract it for special analysis here as well. The critical insight here has been penned well by Wilson and Corbett (2001, p. 64): "The particular strategies used were less important than the underlying belief they symbolized: that every child had to have the in-school support necessary for learning to occur." Or through the eyes of a student, "The most important resource she provided was the assurance that if [he] invested, learning would take place" (Muller et al., 1999, p. 319). We also reemphasize the keystone place that support enjoys in nourishing student engagement (Boekaerts, 1993; Midgley et al., 1989): "When teachers provide appropriate learning support, students are more likely to succeed instead of becoming frustrated and withdrawing" (Bru et al.,

2002, p. 290). "Both the students' attitudes about favorite teachers and their advice to teachers reveal that students invest in teachers who care enough to do whatever is necessary to facilitate learning" (Muller et al., 1999, p. 316), both for individuals and for communities of learners (Howard, 2001).

Looking again through student eyes, we can capture the essence of pedagogical support in two buckets: push and help. On one front, push is about conveying the seriousness of school work to youngsters (Cooper et al., 2005; Fine et al., 2007). It is about challenging youngsters and demanding that each of them bring her or his "A game" to the work (Bru et al., 2002; Lipman, 1995); it is about motivation and encouragement (Flutter & Rudduck, 2004; Rodriguez, 2008).

> We interpreted students to be saying that these effective teachers adhere to a 'no excuses' policy. That is, there were no acceptable reasons why every student eventually could not complete his or her work, and there were no acceptable reasons why a teacher would 'give up' on a child. (Flutter & Rudduck, 2004, p. 83)

In her work, Lee (1999, p. 230) concluded that "students said they wanted, and needed, teachers to 'keep on them,' to continually push them to do their work." In addressing "the push factor," Rodriguez (2008, p. 71) reached a similar conclusion: "A significant number of students spoke about the role that encouragement or being 'pushed' played in their engagement with school." And from Wilson and Corbett's work with children,

> Students said they wanted to learn; they just did not act like it. It fell to the teacher to continually stay on them to do otherwise. (p. 34)

> This student's preference was typical of most of the students we interviewed. With rare exceptions, they wanted a teacher who nudged them along and made sure that they worked. Students felt that few of them had the confidence, drive, perseverance,

or determination to do it on their own. They wanted and expected to be motivated to learn. And that unwavering push usually had to come from their teachers. (p. 70)

In short, students judged teachers as effective when those teachers "pushed them to excel" (Murdock et al., 2000, p. 329) and when they saw those demands "as coming from a place of teacher concern about students themselves" (Patterson et al., 2007, p. 136).

Students also talk about the importance in their "getting to understanding" narrative of teachers providing assistance to turn push into success (Hayes et al., 1994; Kershner, 1996; Miron & Lauria, 1998), a ferocious willingness to help struggling students. "What I am saying is if teachers took that extra time and really tried to pull you in, some things could be different. That's all I'm saying" (Student, cited in Sanon, Baxter, Fortune, & Opotow, 2001, p. 77):

Her message suggested that if a student did not understand the subject matter, then she assumed the problem was not caused by a deficit in the student; she merely needed to find an additional way of conveying the information to the student. (Thompson, 2004, pp. 60–61)

Students see this academic care as an avenue "to cope with academic stressors" (Wenz-Gross & Siperstein, 1998, p. 97). They equate it with proficiency (Wilson & Corbett, 2001). They are generally responsive and grateful for it as well (Howard, 2001; Wallace, 1996a).

SIX

CONSTRUCTED LEARNING

> To our respondents, the process of learning would not seem to be defined by the acquisition of new understanding or insight but rather by brute completion of assigned tasks. (Mergendoller & Packer, 1985, p. 586)
>
> Much has changed since the late 1960s in the way learning is organized in schools, but not in the direction that young people had advocated. (Burke & Grosvenor, 2003, p. 70)

In Chapter 5, we centered the spotlight on engaged teaching. Here we illuminate the work that unfolds in classrooms, again informed by and seen through the eyes of students. We acknowledge that distinction between these two broad categories is somewhat artificial but nevertheless necessary for analysis. Inside the category of constructed learning, we find seven core concepts: work that is intellectually challenging, cooperative, empowering, meaningful, authentic, student centered, and mastery oriented. As we will see, these elements of constructed work share considerable space. One piece of good news to begin the analysis of these core concepts is that "students' views on good learning reinforce[s] educational findings on effective learning strategies" (Lodge, 2005, p. 141), "practices that closely match those outlined in the best practice literature" as well (Storz, 2008, p. 250). A second is that students have a good deal to say on the work going on—or not going on—in schools. A third is that the nuggets excavated from the research and the narratives of students collectively reveal actions that are especially helpful for children placed at risk by society.

INTELLECTUALLY CHALLENGING WORK

The first pillar of constructed work is challenge, what practitioners and scholars label "critical demandingness." Challenge is particularly relevant when embedded in interesting tasks, "providing kids with interesting and challenging things to do" (Rogers, 1994, p. 41). Flutter and Rudduck (2004, p. 81) present what students told them on this pillar as follows: "Good lessons are ones which challenge you and make you think . . . and therefore help you to learn." The efforts of these scholars to hear what children have to say leads them to conclude that "pupils of all ages like to feel a sense of challenge in their learning" (p. 118).

Analysts of student perspective are quite diligent in teasing out the subconcepts that define challenge. Level of task is critical (Wallace, 1996b). While students caution against work that is too complex, or "too distant or destabilising" (Flutter & Rudduck, 2004, p. 113)—or beyond the zone of proximal development, they much more routinely underscore the fact that much of what unfolds in their classrooms lacks challenge, that they are routinely bored with the work that they are assigned. Students also tell us that challenge "is about learning and not just performing" (Maehr & Midgley, 1996, p. 188). Challenge is also marked by a thread of risk taking, an "academic venturesomeness" (Maehr & Midgley, 1996, p. 30), and by higher levels of cognition (Steele et al., 1971). A touch of novelty is often seen in portraits of challenge as well (Flutter & Rudduck, 2004). It is characterized by "opportunities to expand knowledge and competencies" (Bandura, 1993, p. 130) and by the press we spoke about previously (Moos, 1978).

Because "the principle of intellectual challenge . . . helps students to experience learning as a dynamic, engaging and empowering activity" (Rudduck & Flutter, 2004, p. 136), those who track student perspectives on this aspect of constructed work hear about outcomes such as commitment to work, a positive work ethic (Rudduck & Flutter, 2004). "Tasks that are perceived by students as relevant and appropriately challenging are associated with increased intrinsic interest" (Davis, 2003, p. 226) and motivation (Bandura, 1993). "Optimal challenge" is, in turn, linked to "optimal engagement" (Connell & Wellborn, 1991, p. 70).

COOPERATIVE WORK

Students consistently report that they value collaborative work (Lodge, 2005; Nolen & Nicholls, 1993), "more group work" (Lee, 1999, p. 238): "They particularly enjoy working with their peers" (Poplin & Weeres, 1994, p. 32). They express "an overall preference for small-group discussions over whole-group discussions" (Alvermann et al., 1996, p. 254), "contexts for learning that facilitate collaboration among peers" (McIntyre, Pedder, & Rudduck, 2005, p. 154). Students also "report that they work better and learn more in groups" (Thomson & Gunter, 2006, p. 849), that creating "social contexts amenable to collaborative learning are helpful to learning" (McIntyre et al., 2005, p. 149). Fortunately, this felt need and preference by students fits what the research tells us about meaningful work and learning (Shade et al., 1997), that it is "a social process" (Flutter & Rudduck, 2004, p. 11), one that "emphasizes communality" (Smerdon, 2002, p. 289) and "stimulates social connections and collective identity" (p. 289). Thus, according to Cabello and Terrell (1994, p. 20), "lesson excerpts and interviews show that exemplary teachers as a whole strongly emphasize teaching students how to work collaboratively."

Students and those who help us see through their eyes reveal information about the forms of and ingredients in collaborative work. On the form or strategy front, we learn of a variety of ways for students to work collectively (Mergendoller & Packer, 1985) and of a variety of "collaborative techniques" (Flutter & Rudduck, 2004, p. 33). Cooperative learning stands out (Wilson & Corbett, 2001). "Pupil-to-pupil support schemes" (Flutter & Rudduck, 2004, p. 123), such as peer mentoring (Cabello & Terrell, 1994), fit here as well, as does "heterogeneous grouping that resembles a family" (Shade et al., 1992, p. 89). On the DNA or principle front, we find that "students share the responsibilities not only of their own learning but also for promoting others' learning" (Davis, 2003, p. 227). Cooperative work includes "the establishment of democratic principles and the promotion of interdependence" (Howard, 2001, p. 146). It includes "peer-led small group discussions" (Alvermann et al.,

1996, p. 154) and "depends heavily on the establishment of a discourse community . . . , an atmosphere where students feel their ideas are taken seriously" (Ellwood, 1993, p. 74). The DNA of collaborative work features what Brewster and Fager (2000, p. 15) refer to as "reciprocal relationships," learning opportunities "where each student's knowledge is needed by others in the group to complete an assignment" (p. 15). The focus is on "collectivity rather than individualism" (Shade et al., 1997, p. 55). "Group discussions [that] foster material respect and understanding among members" (Alvermann et al., 1996, p. 264) are important. So too are values such as "the importance of contributing to the discussion, listening to others, being tolerant, and staying on topic" (p. 264). Within this social dynamic, qualities needed to be a productive working partner are important as well. "Being prepared to listen was seen as important, caring about school work, being able to explain things, being funny and tolerant—and being ready to help when you are having difficulties" (Rudduck & Flutter, 2004, p. 97).

> They noted group members' responsibilities toward each other such as initiating talk, getting others involved through questioning, and keeping order. Demonstrating responsibility for their own behavior included actions such as offering pertinent points about a topic, sharing personal beliefs, and working to fulfill the academic task. (Alvermann et al., 1996, p. 257)

Opportunities for self-management are also key to good collaborative work. As was the case with intellectual challenge, positive consequences are yoked to collaborative work. We discover from both students themselves and researchers and practitioners who study schooling through student eyes that cooperative work is a valuable experience (Flutter & Rudduck, 2004). It often improves social relations (Johnson, 2009; McLaughlin, 1994). It leads to "improved liking of classmates" (Wilson, Karimpour, & Rodkin, 2011, p. 97). It strengthens "interethnic relations" (Zanger, 1991, p. 29) in racially and culturally diverse classrooms. Cooperative student effort is a catalyst that helps nurture the growth of core dynamics such as active learning, meaning, and ownership (Kershner, 1996; Wigfield, Eccles, & Rodriguez, 1998). For individuals, "caring attitudes" (Wilson et al., 2011, p. 90) among students are enriched as well (Anderman, 2003; Wilson & Corbett, 2001).

Collaborative work is seen by students as strengthening aspects "in the process of learning" (Wigfield et al., 1998, p. 100) too. There is also considerable agreement that "grouping students to engage in sustained collaborative tasks is associated with boosts in students' self-esteem" (Wilson et al., 2011, p. 92). Cooperative work has also been connected to enhanced student responsibility (Ellwood, 1993) and increases in motivation (Kershner, 1996; Nolen & Nicholls, 1993), expectations for success (Wigfield et al., 1998), and self-confidence (Bragg, 2007; Flutter & Rudduck, 2004). Finally, the chain of evidence reveals that collaborative work ends with stronger learning outcomes. These are discussed, not surprisingly, in terms of academic performance (Thompson, 2004; Wilson et al., 2011)— "positive, work-oriented groups and pairs strengthen achievement" (Rudduck & Flutter, 2004, p. 96). The evidence chain also reveals that cooperative work leads to "new forms of wisdom" (Lincoln, 1995, p. 89) and "understanding" (Alvermann et al., 1996, p. 253). A surprising but important finding is that while academic gains are visible across all students, those placed at peril by race, class, and ethnicity are more advantaged by cooperative work than are mainstream students (Irvine, 1990; Seiler & Elmesky, 2007; Slavin & Oickle, 1981).

Empowering Work

As with most of the aspects of this chapter on constructed learning, there is a fairly large gap between what happens in schools and what students tell us should be unfolding. That is, empowering work is the exception, not the rule, for most students in schools (Rudduck & Flutter, 2004). We also have abundant evidence that "those who arguably most need to control learning appear to experience the least control over their learning, that lower-achieving working class pupils are least likely to feel that they have control over their learning" (Arnot et al., 2004, p. 72). And where children have little influence over their learning, they are often disengaged (Wallace, 1996a). All of this returns us to our starting point on eyes: Students generally express a desire for "greater independence and autonomy in their classroom learning" (McIntyre et al., 2005, p. 154), "increased control over their learning" (Arnot et al., 2004, p. 87).

Empowerment in the literature on student eyes is expressed in a variety of overlapping but somewhat differently nuanced terms. In places, for example, the discussion centers on degrees of autonomy (Brewster & Fager, 2000). When autonomy surfaces, it is often employed as a modifier to such ideas as "thinking" (McIntyre et al., 2005, p. 155) and "self-expression" (Mergendoller & Packer, 1985, p. 591). Empowering work is often defined by the presence of student voice. Here at the most general level we see encouraging students "to be vocal about the things they feel [they] need to be vocal about" (Garcia et al., 1995, p. 141). It is about general respect for students' viewpoints (Johnston & Nicholls, 1995). More specifically, it is about input in "the learning process" (Roeser et al., 2000, p. 466) and greater influence on classroom topics (Lee, 1999), about "involving pupils in making decisions about teaching activities" (Flutter & Rudduck, 2004, p. 11), "suitable discussion topics" (Alvermann et al., 1996, p. 264), and the use of time (Flutter & Rudduck, 2004). The test, of course, is "the establishment of an atmosphere where students feel that their ideas [are] taken seriously" (Ellwood, 1993, p. 74). More tangibly still, voice is about "creating opportunities and encouraging student-centered questioning" (Commeyras, 1995, p. 101) and "opportunities for self-evaluation" of class activities (Flutter & Rudduck, 2004, p. 113).

Empowering work is also about the closely related topic of choice, what Poplin and Weeres (1994, p. 32) refer to as "self-chosen situations," and control over learning (Roeser et al., 2000). One aspect of choice refers to "control over working conditions" (Smerdon, 2002, p. 289). And one piece of this storyline focuses on open as opposed to more constrained or closed activities (Wigfield et al., 1998). Choice and control are associated with the concepts of student ownership and identity (Rudduck & Flutter, 2004), independence (Burke & Grosvenor, 2003; Steele et al., 1971), self-determination (Oldfather et al., 1999), agency (Arnot et al., 2004), peer leadership (Alvermann et al., 1996), student authority (Johnston & Nicholls, 1995), and self-management (Mergendoller & Packer, 1985). All, in turn, are dependent on the "authority structure of the school or class" (Epstein, 1981b, p. 109). Finally, students tell us that empowering work is defined by individual accountability for the results of choice and autonomy (Shade et al., 1997). Agency and ownership mean "that students must begin to take responsibility for their own intellectual performance" (Rudduck & Flutter, 2004, p. 85), what Kershner (1999, p. 68) refers to as "a strong sense of personal responsibility for working and learning in school" as well as their own behavior (Dillon, 1989).

MEANINGFUL WORK

Given the development of the narrative to this stage, we should not be surprised to learn that youngsters in schools find much of what they do without meaning. This is troublesome because in this situation engagement is limited (Crosnoe, 2011; Eckert, 1989; Weis, 1990). Or in alternative form, "It only makes sense that the more interesting an assignment is, the more likely students are to immerse themselves in the task and stick with it through completion" (Mergendoller & Packer, 1985, p. 593).

On the topic of absence of meaning, students often describe work as tedious (Mergendoller & Packer, 1985), as little more than busy work (Miron & Lauria, 1998), and as boring to the point of painfulness (Larkin, 1979; Sanon et al., 2001). From two studies, Thompson (2004, p. 94) informs us that "students complain about a boring curriculum, a boring style of instructional delivery, and low standards . . . busy work that was designed merely to keep students occupied." In a study conducted half a century ago, 59% of students told investigators that more than half of their classes were boring. The most common classroom activities, "listening to teachers explain things [and] doing worksheets" are found to create the most disinterest (Spires et al., 2008, p. 505). Indeed, Flutter and Rudduck (2004, p. 110) document that in children's comments "there are constant references to boredom when students felt that lessons are not presented in imaginative ways and when learning activities are limited to a repetitious format of worksheets and textbooks." A student in the study by Mergendoller and Packer (1985, p. 590) describes this boredom quite nicely:

> He would just talk straight. And that gets boring if the teacher just talks like a machine or a robot or something. It bores you to death and you're sitting there drifting off into another land or something. (Student, p. A13).

142   **Part Three:** Student Views of the Academic Program

And Nieto (1994, p. 405) tells us that students in his study "had more to say about pedagogy than about anything else, and they were especially critical of the lack of imagination that led to boring classes."

One element of the poor news here is that the organizational system of schooling and the framework for learning in education have been forged in ways that make boring work the norm in schools (Larkin, 1979; Poplin & Weeres, 1994; Sarason, 1990): "The routines of traditional schooling and particularly the language of reward and punishment indicated a belief that the child will only learn under . . . duress" (Burke & Grosvenor, 2003, p. 68). The second piece of bad news is the abundant evidence that students resist boring activities, work taken under duress, and "busy work" (Miron & Lauria, 1998, p. 207), especially "busy work [seen] as a means of controlling student behavior" (p. 206): "When you are in class and you lose concentration, you are tempted to just leave. That's the boredom thing again. If students are not actively engaged they lose concentration" (Student, cited by Sanon et al., 2001, p. 75). The third piece of bad news is that student withdrawal is a proven recipe for poor learning (Bruggencate, Luyten, Scheerens, & Sleegers, 2012; Feldman & Matjasko, 2005). Or in reverse form, the critical point is that "features of activities that individuals do in school can increase their personal interest in the activities" (Wigfield et al., 1998, p. 78), engagement with work, and social and academic learning (Allensworth & Easton, 2005; Rodriguez, 2008).

On the other hand, when we see things from the perspectives of students, we discover that they derive meaning and enjoyment in "those classes where teachers incorporate fun and interesting materials, presentation styles, and activities" (Lee, 1999, p. 233), when teachers "engage them in learning rather than relegating them to passive tasks that engender boredom" (pp. 233–234). Research on student eyes and voice helps tease out what meaningful work looks and feels like to young persons. Meaningful work is about "experience[ing] school as living rather than more preparation for future living" (Johnston & Nicholls, 1995, p. 97). It is about "interesting and challenging things to do" (Rogers, 1994, p. 41), about getting interesting tasks to undertake or the possibility to make existing work interesting (Hayes, Ryan, & Zseller, 1994; Nolen & Nicholls, 1993):

> To summarize, students expressed preferences for topics that they experienced as likeable, interesting, and debatable.

Most students valued topics that were naturally interesting; some held the teacher responsible for arousing interest in dull topics. (Alvermann et al., 1996, p. 260)

If the topic is not interesting, Tyrone and Nicke [two students] note, then it is the teacher's responsibility to make it sound exciting. In Tyrone's words, "Stress it more, you know. I mean . . . you gotta project it to the students more. Make them want to understand it. (Alvermann et al., 1996. p. 260)

I [a student] think you have to be creative to be a teacher; you have to make it interesting. You can't just go in and say, "Yeah, I'm going to teach the kids just that; I'm gonna teach them right out of the book and that's the way it is, and don't ask questions." Because I know there were plenty of classes where I lost complete interest. But those were all because the teachers just, "Open the books to this page." They never made up problems out of their head. Everything came out of the book. You didn't ask questions. If you asked them questions, then the answer was "in the book." And if you asked the question and the answer wasn't in the book, then you shouldn't have asked that question. (Nieto, 1994, p. 405)

Part of this is about not covering too familiar ground (Arnot et al., 2004). And remember that about 30% of teacher time is spent teaching children what they already know (Hattie, 2009).

Meaningfulness is, according to students, "a curriculum driven by curiosity, adventure and collective endeavour" (Burke & Grosvenor, 2003, p. 70). It is about gearing lessons to meet "the interests and needs of students" (Dillon, 1989, p. 250), including, as we discuss later, their cultural backgrounds. Also, as we emphasize throughout the book, interest for students means "undertak[ing] valued challenges with the guidance and support of trusted adults" (Mitra & Gross, 2009, p. 529) and peers. It is, at least to some extent, about "focus[ing] on what students want to talk about" (Moos, 1979, p. 150) and a willingness of teachers to delve into interesting topics (Flutter & Rudduck, 2004). It is about a little novelty, variety, and different modalities (Thompson, 2004; Wallace, 1996b). It is about inviting and creative and imaginative work (Mergendoller & Packer, 1985)—about constructed learning (Burke & Grosvenor, 2003; Wilson & Corbett, 2001).

Perhaps the most common, and in some ways powerful, center of meaningfulness provided by students is that work is fun (Spires et al., 2008; Zanger, 1991), time passed uncharted (Csikszentmihalyi & Larson, 1984). A critical "attribute the students described about their teachers was their ability to make learning a fun and exciting process" (Howard, 2001, p. 144). And they tell us,

> I think the only thing that I want teachers to know on behalf of the students and myself is that if they want to be here, we do. If they make the class fun and interesting, maybe we will be more fun to teach. I know that this statement doesn't go for all teachers or students, but we do want to learn. We don't want lectures all day and take notes. We want you to make learning fun and interesting. (Lee, 1979, p. 242)

> I think that the key to success and learning is interest, support, and most importantly enjoyment. (Burke & Grosvenor, 2003, p. 130)

> If it is more exciting it helps you to give it more of a try, like give it a real go. (Flutter & Rudduck, 2004, p. 87)

These youngsters express an overwhelming penchant for enjoyable activities, for excitement, and for fun (Arnot et al., 2004; Poplin & Weeres, 1994). They tell researchers "that making lessons 'fun' was not only important for pupils but it was also important that teachers should enjoy what they were doing" (Flutter & Rudduck, 2004, p. 61).

Students also provide insights into what we think of as the principles and conditions of meaningful work, matters that are mixed with but that carry us beyond issues of excitement, interest, and fun. Youngsters describe meaningful work as integrated and as coherent (Burke & Grosvenor, 2003). They are not clamoring for easy activities (Arnot et al., 2004). They see reaching understanding at the heart of meaningfulness (Dillon, 1989; Sanon et al., 2001), what Arnot and team (2004, p. 14), using student eyes, describe as "clear learning purpose" and what Flutter and Rudduck (2004) refer to as purposeful work. As Kershner (1996, p. 18) tells us from his study, "Pupils' critical understanding of education was demonstrated in the way they were able to make a distinction between school activities that were unpleasant but necessary or worthwhile, and those that seem to them to have little educational value." But at the same time, students are unwilling to decouple understanding from usefulness (Anderman, 2003; Taylor-Dunlop & Norton, 1997). Meaningfulness is defined as "thoughtful engagement" (Arnot et al., 2004, p. 13) and seen as the chance to examine serious issues (Poplin & Weeres, 1994) with which they can become personally identified (Wallace, 1996b).

Students describe the types of activities that are likely to carry the title of meaningful work as well. We examine this line of analysis below when we explore student perspectives on authentic and active work. Here we provide a few notes to help us make that transition. We have already shown students' preferences for multiple approaches to learning and a variety of activities. "Manipulative and 'hands-on-activities'" (Thompson, 2004, p. 617) are described as strategies that permit meaningful work to flourish, "interactive strategies" (Shade et al., 1997, p. 92) that pull students into direct involvement (Sanon et al., 2001). Physical movement seems to be an enhancing factor, "aspects of learning which engage the body as well as the mind" (Arnot et al., 2004, p. 64). This seems to be especially important for kinesthetic learners (Thompson, 2004). Multisensory learning in general scores high with students (Shade et al., 1997). Projects and practical assignments, that is, "tangible 'end product[s]'" (Flutter & Rudduck, 2004, p. 110) open doors to meaningfulness (Lee, 1999; Riley & Docking, 2004), especially projects that have life outside the immediate moment of the classroom (Burke & Grosvenor, 2003). "The positive feelings pupils have about 'practicals' was widespread. Pupils talked enthusiastically not just about doing things for themselves but also about teacher demonstrations of 'what happens if. . . . '" (Wallace, 1996b, p. 57).

There is a sense in the eyes of students that what they see routinely unfolding in schools is not "real life" (Spires et al., 2008). They report meaning when schools draw nourishment from beyond the walls of the school (Shade et al., 1997; Wilson & Corbett, 2011). Students speak favorably of "having more opportunity to learn outside of the school boundaries, to see, touch, smell and feel real artefacts or nature" (Burke & Grosvenor, 2003, p. 69), to get away from "the dead air of the classroom and hurried intellectual abstractions" (p. 69). "Thematic and interdisciplinary units" (Anderman, Maehr, & Midgley, 1999, p. 142) often carry the meaning gene for students as do entertaining episodes of learning (Howard, 2001). Sharing "events, issues, and people in their lives" (Howard, 2002, p. 421) in the community of peers can also enrich the seedbed from which meaning takes root, what Johnston and Nicholls (1995, p. 96) describe as the relevance of personal knowledge. Choice often trumps imposition in nurturing meaning (Johnson, 2009). Finally, students routinely acknowledge the power of "technology-related work" to make school activities meaningful (Spires et al., 2008, p. 507).

> Students ranked using computers in general and doing research on the Internet as the school activities they liked best, and listening to teachers explain things and doing worksheets as activities they liked least. Using computers was the one activity that all ethnicities stated as the activity that they liked best in school. (p. 506)

Authentic Work

The fifth dimension of constructed learning is captured well by the concept of authenticity, an idea that we separate into three parts for analysis: linkages to students as cognitive actors, linkages to the lives of students as culturally defined persons, and linkages of learning to real life. We examine how these ideas unfold in the world of schools. We begin with an important reminder, that authentic work is connected to the social and academic success of young persons: "When school experiences 'fit' students' needs, successful development is enhanced and when they do not, problems ensue" (Roeser et al., 2000, p. 463). The essential ground here is that "pupils do not enter classrooms stripped of . . . their own life-historical circumstances" (Wallace, 1996b, p. 60). They are who they are as learners, as members of society, and as actors in the world they inhabit.

Authenticity means on one front alignment with who students are as cognitive actors, "for relevancy in their intimate relationships with knowledge" (Burke & Grosvenor, 2003, p. 60). Shade and team (1997, p. 18) remind us "that students approach each learning task with [their] own particular history of development and learning—with their own point of view about ideas, the world, and learning tasks." We learn here that a key responsibility is connecting learning "to students' prior knowledge" (Thompson, 2004, p. 591). McIntyre and colleagues (2005, p. 153) refer to this as "contextualizing the

Chapter Six: Constructed Learning 147

learning in appropriate ways, [that is,] learning tasks that connect new ideas with things that were familiar," "learning grounded in students' autobiographical stories of their life experiences" (O'Loughlin, 1995, p. 111). Thus "teachers need to be open to the interests and prior knowledge of their students so they can craft lessons that touch meaningful life events and experiences" (Roeser et al., 2000, p. 466), "put students' questions at the center of classroom discourse" (Commeyras, 1995, p. 105), and create opportunities "for students to draw upon their narrative structures to make sense of material for themselves on their own terms" (O'Loughlin, 1995, p. 109).

> Pupils told us that work became more appropriately contextualised if there were evident connections between the task at hand and their current knowledge and understanding. The connections that pupils seemed to find helpful were sometimes achieved through their teacher's introduction of materials, objects and images that were already familiar to them. (Arnot et al., 2004, p. 14)

Authenticity means "build[ing] on earlier learning, not only in terms of content but also in terms of ways of working" (Rudduck & Flutter, 2004, p. 40). Students find in schools that "information gained through their lives is often split off or subordinated as irrelevant" (Fine, 1986, p. 402). On the other hand, exemplary teachers, students tell us, "frequently give students the opportunity to relate personal experiences to the content at hand" (Cabello & Terrell, 1994, p. 20), to create "personal relevance" (Kershner, 1996, p. 71).

> Pupils seemed to be telling their teachers in concrete ways and with clear examples how the authenticity of their learning experiences could be enhanced by bringing tasks into closer and more striking alignment with the mental and social worlds that they inhabit both inside and outside the classrooms. (McIntyre et al., 2005, p. 154)

The second and closely linked aspect of authenticity attends to the place of cultural relevance and cultural congruence (Dillon, 1989). At a minimum, this means "creat[ing] a schooling environment that is not in conflict with the student's cultural background" (Howard, 2001, p. 145). More forcefully, it means nurturing "an environment that respects students' cultural background" (p. 145). The starting point is that "students bring certain human characteristics that have been shaped by their socializing group to the classroom.... The cultural, social, and historical backgrounds of children have a major impact on how they perceive school and the educational process" (Shade et al., 1997, p. 11). Authentic school work is work that honors students' cultures, that reinforces cultural identity "in a manner compatible with academic pursuit" (Fordham & Ogbu, 1986, p. 203). Before delving into the concept of culturally relevant academic work, we pause to remind ourselves that this hallmark aspect of authenticity has been honored more in the breech than in action. That is, "delegitimizing" (Zanger, 1993, p. 184) is more common, as is disregard for intellectual-cultural capital that rests outside the mainstream culture.

> Using culture as a way of interpreting children's behavior and learning style is not an approach to which teachers are accustomed. Up to this point, the students are judged by the cultural norms of the school or the teacher and are expected to learn in the same way. Any variation is considered inappropriate or deficient. This is a typical response for people who are not acquainted with other ways of functioning or who see the world only from their perspective. (Shade et al., 1997, p. 19)

We also remind ourselves of a key conclusion in Chapter 5, that is, this deficit-based understanding of knowledge and the resultant marginalization place students at academic peril.

Culturally congruent academic focus, on the other hand,

> is an attempt to create a schooling experience that enables students to pursue academic excellence without abandoning their cultural integrity. Thus, the ways of communicating

Chapter Six: Constructed Learning 149

conceptions of knowledge, methods of learning, and the overall context of the educative process are situated within a framework that is consistent with the students' cultural background. (Howard, 2001, p. 136)

It is constructed learning designed "to meet the challenge of teaching to individual differences with a particular emphasis on the variation that occurs because of a student's cultural background" (Shade et al., 1997, p. 9). "Cultural integrity and support for academic excellence" (Lipman, 1995, p. 205) are ribboned together. "Features of the students' cultural capital are incorporated into pedagogical practices" (Howard, 2001, p. 145). The pathway from "acknowledging the culturally constituted nature of students' lives" (O'Loughlin, 1985, p. 111) to culturally relevant learning has been well laid out for African American children by Howard (2001, p. 147).

> Teachers need to abandon the deficit-based thinking about the cognitive capacity, sociocultural backgrounds, and overall learning potential of students. Second, there must be a willingness on behalf of teachers to make modifications in their teaching styles to align them more closely with students' ways of knowing, communicating, and being. Finally, teachers must have the will and the courage to learn about the culture, life, and history of African-American people. The acquisition of this knowledge requires more than reading various literature about the African-American experience. It entails talking to parents, students, and community members and immersing oneself in various facets of the day-to-day environment that students experience.

More tangibly, three avenues of effort are viable: recognizing and understanding ways of knowing of nonmainstream children; "build[ing] cultural bridges between the school culture and the culture of the community from which children come" (Shade et al., 1997, p. 81); and using materials that reflect the contributions of diverse cultures.

On the first point, we know that what is appropriate at home in some cultures is inconsistent with the norms of conducting the business of learning in classrooms (Shade et al., 1997). Authenticity is nurtured when both congruencies and differences between home cultures and school cultures are acknowledged, respected, and employed in the learning process (Tyson, 2002; Zanger, 1993), "when cultural communication styles are incorporated into instruction" (Shade et al., 1997, p. 92). The second point links authenticity to a framework that seeks to establish cultural continuity between home and the school "using various directives, monitoring, interactional styles, and participation structures within the classroom that were congruent with the interaction and learning situations commonly found in the students' homes" (Howard, 2001, p. 135).

> The litmus test for the accessibility of an educational system is the degree to which the instructional language and teaching practices match the unofficial teaching practices and informal communication systems of the students' homes and communities. It would appear that if we are to hear students' voices, we must be willing to explore culturally relevant forms of teaching. (O'Loughlin, 1995, p. 110)

The third point shows us that authenticity is deepened when "culture specific" (Shade et al., 1997, p. 120) artifacts and materials and "cultural specific information" (p. 90) are employed to "ensure that the curriculum and materials reflect contributions of a variety of people" (Cabello & Terrell, 1994, p. 22).

Authenticity also has a good deal to do with what students describe as real world relevance (McIntyre et al., 2005). One thick thread here holds together the importance of the "here and now" as opposed to some undetermined time (Kershner, 1996, p. 72), what Spires and team (2008, p. 510) refer to as "real world anchors" as opposed to children's work. An additional piece of the narrative here underscores "the kinds of knowledge that are required for real life in the world outside the school gates" (Flutter & Rudduck, 2004, p. 115). Also found here is schoolwork that "provide[s] opportunities to explore the community and have experiences that broaden their understanding of the broader community" (Shade et al., 1997, p. 89), the idea that "the school would be much more integrated into the wider community" (Burke & Grosvenor, 2003, p. 63). That is,

Chapter Six: Constructed Learning   151

"contextualising learning appropriately involve[s] designing and using tasks that authentically resonate with pupils' wider concerns, experiences and aspirations ... outside the school gate and beyond their learning careers at school" (Arnot et al., 2004, p. 15). On this last point, we learn relevance for students has to do with topics "important for their future lives" (Flutter & Rudduck, 2004, p. 118). "Specifically, students would like school experiences to be more directly related to careers that they might have in the future" (Spires, 2008, p. 509). They would like a chance to address "difficult, contentious, or conflicting issues" (Nieto, 1994, p. 400) in the larger world that confronts them, that is, "the difficulties facing the community and society" (Shade et al., 1997, p. 89). Embedded in this piece of the authenticity storyline are the ideas that "the work must have some value beyond the workplace" (Smerdon, 2002, p. 289) and that students must nurture a sense of responsibility for their work (Shade et al., 1997).

Finally, we learn from students that authentic work is viewed playing out in certain ways in their classrooms. There is emphasis, for example, on blended or integrated subject matter and knowledge that is not divorced from application (Burke & Grosvenor, 2003). There is acknowledgment and use of students' primary language (Shade et al., 1997). There is also attention to "selecting materials that closely match students' interests" (Dillon, 1989, p. 243), to "personal relevance" (Wigfield et al., 1998, p. 77)—in "pursuing a curriculum that is relevant and that connects to young lives" (Smyth, 2006, p. 282) and to interrupting "cultural discontinuity" in the classroom (Zanger, 1991, p. 7). Learning here "flows from exciting, rich, significant experiences" (Bragg, 2007, p. 676).

> Most students desire more interesting and relevant choices in the content and process of instruction. They enjoy classes where assignments require them to think about issues for themselves, involve critical issues embedded with values and controversy, and allow them to talk with peers. They particularly enjoy and learn from experiential activities.... Descriptions of the most boring, least relevant school activities suggest that the more standardized the curriculum, text and assignment, the more disengaged the students. (Poplin & Weeres, 1994, p. 32)

And, as we discussed in Chapter 4, relevance here has as much to do with the pedagogy as with the "tasks teachers present and the topics or subject matter they assign" (Alvermann et al., 1996, p. 253) and includes attention to the work orientations of different groups of students (First & Carrera, 1988). The take-away message runs as follows: In effective classrooms, "teachers make relevant connections and consider subject matter through the eyes of learners" (McLaughlin, 1994, p. 10).

> Insights into what children value and care about help us structure the classroom worlds in which children are most apt to learn. They suggest that we pay attention to what children value as learners and consider children's voices if we are to genuinely support children's learning. (Dahl, 1995, p. 129)

STUDENT-CENTERED WORK

Laced throughout the analysis in this chapter is the following maxim: Engaging work is student focused and student built. That is, creating work that is more meaningful and authentic "require[s] the use of strategies that are more interactive [and] student centered" (Shade et al., 1997, p. 129), strategies that are prized by students and that are effective in promoting learning.

> Students at all achievement levels told us that they prefer classrooms where they can take an active part in their own learning, classrooms where they can work interactively with their teachers to construct knowledge and understanding. We found these active student roles to be particularly important to the engagement and academic success of non-traditional students, who generally failed to thrive in teacher-dominated classrooms. (McLaughlin, 1994, p. 10)

Chapter Six: Constructed Learning 153

For purposes of analysis we separate student-centered work into two lines of discussion, the elements of constructive work and the characteristics of active, participatory work. The status quo from the perspective of students leaves a good deal to be desired. O'Loughlin (1995, p. 109) captures this reality quite accurately, reporting that since many "teachers are usually preoccupied with 'covering' the curriculum, there is little opportunity in school for students to draw upon their own narrative structures to make sense of the material for themselves on their own terms." Commeyras (1995, p. 102) adds confirmation here, documenting that "discussions that revolve around student-generated questions do not typically occur in most classrooms in the United States.... In classroom discourse, students rarely use questioning to seek knowledge, explanations, or understanding." The norms in schools are "teacher-in-control" and "student-as-passive learner" (Dillon, 1989, p. 254). And we would do well to remember that "according to student descriptions of the most boring and least relevant schoolwork, they include activities which stick closely to standardized materials and traditional transmission teaching methods" (Poplin & Weeres, 1994, p. 15).

The elements of constructed work are less complex than often argued. We begin with the material outlined earlier in our analysis on engaged work. We add the idea of students "working under their own initiative ... with the teacher acting as a guide and source of support" (Flutter & Rudduck, 2004, p. 36). Student-centered work entails "emphasis on ownership of ideas and personal construction of knowledge" (O'Loughlin, 1995, p. 108). It underscores an "abandonment" of the nearly exclusive focus on "teacher-centered instructional methods" (Lee, 1999, p. 238) and movement toward a more balanced portfolio of teacher-directed and student-focused learning activities, a movement away from "instructional models in which the flow of information is unidirectional" (Harter et al., 1997, p. 170) and a movement toward "self-regulated learning" (Maehr & Midgley, 1996, p. 31) and a "psychology of inquiry" (Commeyras, 1995, p. 102)—"a dialectical process in which teachers seek students' questions and fashion their teaching in response to students' interests and queries" (p. 102). Attention is devoted to the "notion that we need to connect students' experience with the concepts and organizing principles of the academic disciplines" (Ellwood, 1993, p. 68). In student-centered work, "both the teacher and students share the responsibility for teaching, learning, and interacting, including defining what constitutes a motivating curriculum" (Davis, 2003, p. 220). Constructivism "privileges students' natural questions, and the questions become the center of teaching and learning experiences" (Commeyras, 1995, p. 105).

As should be clear at this stage of our analysis, student-centered work suggests "major changes in the traditional patterns of schooling . . . a major teaching function [here] is to guide students in a well-informed exploration of areas meaningful to them" (Noddings, 1988, p. 221). There is a commitment to the "mutuality" of work: "Teachers have an obligation to support, anticipate, evaluate, and encourage worthwhile activities, and students have a right to pursue projects mutually constructed and approved" (p. 221). This is what Cook-Sather (2006a, p. 354) refers to as a "more reciprocal, mutually informing teaching and learning dynamic," which means, of course, that students have a more "significant role in the teaching–learning process" (Shade et al., 1997, p. 90) or more powerfully, "The 'somethings' the student say become the stuff of the curriculum" (Johnston & Nicholls, 1995, p. 94). "Students construct their own vision of the concepts, ideas, and events" (Shade et al, 1997, p. 129), a construction process facilitated by their teachers (Alvermann et al., 1996).

> Did the instructor make changes during the class that were responsive to learning needs expressed by students? If addressing this question, and providing evidence of change based on its answers, were not only legitimate but required, the structures that currently support the exclusion of student perspectives from conversations about educational policy and practice would be changed. This move in education would be in keeping with the recognition among other service professionals that they have failed to attend sufficiently to the experiences and perspectives of those they aim to serve, and [they would revise] their professional practices to include clients' perspectives to rectify this failure. (Cook-Sather, 2002, p. 11)

The second strand of student-centered work attends to the active, interactive, and participatory nature of student engagement.

Chapter Six: Constructed Learning   155

The core messages are as follows: "It is important to engage students actively in the learning process, rather than expect them passively to receive information" (Shade et al., 1997, p. 115). That is, "most critical is the active involvement of pupils" (McIntyre et al., 2005, p. 153). Students need to be "knowledgeable participants in the life of classrooms" (Arnot et al., 2004, p. 20). "Good lessons are about participation and engagement" (Rudduck & Flutter, 204, p. 79); "good lessons include activity" (p. 80).

We know that pupils see schools as "student 'talk-deprived'" places (Alvermann et al., 1996, p. 264), places lacking in interaction and participatory work. They often characterize classrooms as oppressive venues of teacher talk and student boredom (Arnot et al., 2004; Wallace, 1996b). Analysts, in turn, document that teachers' perceptions of institutional pressures, such as "institutionally sanctioned curriculum, subvert their attempts to engage students in genuine acts of learning" (Zamel, 1990, p. 96) and encourage them to define students in passive and subordinate roles (Bragg, 2007).

> Students go along with their teachers' requests, pay attention, and do not challenge the teachers' authority. It is through this apparent passivity that they, in fact, are able to take control of their future (obtaining passing grades and ultimately graduating). (Miron & Lauria, 1998, p. 197)

Classes were dominated by the teachers, leaving students in the role of spectators most of the time. (Hamilton, 1983, p. 319)

These same young people are, on the other hand, often direct and vocal in their request for greater student action and participation in schools (Rudduck & Flutter, 2004; Sanon et al., 2001), "for more active learning" (Chaplain, 1996a, p. 108). "For these students, education isn't just about learning math, social studies, or science; it is about being active partners in learning—contributing their ideas, being listened to, making choices in their studies" (Cook-Sather & Shultz, 2001, p. 5). It is about "participation in the teaching/learning process" (Poplin & Weeres, 1994, p. 32) and "taking more responsibility for themselves" (Arnot et al., 2004, p. 16).

> Pupils seemed to be calling for classroom learning to be driven by a different kind of dynamic: one that gave less prominence to the textbook or worksheets and the skills of reading and discursive note-taking and greater prominence to their own active involvement and decision-making. (Arnot et al., 2004, p. 13)

A particularly important dimension of active learning is what Boomer (cited in Oldfather et al., 1999, p. 293) labels the "elsewhereness" of knowledge. Turning knowledge into first hand activity is an important epistemological shift that can have significant impact on students' views of themselves.

"Giving pupils opportunity to participate more actively in the learning process is important" (Flutter & Rudduck, 2004, p. 11). "Interactive teaching for understanding" (McIntyre et al., 2005, p. 153) and "activity structures" (Hamilton, 1983, p. 326) pull youngsters into the learning work (Epstein, 1981a; Sanon et al., 2001); it is "almost synonymous with being engaged" (Rudduck & Flutter, 2004, p. 79). In addition to being greatly appreciated by students, it fosters a "sense of agency and ownership" (McIntyre et al., 2005, p. 149). It can also "lead to classroom teaching of enhanced quality" (Arnot et al., 2004, p. 41) and "have a positive impact on pupils' attainment" (Flutter & Rudduck, 2004, p. 40):

> Indeed students of teachers who spend more time scaffolding student responses, encouraging risk taking, and transferring control to students make greater gains in reading compared to students of teachers who spend less time using these interactive strategies and more time evaluating students. (McMahon, Wernsman, & Rose, 2009, p. 281)

The research illustrates "action and participation" in classrooms, some of which we discussed in earlier sections. When we turn to students for answers here, they often talk of "extensive use of problem solving and discovery methods in classroom work" (Shade et al., 1997, p. 94). They also highlight "attempts to generate knowledge that is both valuable and might form a basis for action" (Atweh

& Burton, 1995, p. 562). The importance of discussions is underscored as well (Alvermann et al., 1996; Oldfather et al., 1999), especially discussions featuring the sharing of one's own ideas.

> Students' perceptions in this study support some long-held beliefs about the benefits of discussion. Our findings indicate that discussion allows students to become engaged with ideas, to construct meaning, to take responsibility for their own learning, and to negotiate complex cognitive and social relationships. (Arnot et al., 2004, p. 264)

Dillon (1989, pp. 244–245), in turn, lists

several actions that promote students' active, meaningful learning. These include allowing students to use their natural language during lesson interactions and transforming his [the teacher's] language to that of his students, anticipating possible difficulties students may have with assignments and adapting lessons to meet the needs of students, and bridging gaps between background knowledge students have and new concepts and materials they are to learn.

Scholars document that working "in groups or pairs . . . finding things out from sources outside the classroom or designing solutions to problems that matter" (Rudduck & Flutter, 2004, p. 79) fuel active learning. So also can "involvement in curriculum development" (McLean-Donaldson, 1994, p. 28) and engagement "in self assessment or peer assessment strategies" (Flutter & Rudduck, 2004, p. 11), particularly evaluation that conveys "knowing by demonstration" (Arnot et al., 2004, p. 18). Finally, we learn that physical activity can promote interactive learning (Flutter & Rudduck, 2004) as can "an increased use of hands-on and experimental learning opportunities, more classroom discussion that models and discusses reasoning, the problem solving approach, and more frequent use of cooperative groups and peer support systems" (Shade et al., 1997, p. 93).

158   **Part Three:** Student Views of the Academic Program

Task-Oriented Work

The seventh and final dimension of constructed learning is what researchers describe as "task orientation." The essential matter is the difference between task-centered and ability-oriented learning platforms, or the importance of "mastery expectations" (Sagor, 1996, p. 32). Analysts portray "a task-oriented classroom environment as one in which personal improvement, effort, and progress are emphasized as both the purpose of academic tasks and the measure of success" (Anderman, 2003, p. 7). Relatedly, researchers refer to the difference between mastery and performance goals, goals that "significantly modify the students' approach to learning" (Maehr & Fyans, 1989, p. 243).

> Mastery goals orient the student toward learning and understanding, developing new skills, and a focus on self-improvement using self-referenced standards. In contrast, performance goals represent a concern with demonstrating ability, obtaining recognition of high ability, protecting self-work, and a focus on comparative standards relative to other students and attempting to best or surpass others. (Pintrich, 2003, p. 676)
>
> When students are oriented to task goals they are mainly concerned with learning for the sake of learning, and striving to master tasks, to improve, and to develop intellectually. Such students are interested in problem solving, novel tasks, and challenging situations. Task-focused students are likely to attribute their success to effort. In contrast, when students are oriented to performance goals, they are mainly concerned with demonstrating their ability or concealing a lack of ability. (Anderman et al., 1999, p. 132)

An essential point here is that in a task-oriented classroom, students come to "judge their capabilities more in terms of personal improvement than by comparison against the achievement of others" (Bandura, 1993, p. 120). In creating items around these two goal dimensions, Anderman and team (1999, p. 136) include items assessing the use of interesting and challenging materials, concern with involving all students in decisions and in discussions, and making work meaningful to students. Our scale assessing a performance goal structure includes items assessing an emphasis on relative ability, the importance of correct answers, and moving through the work regardless of the level of understanding.

Or, as Wigfield and colleagues (1998, p. 79) tell us

With ego-involved (or performance) goals, children try to outperform others, and they are more likely to engage in tasks they know they can do. Task-involved (or mastery-oriented) children choose challenging tasks and are more concerned with their own progress than with outperforming others.

In addition to goal structure and learning framework, analysts capture the importance of task-oriented work in terms of engagement, differentiating between engendered and instrumental work. "The first kind of engagement, engendered by school work which offers interest, novelty, challenge and significant personal control over the process, is qualitatively different from instrumental covering of syllabuses and rote learning for examinations" (Bandura, 1993, p. 125).

Important conclusions emerge from analysts in this area. Findings confirm that task-orientation in the domain of goals and classroom actions is not the norm in schools. The reality is "competitive individualism" (Wallace, 1996b, p. 63), a norm that steadily increases in saliency as children age (Feldlaufer et al., 1988). Researchers also report that ability and performance frameworks exact real costs on students. They reveal that competitive frames "promote an ego goal orientation in students" and show that "such practices can contribute to the declines in students' academic competence, beliefs, interest, and intrinsic motivation" (Wigfield et al., 1998, p. 97). "Emphasis on social comparison in classrooms decreases task or intrinsic involvement" (Nolen & Nicholls, 1993, p. 415) and has the "detrimental effect of lowering self-image and reducing efforts" (Chaplain, 1996b, p. 124). When "control over grades" trumps "control over learning," work becomes highly instrumental, and we know "that work done for instrumental reasons alone achieves little more than relief when the end is finally reached"

(Wallace, 1996b, p. 62). Youngsters "become oriented toward avoiding failure . . . and eventually will become less achievement oriented" (Moos, 1979, p. 199).

> School emphasis on ability goals makes it virtually inevitable that a large group of children will develop all too many misgivings regarding their competence to learn. In particular, children who come to school with little preparation and with no continuing support will begin to view themselves not only as different, but also dumb and, worse, of lesser value. The rewards in the ability-oriented school lie in doing better than others regardless of the opportunities or resources you have been granted. It is a race with the participants starting at different points on the track and with those behind having little or no chance to catch up. So it does little good to hug or praise when the whole environment is sending a message that winners—not learners—count. (Maehr & Midgley, 1996, pp. 44–45)

Maehr and Midgley (1996) and other scholars also document how performance architecture leads naturally to ability grouping in schools, a practice that presents many hazards. "In particular, it most often serves to reinforce the idea that school is concerned more with establishing ability hierarchies than fostering the personal and intellectual development of all students" (Maehr & Midgley, 1996, p. 121). Analysts also shed light on the connections between ability goals and assessment in schools. Pupils come "to see assessment as a measurement of their ability rather than attainment and they seem to feel that grades and marks effectively define their potential" (Flutter & Rudduck, 2004, p. 99).

Finally, investigators have unearthed an assortment of benefits that accompany the task-oriented work that students tell us they prefer. Although not deeply explored, there is a sense that task-oriented work is linked to enhanced fairness and equity in schools (McMahon et al., 2009), that the broad notion of justice is enhanced as the deeply entrenched norms discussed above that "reinforce inequality" (Roeser et al., 2000, p. 463) are eliminated. We also know that mastery focus accents gains rather than uncovering deficiencies. In turn, "accenting the gains achieved enhances perceived self-efficacy, aspirations, efficient analytic thinking, self-satisfaction, and performance accomplishments" (Bandura, 1993, p. 125). "Perceived goals of the classroom significantly modify the students' approach to learning. Thus when Mastery goals are more salient than Performance goals, students are likely to be more inclined toward academic challenge and learning for its own sake" (Maehr & Fyans, 1989, p. 243). Not surprisingly, "the task-focused instructional practice leads to improved student motivation" (Anderman et al., 1999, p. 134). We see evidence of "more adaptive psychological and behavioral adjustment" (McMahon et al., 2009, p. 268) when task-oriented goals and classroom environments are ascendant. Bandura (1993, p. 125) also finds that

> learning environments that construe ability as an acquirable skill, deemphasize competitive social comparison, and highlight self comparison of progress and personal accomplishments are well suited for building a sense of efficacy that promotes academic achievement.

Wigfield and team (1998, p. 94) also conclude that "in mastery-oriented classrooms, everyone who performs adequately can experience success. As a result, youngsters in mastery-oriented rooms are more likely to focus on self-improvement than social comparison, to perceive themselves as able, and to have high expectations for success." In turn, Anderman (2003, p. 7) shows that

> middle school students' reported perceptions that their teachers emphasize a task goal orientation have been shown to predict more positive school-related affect. It seems likely that this type of learning environment might also predict higher levels of school belonging for students. That is, students who perceive their teachers as promoting personal improvement and mastery of content might be more likely to maintain a sense of acceptance and validity in their school.

Thus, task-focused work "underscores personal capabilities" (Bandura, 1993, p. 125), "personal competence" (Sagor, 1996, p. 39), "and commitment to life-long learning" (Maehr & Midgley, 1996, p. 91) as well as enhancing "sense of community" (Anderman, 2003, p. 20).

PART FOUR

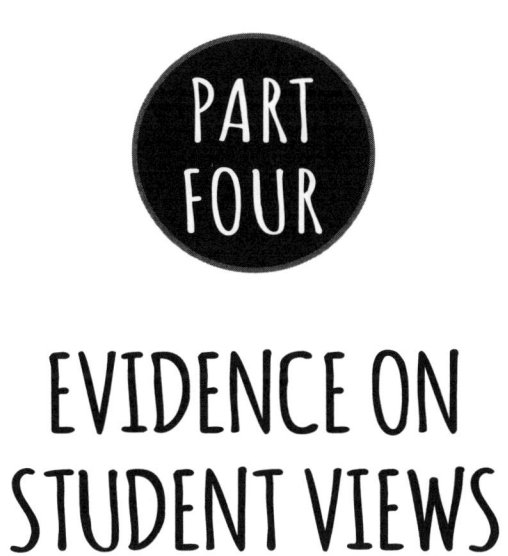

EVIDENCE ON STUDENT VIEWS

High School #1

Nothing better to do

Going through the motions

Moving between the unknown and
    the marginal elite

Invisible actors in our play
    the language inaudible
    the grammar inaccessible

Useless stuff

Constrained options

Unalterable landscapes

A quiet grayness

A scent of unfairness

An edgy sense of powerlessness

Walling off indignities

Unbeaten

SEVEN

STUDENTS HAVE IT RIGHT

> The emergent picture of the classroom where students report a great deal of content learning combines an affective concern with students as people with an emphasis on students working hard. (Trickett & Moos, 1974, p. 8)
>
> Measures of student perception of classroom environment predict gains in cognitive, affective, and behavioral learning criteria, even after differences in achievement, interest in the subject, and IQ are extracted. (Steele et al., 1971, p. 448)
>
> These are not *just* perceptions; they are perceptions that make a difference. (Maehr & Midgley, 1996, p. 78)

GETTING STARTED

Recentering the Work

The task in this chapter is to discern if looking at quality schooling through the eyes of students matters, and, if so, in what ways and how much. We undertake that assignment by employing the practices reported by students in Chapters 3 through 6. In Chapter 1, we began our journey by examining the central role of student–teacher relationships. We saw there that "child–teacher relationships serve a regulatory function with respect to emotional and academic skill development. In so doing, they have enormous influence on a child's competence in childhood" (Pianta, 1999, p. 8), and, as we reveal below, and beyond schooling. These "relationships are the route to intellectual development" (Goldstein, 1999, p. 653) and "appropriate social behavior" (Davis, 2001, p. 435), and "difficult relationships may act as an obstacle to . . . success" as well (Davis, 2001, p. 432). Relationships provide a form of social capital that can promote success (Rodriguez, 2008). "Thus [because] how students feel about and do in schools is, in large part, determined by their relationship with teachers" (Johnson, 2009, p. 101), "time taken in establishing a personal quality to relationships is time well spent" (Rak & Patterson, 1999, p. 372).

We also reported that these relationships unfold in two spheres, in the academic domain in which teachers and students engage (academic press) and in the culture in which they are ensconced (care and support). That is, "although the study of student perceptions is quite varied, investigations can be subdivided into two broad groups: those with primarily instructional concerns and those with primarily social concerns" (Rohrkemper, 1985, p. 29). We saw that when good results accrue, each sphere individually works well, and the two spheres in integrated fashion work well. That is, "success at social tasks has important implications for students' success at academic tasks as well" (Davis, 2001, p. 432) and "academic press has effects not only on students' cognitive wellness, such as their academic success, but also on students' affective wellness" (Ma, 2003, p. 348). In short, analysts "emphasize much how school is an interpersonal as well as a cognitive enterprise" (Ryan et al., 1994, p. 244), enterprises that "facilitate cognitive and emotional development in children" (Bosworth & Ferreira, 2000, p. 118).

Analysts employ a variety of concepts to capture positive student outcomes (Oelsner et al., 2011) from perceptions of youngsters in the areas of academic environment and supportive culture: reactions to school life (Epstein, 1981b); social competence (Davis, 2003); human, cultural, and social capital (McNeal, 1999); positive educational trajectories (Gibson et al., 2004); academic and social development (Smerdon, 2002); performance (Maehr & Fyans, 1989); growth development (Mitra & Gross, 2009); student behavior (Bru et al., 2002); change (Rudduck & Flutter, 2004); and achievement (Muller et al., 1999). These scholars also explain that there is a dual drive train at work here, one working to overcome liabilities and the other to build up assets. To begin with then, communities of care "foster productive learning by removing developmentally hazardous conditions" (Felner et al., 2007, p. 210). They suppress factors that undermine hopes for success, such as the formation of dysfunctional and oppositional peer cultures. Press and support damp down aspects of schooling that push students away from engaging the work of "doing school" well. An engaging and supportive learning community provides a "protective power" (Garmezy, 1991, p. 427) while attacking social problems that place students in peril (Christle et al., 2005; Crosnoe, 2011). They help create a "social environment that neutralizes or buffers home stresses" (Alexander & Entwisle, 1996, p. 77) and community problems and individual characteristics that foster social marginalization and academic disengagement (Demaray & Malecki, 2002b; Garmezy, 1991). Challenging and supportive learning environments create assets, social and human capital, to draw youngsters into the hard work that is required to be successful in school (Ancess, 2003; Supovitz, 2002, 2008). They transform schools into places "where the social and pastoral environment nurtures a desire to learn in students" (Blair, 2002, p. 184). Assets such as care and warmth are stockpiled to assist in helping students reach ambitious learning targets (Quint, 2006; Roth & Brooks-Gunn, 2003).

More specifically, teachers use the capital they garner in relationships to protect students from risk (Gonzalez, 1997; Pianta, 1999), factors such as "lack of control over one's life" (Wallerstein & Bernstein, 1988, p. 380). Larkin (1979) shows how relationships can help break patterns of negative spiraling for children in school, preventing faster and faster disintegration. Nichols (2006, p. 257) shows how support "buffers against certain negative or risky behaviors" and unhealthy schooling experiences (Quiroz, 2001). Connell and Wellborn (1991, p 69) expand on this point, arguing that positive student–teacher "relationships may buffer the effects of the problematic competence-belief and allow children to continue engaging in achievement-related behaviors." Quiroz (2001, p. 337) analyzes the power of relationships to head off the "tendency [of students] to look to themselves as the primary cause of failure in school." Kuperminc and colleagues (1997), in turn, remind us that positive relations nurture press and support for youngsters from less advantaged social environments and those at risk for other reasons, such as a lack of social capital outside of school (Croninger & Lee, 2001;

Goddard, 2003) and having previous experiences of poor relations with teachers (Wentzel, 1998). When schools get this protection function right, "the impact on minority children and youth is considerable, if not life-altering" (Stanton-Salazar, 1997, p. 15). The "risk coefficient" is greatly reduced (Pianta, 1999, p. 15): Howard (2001, p. 133), channeling students' insights, reports that "the students stated that teachers who cared for them, made themselves available... and were concerned with helping them deal with their school and personal problems made a difference in the schooling experience."

Caveats and Cautions

Before we enter the discussion of the outcomes of press and support in a more systematic and developed manner, some cautions merit attention. First, more of our review of student perceptions comes from studies of culture than from studies of academic press. While we know that the way the teaching and learning process is managed is a critical factor (Maehr & Midgley, 1996), less information is available on the impact of academic press as students describe it. While our work on seeing schools through the eyes of students tells us that both press and support are "specifiable and ultimately manageable antecedents of motivation and learning" (p. 67), the findings presented here overweigh conclusions from research on cultural support somewhat. Second, most studies do not track the full course of press and support from relationships to intermediate outcomes (e.g., motivation), to engagement, to learning. While we construct this chain below (see Figure 7.1), it is important to remember that we bundle together studies that examine single couplings (e.g., engagement to achievement) as we develop our narrative. Third, our chronicle attends to the general picture. Subnarratives that are "unique to sites and tend to grade level, subject matter, location, and background of participants" (Alvermann et al., 1996, p. 265) are not examined in any detail. This choice, while necessary, compromises the "ability to understand the nuances of individual contexts" (p. 265).

Fourth, we are looking at only one dynamic in the explanatory framework of student outcomes: student–teacher relationships focused on the academic and cultural spheres of classrooms. Many other issues influence the outcomes shown in Figure 7.1, both in school and externally. For example, the effects here depend on the

Chapter Seven: Students Have It Right 169

goals and preferences of the children (Moos & David, 1981) and student background (Moos & Moos, 1978). We also discover that "students' views of the larger economic world may predict their behavior related to schools" (Murdock et al., 2000, p. 346). So too, a student's "willingness to work in class depends on the student's cognitive image of the classroom in which his work yields future rewards" (Stinchcombe, 1964, p. 19). As we report elsewhere, peers are powerfully linked to social and academic outcomes (Li, Lynch, Kalvin, Liu, & Lerner, 2011). Parent–child relationships also shape students' relationships with peers and teachers (Connell & Wellborn, 1991). The size of the school (Midgley et al., 1989) and the characteristics of the school do so as well (Willms, 2003). "The larger psychological environment of the school is not an irrelevant variable" either (Maehr & Fyans, 1989, p. 244). Crosnoe and associates (2004, p. 71) portray this larger storyline here by reminding us that "research recognizes the value of approaching social issues at the intersection of interpersonal and institutional contexts. Individual behavior is closely related to personal relationships, but such relationships are dependent, in part, on the institutions in which they take place."

Fifth, for purposes of analysis we primarily follow the links of the chain in Figure 7.1 from left to right (e.g., motivation to engagement). It is essential to note, however, that energy between the links

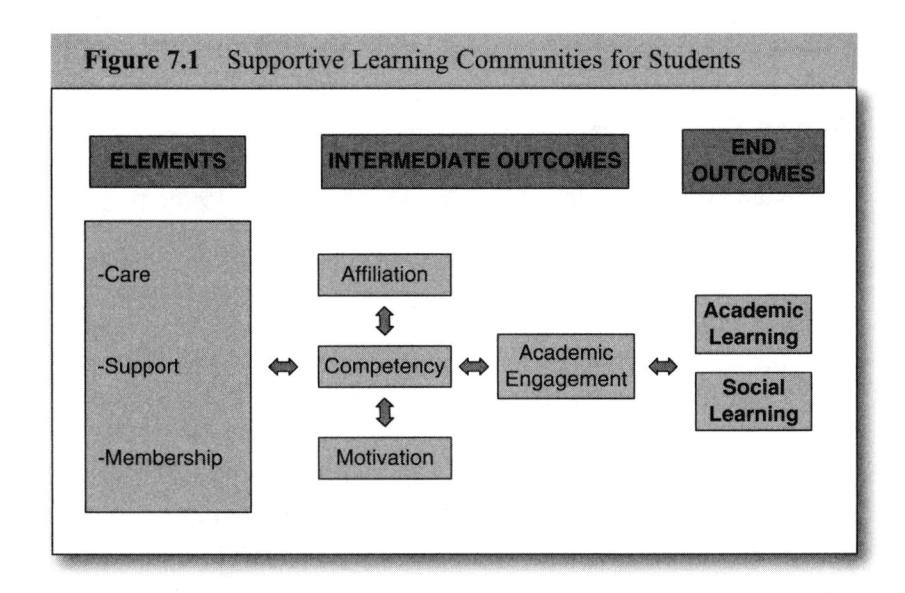

Figure 7.1 Supportive Learning Communities for Students

ELEMENTS	INTERMEDIATE OUTCOMES	END OUTCOMES
-Care -Support -Membership	Affiliation ⇕ Competency ⇕ Motivation ⇔ Academic Engagement	Academic Learning Social Learning

flows in both directions (e.g., engagement to motivation). That is, we know that "the interplay between social and academic variables within the context of schooling almost certainly is reciprocal in nature" (Anderman, 2003, p. 8). Outcomes can be precursors and precursors can be outcomes in our model (Anderman, 2003). More specifically, as an example, "positive self-concept may be both a contributor to and a result of successful school achievement" (Silverstein & Krate, 1975, p. 209).

Sixth, the very notion of connected linkages tells us that the pathway from press and support to learning is indirect (Maehr & Fyans, 1989). You cannot go from support directly to academic achievement. There are mediating links along the voyage. Seventh, as we have underscored throughout the book, context is important (Kuperminc et al., 1997; Weinstein, 1983). For example, analysts tell us that "students' reactions are systematically affected by length of time in participating environments" (Epstein, 1981b, p. 96), especially extended time in negative environments in which "expressive alienation" (Stinchcombe, 1964, p. 49) has accumulated (Larkin, 1979; Murdock et al., 2000), where a "school-alienated life-style among children" is pervasive (Silverstein & Krate, 1975, p. 23). These researchers also inform us that context includes the ethnicity of children (Maehr & Fyans, 1989), "expected occupational destinies" (Stanton-Salazar, 1997, p. 15), student age (Lehr, Sinclair, & Christenson, 2004), and socioeconomic conditions (Willms, 2003)—for example, working-class minority students who are "not competent cultural decoders within mainstream institutions including the school" (Stanton-Salazar, 1997, p. 25). Finally, our work is focused on explanations, showing what is, and on opening pathways of improvement. However, as Maehr and Midgley (1996, p. 125) remind us, improvement "will not happen automatically. Even knowing what to do does not ensure that something will be done."

Modeling Effects: Social Integration, Sense of Self, and Motivation

The first links in the chain of outcomes from supportive culture and academic press can be seen in Figure 7.1. They are the most immediate outcomes of the press and support, are important, and deserve attention (Willms, 2003).

Social Integration

The Construct

> Identification represents the extent to which a student has bonded with school and incorporated it as a significant part of his or her self-concept and lifestyle. (Voelkl, 1997, p. 296)

Consistent with our storyline to date, we acknowledge that "when schools become communities they fulfill a basic human need—belonging" (Bosworth & Ferreira, 2000, p. 123). More specifically, we confirm that integration or "school membership is created through reciprocal relationships between the pupils and the adults representing the institution" (Kershner, 1996, p. 81): "Students who perceive more teacher support feel a stronger sense of belonging in the school community" (Murdock & Miller, 2003, p. 385). In their analysis, for example, Roeser and team (2000, p. 464) found that when "adolescents perceive supportive and respectful teachers they were more likely to bond with the school." That is, "students who felt they belonged gave primary interpersonal reasons" (Nichols, 2006, p. 263). And, as we have highlighted throughout the book, these bondings are especially essential for students who have been placed at risk by race, ethnicity, gender, and SES (Feldman & Matjasko, 2005; Gibson et al., 2004; Marsh & Kleitman, 2002). One African American male student explains this reality as follows:

> We got squeaky wheels and flat tires.... Some smooth white walls rollin' their way right to college, gettin' oil all the way. And then the rest of us ... flat tires! Bumpin' on down the road, making all sorts of crude noises. Probably fall off real soon anyway. Ain't worth the grease. (Silva, 2001, p. 95)

We also see through the work of Kosciw and colleagues (2012, p. xvii) that LGBT children "with a greater number of supportive staff had a greater sense of being in the school community than other students." Across the literature on social integration, we are reminded of the healing power of student–teacher linkages in terms of support and press: "Teachers and programs are in the position to restore student engagement with the school by creating an environment to which students feel bonded. A primary way to do this is by nurturing meaningful interactions between students and teachers" (Kennedy, 2011, p. 8). Smerdon's (2002, p. 298) work "suggests that differences in the quality of educational experiences . . . are associated with significant variations in students' perceptions of membership," and Anderman (2003, p. 19) determined that "students who perceived their classes as more task oriented reported higher levels of belonging than did others."

One recurring insight in our work is that all of the concepts we examine in this volume share space with each other. We see, for example, that this is the case for the norm of "membership" we examined during our analysis of supportive school culture in Chapter 3 and the intermediate outcome "social integration." Scholars across the disciplines often use the concepts synonymously (Johnson, 2009). For us, we think of membership as "being in" the community. Social integration also includes the idea of "a psychological sense of belonging" (Goodenow & Grady, 1993, p. 66) on the part of the student. It is "a psychological need that plays a vital role in the transmission of an internalization of values and cultural norms" (Johnson, 2009, p. 101). It entails responses to group membership (Smerdon, 2002).

Social integration, or the sense of being integrated into the school community, (Pavri & Monda-Amaya, 2001) as described in the research includes such things as "social and personal connections to others at the school and a . . . belief that others in the school [are] there *for* them" (Goodenow & Grady, 1993, p. 67). It represents an essential need for connections with others ((McMahon & Wernsman, 2009). It includes identification with and a feeling of fitting in (Gibson et al., 2004; Willms, 2003), a sense of identification and social bonding (Kennedy, 2011; Kroeger, 2004). Connell and Wellborn (1991) add the elements of emotional security and closeness. Cabello and Terrell (1994) layer in the idea of relatedness. Social integration is about meaningful connections that bring a psychological sense of belonging to life, (Bru et al., 2002; Nieto, 1994), "the feeling of a sense of . . . connection to others and being part of the larger social world" (Oldfather et al., 1999, p. 287), about "solidarity and . . . a sense of belonging to a collective culture" (Burke & Grosvenor, 2003, p. 70)—"an affectional bond with significant others" (Cotterell, 1992, p. 30). Social integration is a sense of being part of the school, of being valued by the institution, of "feeling oneself to be an important part of the life and activity of the class" (Goodenow & Grady, 1993, p. 25) and the school (Gonzalez & Padilla, 1997; Roth & Brooks-Gunn, 2003; Scanlan & Lopez, 2012). It is about affinity

(Conchas, 2001), acceptance (Judson, Cohen-Dan, Leonard, Stinson, & Colston, 2001), inclusion (McMahon & Wernsman, 2009), membership (Eckert, 1989; Gonzalez & Padilla, 1997), belonging (Battistich et al., 1995; Fredricks et al., 2004), affiliation (Newmann, 1981, O'Connor, 1997), attachment (Alexander et al., 1997; Conchas, 2001), inclusion (Ma, 203; Voelkl, 1997), and connection (Feldman & Matjasko, 2005; Roth & Brooks-Gunn, 2003).

Muted support, on the other hand, is an invitation to weak student identification with and/or possible disaffiliation with the school, "an absence of highly developed feelings of valuing and belonging" (Voelkl, 1997, p. 296). Students in such schools are often portrayed as "just passing through" (Eckert, 1989, p. 65). Rather than being bonded to the school, they are independent actors, ones who often feel a sense of disconnection and alienation toward teachers and peers (Antrop-Gonzalez, 2006; Newmann, 1981). They display what Farrell (1990, p. 112) calls "absenting behavior," a "culture that is dominated by the private as opposed to the institutional" (Eckert, 1989, p. 172). Separation and exclusion are elements of disidentification. So also are estrangement, detachment, and isolation (Newmann, 1981)—"emotional and physical withdrawal" (Voelkl, 1997, p. 294). Interestingly, Willms (2003) discovered in his research that literacy skills as well as isolation are implicated in social integration in schools.

We close this section on definition with two notes. First, children's experiences at home and in the community (Willms, 2003) and race, class, ethnicity, and sexual orientation often play a mediating role in social integration (Fine, 1986; Kosciw et al., 2012; Lee, 1999). Second, there seems to be decline in social integration through the middle school grades (Anderman, 2003), after students leave elementary school.

Impacts of Social Integration

> Researchers also have noted the benefits of social interaction for children's motivation and achievement. (Wigfield et al., 1998, p. 100)
>
> Research points as well to a strong and positive link between students' subjective sense of belonging in school and both their participation and achievement. (Gibson et al., 2004, p. 129)

Having established that social integration is a valuable schooling outcome in its own right (Willms, 2003), one created by academic press but especially supportive culture, we now turn to the dimensions that social integration ignites. Within the narrative underscored in the model in Figure 7.1, we see that social integration links to all the variables in our model, some directly and some in a moderated manner, that is, through effects on intermediate variables. Goodenow and Grady (1993, p. 70) make this point in the negative across all the stages of the model when they confirm that "the *result* of a failure to attain a full and legitimate sense of ownership in the school as a social system may be, for many students, lowered motivation, less engagement, ultimately diminished academic achievement." Crosnoe and associates (2004, p. 60), in turn, find that "social integration counterbalances these problems."

We find in the research that social integration can promote outcomes for both students and the organization. Focusing on students, at the broadest level, there is capital imbedded in relationships between students and teachers (Gibson et al., 2004; McNeal, 1999). Social integration impacts students' "ability to access the benefits of human, social, and cultural capital" (McNeal, 1999, p. 293) and their achievement of "intergenerational bonding" (Crosnoe et al., 2004, p. 61), and it enhances their social and emotional health (Pavri & Monda-Amaya, 2001) as well as longer term health and well-being (Willms, 2003). Social integration "plays a vital role in the transmission of values and cultural norms" (Johnson, 2009, p. 101). It "raises the costs of problem behavior" (Crosnoe et al., 2004, p. 61). As noted throughout our discussion, social integration is especially powerful for students placed at risk by society; that is, sense of belonging is a critical element in any educational program for children placed at risk by society (Ma, 2003).

Identification (or disidentification) impacts commitment to the school and a sense of obligation to those at the school (Gamoran, 1996). Positive identification helps build a sense of legitimacy around the school and a valuing of the institution (Fredricks et al., 2004; Goodenow & Grady, 1993). According to Voelkl (1997, p. 296), the idea of valuing schooling

> include[s] the recognition of the value of the school as both a social institution and a tool for facilitating personal advancement. That is, the youngster regards school as a central institution in society and feels that what is learned in

class is important in its own right and that school is instrumental in obtaining his or her personal life objectives . . . the belief that schoolwork is both interesting and important.

Valuing also leads to a "commitment to and identification with the goals of the institution" (Eckert, 1989, p. 103); its values and purposes (Ancess, 2003; Baker et al., 1997; Marsh & Kleitman, 1992); its norms and practices (Battistich et al., 1995, 1997; Voelkl, 1997); the avenues it establishes for members to pursue goals (Newmann et al., 1992), that is, its structures, policies, and practices (Hallinan & Kubitschek, 1999); and its sanctioned outcomes (Marsh & Kleitman, 2002; Voelkl, 1997). In schools with strong pastoral care, youngsters become invested in the activities of the classroom (Freiberg et al., 2009) and school (Marsh & Kleitman, 2002).

There is considerable support for the conclusion that social integration in schools leads to enhanced sense of self for students (Goodenow & Grady, 1993; Kuperminc et al., 1997), or what Anderman (2003, p. 6) calls "school related affect." More specifically, McMahon and Wernsman (2009, p. 270) have established that "sense of school belonging is positively related to commitment to school goals, expectations, and academic self-efficacy." Gibson and team (2004) add self-esteem to this list of outcomes. Murdock and Miller (2003, p. 385), in turn, show that "students' feelings of belonging predict positive school affect." Pavri and Monda-Amaya (2001) confirm the connection between social integration and positive self-concept. Goodenow and Grady (1993) note linkages to expectancy of success.

Data from an assortment of studies reveal strong bridges between social integration and student motivation (Murdock et al., 2000; Oelsner et al., 2011; Wilson et al., 2011), what Anderman (2003, p. 6) labels "adaptive patterns of academic motivation" and Goodenow and Grady (1993, p. 68) call "general school motivation." Gibson and team's (2004, p. 136) conclusion that "students who fail to attain a full membership in the community are likely to be . . . less motivated academically" (Booker, 2006, p. 4) reinforces this point. Grady (1993, p. 61) reports in his review that "disconnection and diminished sense of belonging result in decreased student motivation." On the positive side of the ledger, Goodenow and Grady (1993, p. 61) concluded that "sense of membership heavily influenced students' commitment to schooling," and Gonzalez and Padilla (1997) discovered in their analysis that sense of belonging is a significant predictor of resilience.

Turning to the tail end of the model, we find that social integration has important effects on engagement (Phelan et al., 1992; Quiroz, 2001). Goodenow and Grady (1993, p. 67) confirm this finding, concluding that "students who do have a high sense of belonging in school are also more likely to be academically engaged than those whose sense of belonging is low." Conceptual analysis of engagement helps us see that it includes key ideas such as alienation, delinquency, off-task behavior, attendance problems, and dropping out (Crosnoe et al., 2004; Gibson et al., 2004; Lehr et al., 2004). For example, Goff and Goddard (1999, p. 47) note that "according to several theories, delinquency is related directly or indirectly, to ... sense of belonging." Gonzalez and Padilla (1997, p. 302) hold that "a sense of belonging may reduce students' feeling of disengagement, which may lead to dropping out." Conversely, "a student who feels a sense of belonging may become more engaged and exhibit greater effort on academic tasks" (p. 302). Lack of social integration is also linked to off-task behavior such as acting out in class (Gibson et al., 2004) or simply turning into a tourist in the classroom (Murphy & Torre, 2014).

Finally, we have evidence that social integration predicts academic achievement (Davis, 2003; Gibson et al., 2004; Murdock et al., 2000; Wigfield et al., 1998)—academic behavior (Johnson, 2009), academic performance (Booker, 2006), and academic outcomes (Gonzalez & Padilla, 1997) across an array of indicators, and along the way "the pursuit of task goals and the pursuit of prosocial academic and peer goals" (Davis, 2003, p. 213). That is, children who display high levels of membership exhibit increased levels of achievement (Booker, 2006) measured in terms such as student grades, minutes spent doing homework, teacher rating of competence, and standardized achievement tests (Booker, 2006; Davis, 2003; Gonzalez & Padilla, 1997). That is, "regardless of how school bonding is conceptualized, high levels of school bonding have been consistently associated with positive youth outcomes, including academic outcomes, such as increased academic motivation, self-efficacy, and higher grade point averages" (Oelsner et al., 2011, p. 465). Social integration is also linked to "positive educational trajectories" (Gibson et al., 2004, p. 138). Absence of social integration, not surprisingly, "contributed to academic problems on the individual and institutional level" (Crosnoe et al., 2004, p. 60) and deceased achievement (Booker, 2006). The summative message here is that "the evidence for the relationship between belonging and achievement is convincing even when the other school-related psychological variables are taken into account" (Booker, 2006, p. 2).

We close this section with two reminders. First, as shown in Figure 7.1, social linkage to achievement is almost always mediated by engagement (Gibson et al., 2004). Second, the relationship between social integration and achievement is reciprocal. That is, achievement is associated with increases in engagement and then social integration (McNeely et al., 2002).

Sense of Self

The Construct

The challenge before us in this section is clear: we must "pinpoint the determinants of self-concept as well as those factors that we believe the self-concept, in turn, impacts" (Harter, 1990, p. 322). We begin that work in the same manner we did for social integration, with an effort to corral the construct. There are a number of ideas that flow from or compose the concept of sense of self or "psychological well-being" (Cotterell, 1992, p. 32) or psychological health. We see self-esteem here, which itself is a complex concept and includes many elements (Nieto, 1994), a concept that is composed of "distinct developmentally and ecologically keyed dimensions" (DuBois, Felner, Brand, & Phillips, 1996, p. 569), that is, it is shaped by biology and environment. According to Saunders and colleagues (2004, p. 84), "Self-esteem refers to how individuals feel about themselves in a comprehensive or global manner." Scholars also remind us that "racial self-esteem . . . how the individual feels about his racial group membership" (p. 84) is an important element in the domain of "student identity" (Quiroz, 2001, p. 340).

When I entered the New York City school system, I came upon a world unknown to me, a language that I did not understand, and a school administration which made ugly faces at me every time that I spoke Spanish. Stereotyping and racial comments were a daily routine. Bilingual students were made

(Continued)

> (Continued)
>
> to feel inferior and often portrayed as slow and stupid. Many teachers referred to us as animals. Believe me, maintaining a half-decent image of yourself wasn't an easy thing. I feel that I had enough strength of character to withstand the many school personnel who tried to destroy my motivation. But many of my classmates didn't make it. (Student, cited by First & Carrera, 1988, p. 51)
>
> Insofar as students' narratives represent more general struggles surrounding Latino ethnicity, they alert us to the difficulty of achievement of any kind when children demonstrate ambivalence regarding a fundamental—and unchangeable—element of their identity. Without an awareness of ethnicity, how it operates in our society, and how children are situated because of it, it is impossible to create liberating learning environments that allow children to successfully transition from family and community to the unfamiliar world of school. And, as Davidson (1996) points out in her examination of student narratives, schools are "cultural arenas" that have a significant and direct impact on the creation and re-creation of students' ethnic and racial identities. (Quiroz, 2001, p. 336)

So too is gender (Harter et al., 1997) and sexual identity (Kosciw et al., 2012; Thompson, 2004). There are "distinct and uniquely influential components of the self system" (DuBois et al., 1996, p. 544), or what we have labeled "sense of self." We also find in the larger construct "social sense concepts, a type of expectancy belief because they contain our beliefs about ways relationships operate and our estimate about the likelihood of positive social interaction" (Davis, 2001, p. 433). Self-efficacy, in turn, "is concerned with individuals' belief in their competence to accomplish specific tasks—a basic need to feel effective in their interactions with the world" (Chaplain, 1996b, p. 116), "a belief in one's capabilities to exercise control over his or her level of functioning and environmental demands" (McMahon & Wernsman, 2009, p. 270).

The idea that is most salient here is "academic self-concept" (Shade et al., 1997, p. 54). "Academic self-efficacy includes how the individual feels about his/her academic capabilities" (Saunders et al., 2004, p. 85) and "the belief that students have control over their performance in a specific subject" (McMahon & Wernsman, 2009, p. 270) and "the extent to which students believe that with effort they can master the material they are learning in school" (Murdock & Miller, 2003, p. 386), what Kershner (1996) refers to as the "do-ability" of specific tasks. Eccles-Parsons and team (1983, p. 82) label this "self-concept of ability, defined as the assortment of one's own competency to perform specific tasks or to carry out role-appropriate behaviors," and Shade and associates (1997, p. 54) describe it as "whether or not students are able to handle the work school asks of them"—"adolescents perceiving themselves as academically competent and able to master school-related tasks" (Roeser et al., 2000, p. 452).

> Those who have a high sense of efficacy visualize success scenarios that provide positive guides and supports for performance. Those who doubt their efficacy visualize failure scenarios and dwell on the many things that can go wrong. It is difficult to achieve much while fighting self-doubt. (Bandura, 1993, p. 118)

Bandura (1993, p. 119) continues telling us of the importance of self-efficacy when he notes that "a person with the same knowledge and skills may perform poorly, adequately, or extraordinarily depending on fluctuations in self-efficacy thinking." Embedded in our chronicle of self-efficacy around children are the "need for competence" (Newmann et al., 1989, p. 34), "perceptions of competence" (Pintrich, 2003, p. 671), and the ability "to think of themselves as competent at many things that the school demands" (Maehr & Midgley, 1996, p. 44). Closely related to the notion of "achievement expectancies" (Johnson, 2009, p. 101) are the constructs of self-confidence (Masten, Best, & Garmezy, 1990; Rudduck, 2007) and capability (Saunders et al., 2004).

Before we proceed to review the antecedents and take up the question of the outcomes of sense of self in general and academic efficacy in particular, a few notes warrant attention. The first returns us to a theme laced through this volume, the "direction of causality" (Skaalvik & Hagtvet, 1990, p. 302). We know with some certainty that reciprocal relationships mark all the variables in our model. In this case, this means that self esteem grows from a culture of care and an environment of academic press, is influenced by social integration, and influences motivation and engagement. Second, researchers also help us understand that "the process leading to high global or academic self esteem is different than that leading to high self esteem in a particular discipline" (Hoge et al., 1990, p. 126). "For global and academic self-esteem, the most important aspects of school are school climate and the feedback from teachers. For self-esteem in a specific discipline, the most important aspect is grades in that discipline" (Hoge et al., 1990, p. 126). Third, we also will not be surprised to learn that a mix of school factors, family conditions, and innate intelligence appears to be essential for self-esteem during the school year (Hoge et al., 1990). Research indicates that "the reasons why some people develop poor self-image are complex and are likely to include factors outside the school gates" (Flutter & Rudduck, 2004, p. 120). We need to be clear that our focus is only on the school factors here. Fourth, this means that the outcomes tend to underplay major personal effects of a sense of self, effects which have been linked to troublesome conditions such as hopelessness and depression (Harter et al., 1997). Fifth, the connection between sense of self in general and academic self efficacy in particular is likely to change as a result of development (Skaalvik & Hagtvet, 1990). Finally, we underscore "two strategies for enhancing one's self esteem. One can reduce discrepancy by either increasing one's competence or by discounting the importance of the domain" (Harter, 1996, p. 26). Both strategies are visible in the analysis below.

Antecedents and Outcomes

In the chapters on academic press and supportive culture and in our just completed analysis of social integration, we concomitantly established the antecedents of sense of self. That scaffolding work is "strong support for [two] sources of self esteem, namely perceptions of success in areas where one has aspirations for success and the internalization of the approval (or disapproval) of significant others" (Harter, 1996, p. 25). In short, we learned that supportive care and academic press nurtured through meaningful student–teacher relationships are complicit in nourishing, or damaging, the intermediate variables in our model (Jackson & Warren, 2000; Nieto, 1994), or as Davis (2003, p. 228) captures it, "student identity." Drilling down a bit, "child–teacher relationships play an important role in developing school competence such as self esteem" (Pianta, 1999, p. 67) and understandings about ability and control (Wentzel, 2002), and "the classroom environment can be a determinant in children's beliefs about their academic self-efficacy" (Moos & Trickett, 1987, p. 36).

On the supportive culture side of the ledger, researchers have regularly documented that "perceived teacher caring is positively associated with . . . academic self efficacy" (Murdock & Miller, 2003, p. 390) and "students' internal control beliefs" (Johnson, 2009, p. 101). There is a strong connection between felt teacher support and student self-worth (Ryan et al., 1994), as well as positive self-image (Davidson & Lang, 1960; Weinstein, 1983), self-esteem (Harter, 1996), and self-concept (Fine, 1986)—all aspects of our larger concept, sense of self. We know that the major quest for youngsters is for personal identity (Csikszentmihalyi & Larson, 1984; Farrell, 1990), what Crosnoe (2011) calls identity work and Feldman and Matjasko (2005) talk about as learning to understand oneself. Analysts also document that identity and self-esteem are tightly yoked. Each student's self concept is forged in good measure through the sense of community he or she feels at school, by the relationships forged with teachers and peers (Battistich, 1997; Guest & Schneider, 2003; Marsh & Kleitman, 2002). That is, students "come to an understanding of their own social worth by seeing how they are treated by others" (Crosnoe, 2011, p. 139). Supportive communities help nourish the formation of healthy self-concept and stronger self-esteem (Demaray & Malecki, 2002a; Pounder, 1999), thus positively shaping the nature of students' developmental pathways (Feldman & Matjasko, 2005) and, consequently, prosocial attitudes and actions (Battistich et al., 1997; Rothman & Cosden, 1995). Nonsupportive communities for students, on the other hand, can lead to reduced self-esteem, nonproductive developmental pathways, and counterproductive attitudes and behaviors (Crosnoe, 2011). These behaviors and attitudes, in turn, are related to engagement and school success (Finn & Rock, 1997; Mulford & Silins, 2003; Rumberger, 2011)—for better or worse.

In total then, "children's perception of their teachers' feelings toward them are correlated positively and significantly with self-perception" (Davidson & Lang, 1960, p. 116). We also learn that the flows between press and support and sense of self are influenced by the students' existing assessments. For example, preexisting assessment of self-concept plays an important role (Rudduck, 2007): "The children who had a more favorable or a more adequate self concept, that is, those who achieved a higher self perception score also perceived their teachers' feelings toward them more favorably" (Davidson & Lang, 1960, p. 109). This is important in general and particularly when we recall that there is a lowering of self-concept as one moves from elementary to middle school (Maehr & Midgley, 1996). That is, "systematic differences exist between pre- and post-transition classrooms.... These differences in classroom environment may contribute to negative changes in student beliefs" (Feldlaufer et al., 1988, p. 134). We also know that these flows from culture and press lead to both positive and negative outcomes in sense of self (Chaplain, 1996b; Dillon, 1989). Students' negative assessment of press and support produce negative beliefs about themselves (Harter et al., 1997), and poor academic self-concepts specifically (Murdock et al., 2000). Thus, at times, teachers are "complicit in creating negative self-esteem" (Nieto, 1994, p. 414).

The research on the impact of press and supportive culture can be further refined. That is, we also look for links from the subelements of challenge and care to sense of self. Examining care, for example, researchers have discovered linkages between voice and self-esteem (Harter, 1990), self-confidence (Rudduck, 2007), and self-efficacy (Morgan & Streb, 2001). On the press side, these analysts have documented linkages between student perceptions of cooperative and participatory learning platforms and student interdependence rather than individual competition (Hoge et al., 1990) and self-esteem and self-efficacy (Oldfather, 1995; Wigfield et al., 1998). Flutter and Rudduck (2004, p. 123) point out the value of "pupil to pupil support schemes" in this regard. We see the same effects for implementation of an inclusive curriculum (Kosciw et al., 2012), relational trust (Miron & Lauria, 1998), enhanced self-management responsibilities (Weinstein, 1983), teacher efficacy (Eccles et al., 1993), student autonomy (Hoge et al., 1990), interactive pedagogies (Rudduck & Flutter, 2004), and "student choices and creative self

Chapter Seven: Students Have It Right   183

expression" (Hoge et al., 1990, p. 118). We close with the observation that social integration is a causal factor in enhanced self-concept (Smerdon, 2002).

Having reviewed the antecedents of sense of self, we turn to our second question: What are the outcomes of a positive or negative sense of self? We begin with the general storyline around this question and then reveal the linkages between sense of self and the other variables in the model in Figure 7.1. On the general front, "efficacy beliefs contribute significantly to the level and quality of human functioning" (Bandura, 1993, p 145)—"efficacy beliefs influence how people feel, think, motivate themselves, and behave" (p. 118). We learn that self-efficacy provides a "measure of overall well-being for adolescents" (Saunders et al., 2004, p. 88), that "pupils' confidence in their abilities as learners is linked to their general level of self-esteem" (Flutter & Rudduck, 2004, p. 120). Researchers tell us in broad strokes that sense of self is "predictive of better adult outcomes" (Garmezy, 1991, p. 426), academically related actions in general (Eccles-Parsons et al., 1983), and task persistence specifically. "Self efficacy has been demonstrated to influence . . . educational achievement of children and adolescents" (Stajkovic & Luthans, 1998, p. 256). It exerts "a powerful influence on young people's life chances" (Rudduck, 1996b, p. 139). We know that academic competence beliefs impact emotional health (Roeser et al., 2000). A student's level of self-efficacy is a good indicator of ability to cope with stress (Chaplain, 1996a, 1996b).

> Particular problems such as school failures, homelessness, suicide, unemployment, drug use, crime, and single parenthood can be identified as outcomes of a struggle without maps towards identity formation. (Bradley et al., 2004, p. 199)
>
> The impact of most environmental influences on human motivation, affect, and action is heavily mediated through self processes. They give meaning and valence to external events. Self influences thus operate as important proximal determinants at the very heart of causal processes. (Bandura, 1993, p. 118)

Sense of self has an "impact on the child's affective motivational and coping processes" (Harter, 1990, p. 321). "Beliefs about the self exert a powerful influence on interpersonal perception and behavior" (Davis, 2001, p. 433). Analysts also document a relationship between sense of self and patterns of behavior in school (Connell & Wellborn, 1991), especially broad indices of performance (Boekaerts, 1993). This sense of self when high "functions protectively by motivating attempts at adaptation" (Masten et al., 1990, p. 431). When low, it often produces passivity, distancing of oneself, emotional distress (Fine et al., 2007; Harter et al., 1997), and "academic learned helplessness" (Eccles-Parsons et al., 1983, p. 88). "Feelings of self-efficacy increase this likelihood of instrumental behavior" (Masten, 1990, p. 431) and "influence what one perceives to be the opinions of others" (Harter, 1996, p. 29). The big impact for children has been penned by Harter and team (1997, p. 170): "Sense of self provides a firm foundation for their transition to adulthood."

Taking a broader sweep, we see that sense of self and self-efficacy impact and are impacted in return by all the pieces of our model. Ma (2003) and Wentzel (2002) reveal the reciprocal link between students' sense of self and social integration, although the flow seems more powerful from integration to self (Anderman, 2003; McNeal, 1998). Social integration, according to McNeal (1998, p. 184) "contributes to personal development and identity formation." Davis (2003, p. 216) uncovered a powerful effect for social integration, finding that "students' feelings of connectedness to school accounted for between 13% and 18% of the variance in ratings for emotional distress." In their review, McMahon and Wernsman (2009, p. 270) conclude that "sense of school belonging is positively related to commitment to school goals, expectations, and self-efficacy." On the other hand, "lack of a sense that one fits can have a powerful negative effect on self concept" (Rudduck, 1996a, p. 175). Smerdon (2002, p. 289) in a major review found that "belonging has positive effects on academic self efficacy [and] academic self-consciousness." The takeaway message is as follows: "Belonging contributes to self efficacy" (McMahon & Wernsman, 2009, p. 278).

Sense of self is also yoked to motivation, a fact well documented in the research literature (Chaplain, 1996a; Maehr & Midgley, 1996). "Academic self-efficacy and competence perceptions motivate students. . . . When people expect to do well, they tend to try hard, persist, and perform better" (Pintrich, 2003, p. 671). On the other hand, "people who have a low sense of efficacy . . . have low aspirations and weak commitment" (Bandura, 1993, p. 144). We learn that "those who have a strong belief in their capabilities exert greater effort when they fail to master the challenge" (Bandura, 1993, p. 144). Maehr and Midgley (1996, p. 42) portray the center of gravity here: "Sense of self is at the root of motivation to learn." Indeed "decades of research show that children's self perceptions, such as self efficacy, ... are robust mediators of motivation" (Furrer & Skinner, 2003, p. 148).

Researchers have also established that sense of self is linked to student engagement (Connell & Wellborn, 1991). A higher level of self-esteem is associated with higher levels of both behavioral and psychological engagement (Appleton et al., 2008). Control of learning enhances student motivation (Rudduck & Flutter, 2004). Students' "perceptions of self efficacy ... and control are robust self-system predictors of children's engagement in school" (Furrer & Skinner, 2003, p. 151), both positively and negatively. Maehr and Midgley (1996, p. 43) underscore importance for children here when they conclude that "when something as serious as their self esteem is at stake, students do not respond thoughtfully or rationally.... They are creative primarily about avoiding the kind of engagement that is necessary to learn."

There is also abundant evidence that sense of self (i.e., self-concept ability and global self-concept) (Skaalvik & Hagtvet, 1990) is connected to student performance in general and academic achievement specifically (Boekaerts, 1993; Roeser et al., 2000; Saunders et al., 2004), with studies routinely demonstrating both the positive and negative relationships between the efficacy and performance variables (Saunders et al., 2004).

Perceived self-efficacy influences performance both directly and through its strong effects on goal setting and analytic thinking. Personal goals, in turn, enhance performance attainments through analytic strategies. (Bandura, 1983, p. 128)

Decades of research show that children's self-perceptions, such as self-efficacy, goal orientations, or autonomy, are robust predictors of motivation and performance in school both concurrently and over many years. (Furrer & Skinner, 2003, p. 148)

(Continued)

186   **Part Four**: Evidence on Student Views

> (Continued)
>
> As the self-concept becomes better established and more stable, it may be expected to increasingly affect performance expectancies and study behavior, which in turn may affect academic performance. (Skaalvik & Hagtvet, 1990, p. 304)
>
> Similar equations were used to test the relationship of the self-perception variables to the 2nd dependent variable, grade point average. In the 1st equation with the 4 self-perception variables entered, both self esteem and academic self efficacy were significant predictors. (Saunders et al., 2004, p. 86)
>
> When adolescents perceive themselves as academically competent and able to master school-related tasks, they get higher grades, and when they achieve good grades, they feel more competent academically. The negative relation of emotional distress and academic grades corroborates other mental health research that shows emotional distress can impair children's and adolescents' ability to effectively learn in school. (Roeser et al., 2000, p. 452)

For example, Murdock and Miller (2003, p. 394) found in their work that their "middle school students self-efficacy judgments were highly correlated with their relative classroom performance," and Eccles-Parsons and team (1983, p. 83) concluded that "studies suggest that, at least for some students, increases in self confidence can produce increases in achievement." Eccles-Parsons goes on to tell us that by adolescence, expectancies are tightly linked to general achievement performance. Bandura (1993, p. 133) helps us see that "students who have a low sense of efficacy to manage academic demands are especially vulnerable to achievement anxiety." Skaalvik and Hagtvet (1990, pp. 206, 304) have weighed in on the directionality of the relationship here, reporting that, in general, "self concept of ability is a stronger predictor of academic achievement than vice versa [or] . . . self concept has causal predominance over achievement for high school students." And Bandura (1993, p. 137) takes us inside the avenue of influence here, reporting that "increased sense of academic efficacy promotes academic attainment both directly and by heightening aspirations." A few studies provide evidence on the aspects of achievement influenced. For example, in Roeser's (2000, p. 456) work, "all of those student s who achieved good grades also reported a sense of competency and efficacy in the academic domain." And high levels of academic efficacy, control, and self-esteem are related to achievements in life (Silverstein & Krate, 1975).

Motivation

The Construct

The final intermediate outcome in our model in a general sense is students' attitudes or dispositions toward school. The center of gravity here is student motivation. As we examine in some detail below, "the effects of school culture are mediated by motivational variables." More specifically, "perceived culture is associated with certain motivational cognitions that collectively appear to be related to performance" (Maehr & Fyans, 1989, p. 233). Or, using our nomenclature, academic press and a positive school culture of care and support nurture positive attitudes toward school (Birch & Ladd, 1997). Motivation itself "results from some combination of the likelihood that one will achieve a goal (expectancy) and how much that goal is desired or wanted (valued)" (Graham et al., 1998, p. 608). That is, "the definition of motivation involves the combination of the probability of goal attainment and the value associated with the goal" (Booker, 2006, p. 5). Pintrich and De Groot (1990, p. 34) report that when these two conditions are in place, high probability and "beliefs that the task is interesting and important, students will engage in more metacognitive activity, more cognitive strategy use, and more effective effort management."

When we look into the essential components of motivation (Wigfield et al, 1998), three elements are visible: interest (meaningfulness), values, and goals (Pintrich, 2003). The goal of motivation theory is to explain "what gets individuals moving (energization) and toward what activities (direction)" (Pintrich, 2003, p. 669).

We use the term personal investment as an alternative for the common term "motivation." We do so not to make the topic seem easy or esoteric, but because we want to reflect a specific perspective on the nature of motivation. Investment

(Continued)

188   **Part Four**: Evidence on Student Views

> (Continued)
>
> suggests a metaphor regarding what motivation really is like. Referring to motivation as investment suggests an image in which all students have certain resources they may use in different ways. All students have time, energy, and abilities; they bring a history of experience, information, and knowledge to any situation—be it school, a social group, work, or whatever. The primary issue of motivation, then, is not whether students have it. They do. It is a matter of how they choose to invest it. Motivation is like money—it can be used in a variety of ways. The issue is how these resources are invested and with what results. (Maehr & Midgley, 1996, p. 27)

Our first point here is that "motivation of students is a critical component in the learning process" (Maehr & Fyans, 1989, p. 216); "interests, values, and goals mediate students' performance, choices, and efforts" (Wigfield et al., 1998, p. 104); and goals and interests are essential to understanding why students act as they do (Wentzel, 1998).

> [Those] interested in basic questions about how and why some students seem to learn and thrive in school contexts, while other students seem to struggle to develop the knowledge and cognitive resources to be successful academically, must consider the role of motivation. (Pintrich, 2003, p. 667)

Analysts in the area of motivation provide helpful insights on motivation beyond definitional material. To begin with, we are reminded that there are two types of motivation, intrinsic and extrinsic.

Extrinsic rewards. Competence can be rewarded by high grades, admission to higher education, attractive jobs, increased income, social approval, and status. Extrinsic rewards that are powerful for some students, however, may have no effect on the engagement of others. Only when students perceive that academic achievement will lead to rewards they value and, further, believe that their own hard work will result in academic achievement, will their engagement increase.

Intrinsic interest. Students may invest in or withdraw from learning depending on how interesting they find the material, regardless of its connection to extrinsic rewards. Students naturally find some topics and activities more stimulating and enjoyable to work on than others. However, what a student finds interesting often depends not simply upon the subjects or topics themselves but upon the way the topics are presented and the student's prior experience with those concepts. (Newmann, 1989, p. 35)

Second, we also know that intrinsic motivation declines over the school career of children (Harter, 1996; Wallace, 1996), particularly as students make the move to junior high school (Harter, 1996).

> There is good empirical evidence from cross-sectional and longitudinal studies that over the course of the school years, student motivation on the average declines or becomes less adaptive, with a large drop as students enter the junior high or middle school years. This declining motivation generalization is very well supported and seems to be characteristic of most motivational beliefs including efficacy and control constructs as well as values and personal interest. (Pintrich, 2003, p. 680)

Maehr and Midgley (1996, p. 94) find that this decline "can be part attributed to what is going on in the schools and classrooms. . . . The psychological environment of the learning environment . . . is responsible for the kinds of motivation problems that are too readily evident." Feldlaufer and associates (1988, p. 134) help us see what is happening inside classrooms:

> In general, there is limited evidence suggesting that junior high school classrooms, in comparison to elementary school classrooms, offer fewer opportunities for student self-management and choice, and are characterized by a less positive teacher/student relationship, both of which could undermine students' interest in their academic subjects. In

addition, there is some evidence that the shift to junior high school is associated with an increase in whole class task organization, between-classroom ability grouping, and external evaluation; practices that may increase the saliency of social comparison and ability self-assessment. This may have negative effects on some students' confidence in their ability and motivation to achieve; in particular those students who are not highly able or do not perceive themselves as highly able prior to entry into junior high school.

This turn of events is unfortunate, for "there is compelling evidence that students who are more intrinsically than extrinsically motivated fare better" (Brewster & Fager, 2000, p. 18).

Third, we see here as we have throughout the book that belief systems formed early in life can be antithetical to achievement. Given our analysis to date, we discover that these nonsupportive belief systems are associated with children's social and economic hardships, especially students of color and boys.

> For example, sociologists have pointed to the opportunity structure in American society as they have argued that economic and social disadvantage has led many Black students to believe that their efforts in school will have relatively little payoff in terms of economic and social mobility. That is, the perceived barriers imposed by a society that perpetuates inequality along race and class lines communicate to minority youngsters that there is little relationship between their efforts and eventual outcomes. (Graham et al., 1998, p. 607)

Fourth, there is support for the proposition that students' achievement-related motives and dispositions vary by subject area (Feldlaufer et al., 1998). That is, at least to some extent, "the answer to motivation may be in the content" (Maehr & Midgley, 1996, p. 93). We also know that "the investment made by pupils is highly individualized and related to their perceptions of an imagined future painted by their teachers" (Wallace, 1996b, p. 61). Children "come to view the learning environment as taking this or that form and presenting certain possibilities that are grasped by the student and that relate to the ways he will (or will not) invest" (Maehr & Midgley, 1996, p. 67). Fifth, as noted earlier in general, there is a reciprocal relationship between motivation and the other variables in our model (e.g., Figure 7.1). For example, motivation is both influenced by and an influencer of sense of self, and motivation is connected to achievement, which also exerts an influence on motivation (Murdock et al., 2000).

The Elements of Motivation

We reported above that the definition of motivation highlights three concepts—interest, values, and goals. Here we provide a snapshot of each of the pieces. Interest has been well described by Oldfather and team (1999, p. 282) as "a continuing impulse to learn." These scholars tell us that interest "is characterized by intense involvement, curiosity, and a search for understanding" (p. 283). Maehr and Midgley (1996, p. 28) add to our understanding here:

> The point, of course, is that we are all regularly confronted with multiple options, and we do in fact go in some directions and avoid others. This directionality of our behavior over the short and long terms is specifically embraced in the term personal investment. We participate, engage, invest in some activities and acts and not in others. Personal investment implies that an individual does one thing when other possibilities are presumably open to him.

Analysts explain that "taking personal responsibility for their problems in school and life" (Penna & Tallerico, 2005, p. 14) can be considered an aspect of student interest (Kershner, 1996). So too, relatedly, is sense of obligation. "This sense of obligation," scholars conclude "appears to make a difference in what students do; it appears to predictably mediate certain relationships between the person and the environment" (Willems, 1967, p. 1258).

The second "family of social-cognitive constructs that has been a major focus of research on student motivations is goals and goal orientation" (Pintrich, 2003, p. 675), what Wentzel, (2002, p. 291) "calls mastery goal orientation." It can be described as "educational aspirations" (Murdock et al., 2000, p. 341), what youngsters see themselves attempting to accomplish (Wentzel, 2002). It links to student effort

192   **Part Four**: Evidence on Student Views

and investment (Wentzel, 2002). Indeed, Appleton and team (2008, p. 378) report that "investment in education is believed to largely be a function of students' perceptions of task or ability goals."

As was the case with interest, we know that social contexts impact goal adoption (Maehr & Midgley, 1996). Maehr and Midgley go on to report that "goal-adoption is to a significant degree a function of experienced contexts and that the psychological character of these contexts can be changed to affect goal adoption patterns." We close here by acknowledging that "students' perceptions of task and ability goal emphases in classrooms are in fact related [to] qualitatively different motivational orientations and patterns" (Maehr & Midgley, 1996, p. 90).

Finally, we add values to the motivation basket, a construct that blends quite easily with interest and goals. "Unlike achievement-related cognitions which largely center on beliefs about ability, values have to do with desires and preferences . . . and are more directly concerned with the perceived importance, attractiveness, or usefulness of achievement activities" (Graham et al., 1998, p. 606). Eccles and associates (1993, p. 31) define value as follows: "The overall value of any specific task is a function of three major components: (1) the attainment value of the task, (2) the intrinsic or interest value of the task, and (3) the utility of the task for future goals." Davis (2001, p. 434) deepens the narrative, explaining that

> perceived importance refers to the extent to which performance on a task confirms a central aspect of one's self-schema [see section on sense of self]. Perceived utility refers to the usefulness of the task for attaining future goals. Intrinsic interest refers to the amount of pleasure associated with a task.

Eccles-Parsons and team (1983, p. 89) outline two components of goals: "intrinsic or interest value and utility value." The former "is the inherent, immediate enjoyment one gets from engaging in an activity" (p. 89). In some scales it is assessed by measuring students' interest and their perceived importance of coursework (Murdock & Miller, 2003). The latter "is determined by the importance of the task for some future goal that might be somewhat unrelated to the process nature of the task at hand" (Eccles-Parsons et al., 1983, pp. 89–90). Murdock and team (2000) present the two ideas of concrete and abstract values. According to Davis (2001, p. 434), findings in the field "indicate value plays a crucial role in guiding students' choice of achievement activities." In sum, researchers show us, "the value of a particular task to a particular person is a function of both the perceived qualities of the task and the individual's needs, goals, and self perceptions" (Eccles-Parsons et al., 1993, p. 90). As was the case with other aspects of motivation, values are implicated in the underperformance of Black and ethnic minority youngsters. Because some "African American students feel that their efforts to achieve academically will not result in increased economic or social mobility, they opt to devalue the importance of schooling. . . . African American students expect little from school, so they value little in school" (Booker, 2006, p. 5).

Influences and Impacts

In this section, we start with the evidence, from general to specific, that press and support lead to student motivation. We do so first by highlighting major conclusions:

(1) School actions can and do affect a student's level of motivation (Brewster & Fager, 2000).

(2) Motivation develops from a complex web of social and personal relationships (Goodenow & Grady, 1993), that is, "the general quality of the relational environment is a relevant variable" (Birch & Ladd, 1997, p. 76).

(3) Within schooling, the connection that forms between a student and teacher can be a robust motivator (Davis, 2001). Indeed "teachers can have a much greater influence on students' motivation displayed in their classrooms than can parents" (Wentzel, 2002, p. 297).

(4) Youngsters who report stronger connections with their teachers are more motivated in school (Murdock & Miller, 2003), and relatedly "the psychological environment of the learning environment in classrooms and schools is responsible for motivational problems" (Maehr & Midgley, 1996, p. 94).

We present three general notes before we delve into the discussion of how supportive culture and academic press can impact motivation and how motivation in turn influences all the elements in our model (e.g., sense of self, student engagement). "To begin, we see that motivation is an individual phenomenon. School is an oasis for some students and a place of discouragement for others" (Cooper, 1999, p. 263). Second, although "there is an overall relationship between school culture and motivation score, in the case of each of the ethnic groups... the degree of this relationship varies" (Maehr & Fyans, 1989, p. 239). The traffic flows in two directions here. Specifically, "teachers have closer relationships with children who they perceive as having more positive attitudes toward school. Teachers may feel close to children who express school liking and who seem to enjoy most of the activities in the classroom" (Birch & Ladd, 1997, p. 76).

Analysts show that the norms of academic care and supportive culture work individually and in tandem to shape student motivation (Murphy & Torre, 2014). That is, both classroom culture and tasks can foster motivation (Pintrich & De Groot, 1990). On the academic care side of the equation, Epstein's (1981b, p. 82) review "concludes that student participation, student enrichment, and democratic student–teacher control of school activities develop more positive attitude toward school." Motivation is linked to

> student perceptions of the teacher and what goes on in the classroom, including summary judgments of emphasis on task or ability goals and reports of specific instructional and management practices employed by teachers, such as how they group, evaluate, and recognize children and how they organize the learning tasks. (Maehr & Midgley, 1996, p. 45)

More specifically, Davis (2003, p. 213) found that "teachers who successfully manage balancing the need for structure with the need for autonomy increase students'... intrinsic motivation for academic tasks." Similarly, Bru and team (2002, p. 290) concluded that "students who perceive that the classroom climate allows them a degree of autonomy are more intrinsically motivated than students who regard the climate as controlling." In addition to autonomy and voice, cooperative instructional structures lead to attitudes that are more positive in classrooms (Wigfield et al., 1998). "Task-focused instructional practices" enhance motivation as well (Anderman et al., 1999, p. 134). So too does the provision of clear explanations and authentic learning activities (Anderman et al., 1999; Bru et al.,

2002). "Students sense something . . . in the nature of tasks offered that affects not only their will to invest but also *how* they invest in learning" (Anderman et al., 1999, p. 134).

If academic press and care can improve motivation, then their absence can undermine it (Murphy, 2016). "Results suggest that when adolescents perceive their teachers . . . as promoting competition and social comparison among students . . . they are less motivated to learn" (Roeser et al., 2000, p. 460). When students are provided "fewer opportunities to make suggestions regarding what they will learn and how, there is often a negative impact on student motivation" (Feldlaufer et al., 1988, p. 150). We learn that "in classrooms characterized by poor opportunity to learn, low expectations, unimaginative curricula, and teacher control," (Roeser et al., 2000, p. 461) motivation is important negatively (Bru et al., 2002). Youngsters are also less motivated in classrooms that emphasize an ego goal orientation in students rather than underscore mastery goals (Bru et al., 2002; Maehr & Midgley, 1996).

Moving to cultural care, we are informed that there is "confirmation of the idea that the way in which students perceive school culture is related to their motives" (Maehr & Midgley, 1996, p. 72) and that "teacher support is independently related to numerous motivational variables" (Murdock & Miller, 2003, p. 385): That is, "supportive relationships with teachers . . . promote students' motivation to learn" (Davis, 2001, p. 432). Teacher use of targeted caregiving strategies (Wentzel, 2002) helps account for student motivation. We know from studies that "students who experience their teachers as autonomy supportive and warm are more likely to be intrinsically motivated" (Ryan et al., 1994, p. 231). Researchers inform us that "motivation is enhanced in classrooms with teachers who foster the experience of relatedness to socializing others" (p. 226) and who create "psychological environments of small groups" (Maehr & Fyans, 1989, p. 234). Teachers characterized by students "as less caring, warm, friendly, and supportive have a negative impact on motivation" (Feldlaufer et al., 1998, p. 151). So too do teachers who emphasize control-oriented assessment (Bru et al., 2002). Finally, a "mismatch between students' desires and classroom opportunities will result in a decline in motivation" (Eccles et al., 1993, p. 566).

Attending to the essential elements of motivation—interests, goals, and values—adds nuance to the impact of supportive culture via teacher–student relationships. Maehr and Midgley (1996, p. 67) start us on our voyage here by reminding us that "culture consists of perceptions . . . that are useful in defining when and how children will invest in learning." A supportive and caring teacher is also linked to increased interest in school and in subject areas (Davis, 2001; Wigfield et al., 1998). "Feelings of relatedness tapped by measures of school climate and quality of teacher–student relationships . . . [have] been linked to interest in school" (Furrer & Skinner, 2003, p. 149). So too are activities that are more open (Wigfield et al., 1998). On the other hand, "students who perceived math classrooms as putting greater constraints on their preferred level of participation in classroom decision-making . . . showed the largest and most consistent declines in their interest in math between the sixth and seventh grade" (Eccles et al., 1993, p. 566). Classroom environments that "overlooked or negated students' needs and devalued their voices . . . created apathy toward learning" (Rodriguez, 2008, p. 776).

Along with interest, scholars document that school climate in general (Maehr & Midgley, 1996) and students' views of teacher caring (Johnson, 2009) make an important "difference in the bottom line of education which is the investment of students in learning" (Maehr & Midgley, 1996, p. 100). In places "where students believe their voices matter they are more likely to be invested" (Quaglia & Corso, 2014, p. 3).

Moving to the second element of motivation, "schools and classrooms have been shown to vary in how they lead individuals to construe . . . the goals of a situation" (Maehr & Midgley, 1996, p. 48) and in "their achievement goal pursuit" (Davis, 2001, p. 448). "The point . . . is that school culture is likely to significantly shape the individual goals students come to hold" (Maehr & Midgley, 1996, p. 66). Pushing down a bit, we discover that "social contexts affect good attainment" (p. 48). Equally important, we learn from analyses of motivation that youngsters' assessments of general levels of support from teachers define these social contexts (Wentzel, 2002) and that "students with greater feelings of support from teachers are more likely to adopt prosocial goals" (Nichols, 2006, p. 256).

Finally, we find that academic care and supportive culture increase the value students attribute to their learning (Murdock & Miller, 2003). The overall theme here is that "students' perceived task values differ as a result of teachers' instructional practices and support" (Anderman, 2003, p. 8).

Chapter Seven: Students Have It Right 197

In the academic part of the story, we see that having peers as colearners and doing learning in a social context increases value (Wigfield et al., 1998). Midgley and colleagues (1989, p. 984) present the cultural support part of the value narrative as follows:

> As predicted, students whose teachers are perceived to be high in support both years show very little change in their valuing of math across the transition. In both years the students in this group have the most positive perceptions of the value of math of any of the groups. Students who have teachers perceived to be low in support both years suffer a steady decline in their valuing of math across the 2 years and have the most negative perceptions of any of the groups. As predicted, moving from less supportive to more supportive teachers after the transition enhances the intrinsic value of math during the junior high school year. In contrast, students who move from more supportive teachers in elementary school to less supportive teachers in junior high school value math much more before than after the transition. For these students, there is a sharp decline in the intrinsic value of math.

Overall, the research reveals that perceived teacher support is a powerful predictor of values (Murdock & Miller, 2002; Pavri & Monda-Amaya, 2001).

Further assessment of motivation confirms that interests, goals, and values influence the two other psychological states in the model in Figure 7.1. "In this regard, motivation is related to underlying psychological processes" (Appleton et al., 2008, p. 379). Turning first to sense of self, we discern that "higher levels of perceived control are positively related to motivation" (Pintrich, 2003, p. 673) and that "personal goal setting is influenced by self-appraisal capabilities. The stronger the perceived self-efficacy, the higher the goal challenge" (Bandura, 1993, p. 118). "Students who believe they are able and that they can do well are much more likely to be motivated" (Pintrich, 2003, p. 671).

Moving on to social integration exposes similar influences (Anderman, 2003; Rudduck, 2007). "Psychological connections to school play an important role in affecting student motivation" (Appleton et al., 2008, p. 377). Or as Ryan and colleagues (1994, p. 226) express it, "In virtually every domain of human endeavor there is mounting evidence that a network of supportive relationships facilitates an individual's motivation." Belongingness or social integration mediates between student–teacher relationships and motivation (Epstein, 1981a; Nichols, 2006). A "student cannot progress to a subsequent stage of growth and knowledge without feeling a sense of belonging and acceptance from those in the immediate environment" (Booker, 2006, p. 5). "To summarize, longitudinal analyses reveal a pattern of continuing, significant, independent influence of opportunities for participation on students' attitudes toward school" (Epstein, 1981b, p. 99). That is, belonging promotes positive dispositions toward school, or belonging predicts motivation (Nichols, 2006). We also learn that the positive effects of participation on attitudes are ongoing and cumulative (Epstein, 1981b).

Motivation is "a necessary, but not sufficient ingredient in the ignition of engagement" (Appleton et al., 2008, p. 379). We know, for example, that there is a "robust relationship between cognitive engagement and investment in learning" (p. 381) and that "students are more likely to be engaged when they have internalized a value for learning. Indeed, these internalized values are essential to student engagement (Wigfield et al., 1998). Although again we are confronted with the matter of causality, "it appears that the students who choose to become cognitively engaged . . . are those who are interested in and value the tasks they work on in classrooms" (Pintrich & De Groot, 1990, p. 37), that is, they are motivated.

We also see that motivation powers achievement (Roeser, Midgley, & Urdan, 1996; Rudduck & Flutter, 2004). "There is a mutual concurrent effect of attitudes and classroom success" (Epstein, 1981b, p. 103), one that occurs "indirectly and over time" (Epstein, 1981b, p. 103). Maehr and Fyans (1989, p. 216) report that studies by Walberg "have suggested that motivation accounts for between 16%–20% of the variation in student achievement." Later research concluded that "motivation accounted for up to 38% of the student achievement variance" (Maehr & Fyans, 1989, p. 216). Indeed, "there is a large literature that identifies . . . motivation beliefs as critical in understanding students' academic outcomes" (Ryan, 2000, p. 102). That is, "motivation is the key, producing social, cognitive, and academic outcomes" (Wigfield et al., 1998, p. 91). Analysts have established linkages between the elements of motivation and academic achievement, including standardized test scores (Maehr & Midgley, 1996). "Perceived culture is associated with certain motivational cognitions that collectively appear to be related to performance [and] the motivational components are linked in important ways to student cognitive engagement and academic performance in the classroom" (Pintrich & De Groot, 1990, p. 37).

On one front, we see a connection between interest and learning. In his work, for example, Wentzel (2002, p. 295) found that "interest in school was related significantly and positively to academic performance." Smerdon (2002, p. 289) confirms that students' "commitment to academic work . . . is a key factor in explaining and enhancing students' academic success," including grades and test scores (Wentzel, 1998). Goals also influence learning and achievement for students (Pintrich, 2003). Finally, there is a documented connection between student values and learning: "There is a positive relationship between students' valuing of school and school outcomes" (Quiroz, 2001, p. 340), one extending to students' future economic well-being. Scholars conclude that the values in the motivation formula often are "prerequisite to academic learning" (Hamilton, 1983, p. 323) and securing a good education (Roeser et al., 2000). On the other hand, there is a strong linkage between "devaluing the importance of schooling . . . and lower academic performance" (Booker, 2006, p. 5.)

THE STATE OF ENGAGEMENT

Getting Started

We begin here with the argument that student engagement is the door into important educational outcomes (Rudduck & Flutter, 2004). We agree with Connell and Wellborn (1991) that the analysis of engagement in schools needs to be highlighted more forcefully than it has been in the past. To strengthen schools, it is essential, therefore, that increasing student engagement be relocated to the center stage of the school improvement production (Datnow, Park, & Kennedy, 2008; Joselowsky, 2007) and that we work to deepen our understanding of this pivotal construct (Fredricks et al., 2004; Marks, 2000). One important step would "be to expand the priorities of schools to include *engagement* in learning as a central institutional goal along with meeting certain performance standards" (Connell & Wellborn, 1991, p. 70). Our second introductory note should be deeply ingrained by this point in our chronicle: Positive student–teacher relationships nurture engagement and offset the dynamics that promote disengagement (Johnson, 2009; Willms, 2003). "Teachers' behaviors in the classroom continue to impact the level of engagement with class material" (Davis, 2003, p. 211), or as Rodriguez (2008, p. 768) encapsulates the message: "Respectful relationships can significantly mediate academic engagement or disengagement." That is, "engagement is a result of interaction between students, teachers, and the curriculum" (Taylor-Dunlop & Norton, 1997, p. 278). Qualities that "emerge within the relationship between students and teachers prove to be important not only for students' academic engagement . . . but also for students social and emotional development" (Kennedy, 2011, p. 8). On the disengagement theme, Murdock and team (2000, p. 329) conclude that "student–teacher relationships may be the key to understanding the process of alienation from schooling." More specifically, "studies of high school dropouts document poor relationships with teachers and perceived teacher disrespect/unfairness as central to students' decision to leave school" (Murdock et al., 2000, p. 329). "Students who feel unconnected . . . find it harder to become constructively involved in academic activities . . . and should be more likely to be disaffected" (Furrer & Skinner, 2003, p. 149). Researchers who investigate the workings of student engagement and disengagement in classrooms find that disengagement builds up over time and can become so severe that it leads to dropping out of school (Davis, 2003; Murphy & Torre, 2014).

The Construct

There are a variety of ways to build understanding of engagement in schools. A good way to begin is to examine definitions of the concept, acknowledging that there is some fuzziness across the various studies (Dahl, 1995; Marks, 2000). Furrer and Skinner (2003, p. 149) report that

> engagement refers to active, goal-directed, flexible, constructive, persistent, focused interactions with the social and physical environment. In contrast patterns of disaffection, in which individuals are alienated, apathetic, rebellious, frightened, or burned out, turn people away from opportunities for learning.

Newmann (1989, p. 34) provides the following definition:

> Engagement is more than motivation of the general desire to succeed in school. It involves participation, connection, attachment, and integration in particular settings and tasks. As such, engagement is the opposite of alienation: isolation, separation, detachment, and fragmentation. Persons are engaged to a greater or lesser degree with particular other people, tasks, objects, or organizations. Thus, engagement helps to activate underlying motivation and can also generate new motivation. Engagement in academic work is the student's psychological investment in learning, comprehending, and mastering knowledge or skills. Students' level of engagement in academic work can be inferred from the way they complete academic tasks: the amount of time they spend, the intensity of their concentration, the enthusiasm they express, and the degree of care they show.

And Balfanz and colleagues (2007, p. 224) "define school disengagement as a higher order factor composed of correlated subfactors measuring different aspects of the process of detaching from school, disconnecting from its norms and expectations, reducing effort and involvement at school, and withdrawing from a commitment to school and to school completion." Wallace (1999a, p. 52) reminds us engagement "goes beyond compliance to denote a level of emotional involvement in school work." From the street level, a teacher lays it out this way: "Most of all, engagement means that students seem to want to be here and they want to work and learn" (Shade et al., 1997, p. 5). "Engagement requires intention, concentration, and commitment by students" (Taylor-Dunlop & Norton, 1997, p. 278), and is reflected in patterns of "attendance, participation, attention, and behavior" (Kennedy, 2011, p. 7).

Another way to peer into engagement is to review the types of engagement, or perhaps more accurately the components of this "meta construct" (Appleton et al., 2008, p. 381). We understand, to begin with, that engagement is a multifaceted concept (Wallace, 1996a); that is, engagement encapsulates multiple components (Li et al., 2011). Fredricks and associates (2004) provide us with the richest conceptual map of engagement, one that is scaffolded on three core pillars: cognitive engagement, emotional engagement, and behavioral engagement. Cognitive engagement attends to issues of self-regulation. The focus here is on metacognition and cognitive strategy use and investment in learning. It "includes flexibility in problem solving, preference for hard work, and positive coping in the face of failure" (p. 64). Emotional engagement according to these scholars is often cast in terms of student identification with school, including an assortment of "emotions related to the school, schoolwork, and the people at the school" (p. 66). Finally, for Fredricks and colleagues (2004) and other scholars of student engagement (Alexander et al., 1997; Balfanz et al., 2007; Voelkl, 1997), behavioral engagement includes general and specific actions, including work-related and conduct actions such as putting forth effort, attending, participating, paying attention, and demonstrating persistence. More specifically, they define behavioral engagement in three ways:

> The first definition entails positive conduct, such as following the rules and adhering to classroom norms, as well as the absence of disruptive behaviors such as skipping school and getting in trouble. The second definition concerns involvement in learning and academic tasks and includes behaviors such as effort, persistence, concentration, attention, asking questions, and contributing to class discussion. A third definition involves participation in school-related activities such as athletics or school governance. (Fredricks et al., 2004, p. 61)

We start with the fact that engagement and disengagement are two sides of a continuum (Newmann et al., 1992). The job of the school is to get and keep students at the farthest right-hand side of that continuum, where there is full and meaningful engagement in the classroom and the school, "arranging conditions so that people expend energy in ways that enhance engagement with work" (Newmann, 1981, p. 548). As suggested above, the roots of disengagement (or engagement) in schools can be traced to conditions in the larger world of childhood and adolescence, to the alignment between this larger world and the focus and methods of schooling, and to actions specific to schools. At times, schools cause disengagement. More often than not, however, they fail to ameliorate or exacerbate nascent disaffiliation (Baker et al., 1997), either by ignoring the realities of the larger world in which youngsters operate, or ineptly (often thoughtlessly) attempting to force students to fit into prevailing school models (e.g., demonstrating unawareness of or rejecting cultural norms and values of working class and minority cultures) (Crosnoe, 2011; O'Connor, 1997). We also build on Laffey's (1982) sage advice and employ multiple indicators to measure engagement.

It is also instructive to see what is inside these components and to examine how they are measured. Appleton and colleagues (2008, p. 372) provide considerable knowledge here when they explain that

> variables such as time on task, credits earned toward graduation, and homework completion represent indicators of academic engagement, whereas attendance, suspensions, voluntary classroom participation, and extracurricular participation represent indicators of behavioral engagement. Cognitive and psychological engagement are considered less observable and gauged with more internal indicators, including self-regulation, relevance of schoolwork to future endeavors, value of learning, personal goals and autonomy as indicators of cognitive engagement and feelings of identification or belonging, and relationships with teachers and peers as indicators of psychological engagement.

Other scholars point to strategies such as reports of engagement and disengagement by teachers and/or students (Connell & Wellborn, 1991). Still other analysts note the specific tools used to generate reports, such as questionnaires, student writing assignments, and logs of participation and involvement (Furrer & Skinner, 2003; Lodge, 2005).

Relatedly, understanding is enhanced by identifying the indicators assessed in the quest to corral the components of engagement (or disengagement) in schools. One indicator is "graduation from high school with sufficient academic and social skills to partake in post-secondary enrollment options and/or the world of work" (Appleton et al., 2008, p. 372). Ryan (2000, p. 102) adds "participation in classes and time on homework" to the list. Connell and Wellborn (1991, p. 54) provide a number of other indicators of student engagement, including on-task versus off-task behavior, tardiness, and classes skipped. Burke and Grosvenor (2003) add truancy, and Willms (2003) adds frequency of absence, class skipping, and late

204   **Part Four**: Evidence on Student Views

arrival to school. Newmann (1989, p. 34) deepens our list of indicators, reporting that "levels of engagement in academic work can be inferred from the way they complete academic tasks: the amount of time they [students] spend, the intensity of their concentration, the enthusiasm they express, and the degree of care they show."

Levels of Engagement

It is helpful to examine student engagement across the full spectrum or continuum we presented above, from active engagement to active disengagement. The categories we present in Figure 7.2 show the overlapping levels of participation on that scale. The model is heuristic. It shows "levels" of engagement on a continuum, from active disengagement to active engagement. On the positive side of the line, we refer to the lowest level of engagement as "minimalist participation." At this point, students are investing very little in schooling, "doing just enough." Minimal effort, involvement, and

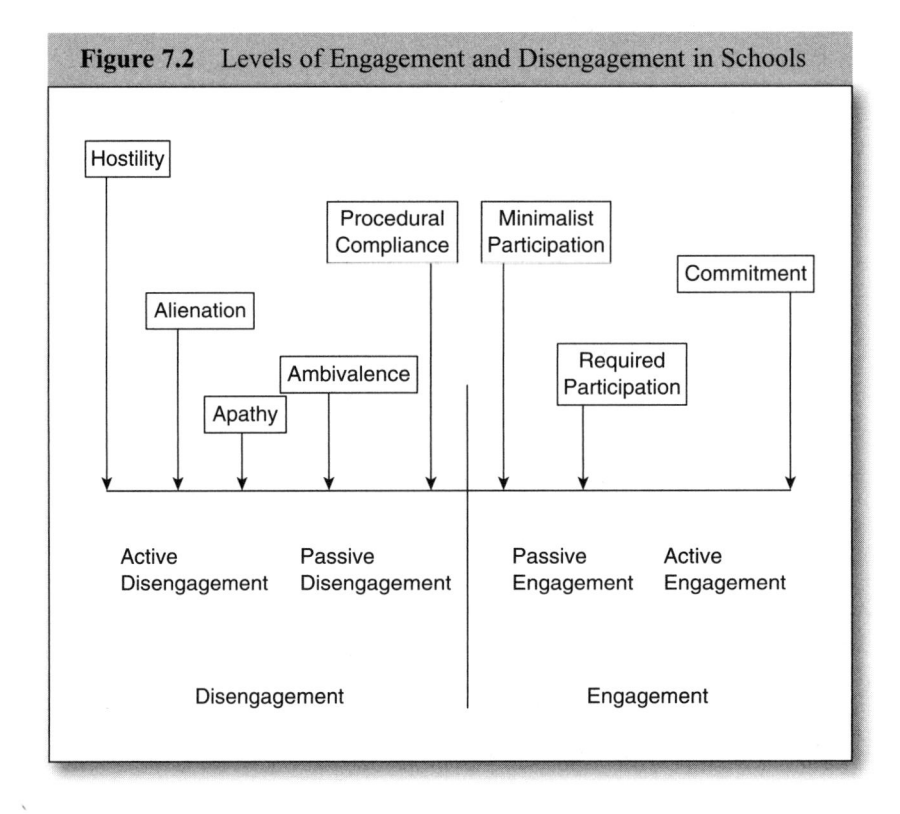

Figure 7.2   Levels of Engagement and Disengagement in Schools

Disengagement		Engagement
Active Disengagement — Passive Disengagement		Passive Engagement — Active Engagement

Labels (disengagement side): Hostility, Alienation, Apathy, Ambivalence, Procedural Compliance

Labels (engagement side): Minimalist Participation, Required Participation, Commitment psychological investment are evident (Eckert, 1989; Newmann et al., 1992; Weis, 1990). This is a marginal form of engagement, overlapping with "procedural compliance" on the disengagement side of the line. They share the gene of passivity, with students "doing what they are told but not consciously doing anything at all" (Weis, 1990, p. 32). These are the RHINOS, students who are there really in name only (Rudduck & Flutter, 2004, p. 6). The middle point on the engagement side of the continuum is best thought of as "required participation," where more than minimum is invested by students. Students exert sufficient energy to meet classroom and school expectations. Students appear to be "on task" here. There is involvement but little psychological investment. The high point on the engagement continuum is "commitment." At this level, we see active involvement and meaningful investment in learning on the part of students. Active involvement "involves psychological investment in learning, comprehending, or mastering knowledge, skills, and crafts, not simply a commitment to complete assigned tasks or to acquire symbols of high performance such as grades or social approval" (Newmann et al., 1992, p. 12).

Five levels define disengagement, "the emotional and physical withdrawal of students from school" (Voelkl, 1997, p. 294), rungs on the ladder of disaffiliation representing degrees of "students' feeling of not belonging in school and not valuing school and school related behaviors" (p. 294). We examine them from passive to active withdrawal. We see first "procedural compliance," which we argue is the modal point of student engagement with schooling today, a reality that is both troubling and sobering for those in the schooling business (Newmann et al., 1992; Voelkl, 1997; Weis, 1990). As we revealed above, it shares space with minimalist participation. Students here work to "get by" (Quiroz, 2001; Weis, 1990). They are not especially interested in the goals of the school (Csikszentmihalyi & Larson, 1984) and demonstrate very little interest in their education (Crosnoe, 2011; Weis, 1990). They have mastered the art of appearances, however. They have learned how to get along by going along. By and large, they "do not engage in overt or calculated rejection of school" (Weis, 1990, p. 18) or its values and norms. They participate in the form but not the substance of education (Eckert, 1989; Farrell, 1990). Here, as Weis (1990, pp. 32–33) documents, engagement "plays itself out largely in student participation in the maintenance of the appearance of order and a willingness to hand something in in order to pass courses." There is adherence to school routines and little more than perfunctory effort (Ancess, 2003; Newmann et al., 1992). "Students just sit in class and do what they are told" (Weis, 1990, p. 30).

On the next two rungs down the ladder of engagement, we see "ambivalence" and "apathy." They overlap and share a few defining elements with procedural compliance as well. They key difference between them and their lethargic cousin is that some active resistance to schooling—to its goals, values, norms, procedures, and ways of operating—begins to appear. Going along to get along is supplemented at times by even less positive and more negative energy and push back on school routines and structures, although it is more implicit and less subversive than we find further down the continuum (Crosnoe, 2011; Farrell, 1990).

"Alienation" represents a still more robust form of disengagement. It includes withdrawal of personal agency and withdrawal from accepted forms of community in school (Ancess, 2003; Kohl, 1991), a deepening estrangement (Newmann, 1981). The resistance gene is enriched and becomes increasingly explicit (Eckert, 1989; Zanger, 1993). School goals and values are not simply rejected but often trampled upon. The most vigorous form of disengagement is "hostility." Getting by and going along to get along are rejected as personally demeaning actions (Ogbu, 1974; Quiroz, 2001). Counterproductive (from the schools' perspective) values formed on "ways of being" at school are on display (Crosnoe, 2011; Eckert, 1989). Controlled battles with teachers are engaged, and sometimes sought out. Maladjustment becomes a viable protective faction in the short term (Jackson & Warren, 2000; Wilson et al., 2011). "Delinquent" subcultures often materialize based on this hostility to school (Eckert, 1989).

Overall the theme here is that what students tell us "does not reflect well on the ability of school to attract the investment of children in learning" (Maehr & Midgley, 1996, p. 24). Rudduck and Flutter (2004, p. 233) probably have it right when they tell us that "the most immediate and persistent issue in school is not so much low achievement but students who are disengaged." In his study, Jackson (cited in O'Loughlin, 1995) concluded in 1968 that the majority of students were bored and waiting for something to happen. In 1971, Steele and team (p. 462) arrived at the same conclusion: "The most striking characteristic of average classes is the lack of enthusiasm. In over half of the average classes students are negative and uninterested in class activities." In 1974, Bronfenbrenner (cited in Johnson, 2009, p. 99) "described high schools as potent breeding grounds of alienation." Larkin in his 1979 (p. 139) report of a suburban high school tells us this about student engagement:

> Boredom is the universal element that transcends all social divisions at Utopia High. Throughout the study, the theme of boredom recurred. For the active students, engrossing themselves in projects and events provided a bulwark against it. For the more passive, it has become a way of life. Boredom hung over Utopia like a thick fog. It was something everyone had to cope with: a fact of life even for those who chose to avoid it.... Boredom was manifested at Utopia High in the following ways: hanging out, the "nothing-to-do-syndrome," disdainful views of Pleasant Valley, cynicism, despair, cruising, fantasies of leaving the area, and restlessness.

In 2009, Mitra and Gross (p. 522) concluded that "alienation results in 25–70% of students being disengaged from high schools." Similarly, other recent students "report that as many as 40–60 percent of high school students are consistently unengaged, chronically inattentive, and bored" (Johnson, 2009, p. 100). The takeaway point is that in general youngsters are unengaged in the academic business of schooling (Tyson, 2002; Sedlak, Wheeler, Pullin, & Cusick, 1986). Many have nothing "to do with the school, except the fact that they go there" (Mitra & Gross, 2009, p. 528).

On the school side of the issue, the causes for such lack of engagement are multiple and not difficult to find (Lee, 1999; Ogbu, 1974). According to students, school is often a "stifling experience" (Cook-Sather & Shultz, 2001, p. xi). We also learn that the core dynamics of schooling inhibit student engagement (Newmann, 1989). Most of these elements run counter to the dimensions of academic press we examined in Chapters 3 and 4. "Teaching is essentially coercive" (Newmann, 1989, p. 34).

"In over half of the average classes the teacher talks from 75 to 90% of the time.... The focus is on the teacher as information giver, with a limited amount of active involvement of students" (Steele et al., 1971, p. 46). A note from a student feels appropriate here:

The majority of the kids who were there didn't want to be. So, you've got all these kids crammed into this room, learning material that they either already know or don't care about. They don't want to be there in the first place. It just wasn't a good environment for people. (Johnson, 2009, p. 109)

And "a considerable body of evidence shows that disadvantaged students receive the least interesting, most passive forms of instruction, and are given the least opportunity to participate actively in their own education" (Levin, 2000, p. 164). Most classes are set up to make it difficult for the types of care and support we discussed in Chapters 3 and 4 to materialize, especially in schools in which a large number of children are in peril from conditions in society (Ogbu, 1974; Silverstein & Krate, 1975).

> And the consequences are profound, particularly for low-achieving students. While high-achieving students turn frequently to their friends and parents for assistance, low achievers withdraw or allow priorities other than schoolwork to take precedence. As a consequence, they fall further and further behind. In schools where alternative resources are available (for example, peer tutoring programs), some low-achieving students reach out for help. However, continued frustration and failure lead many of them to disengage from learning. (Phelan et al., 1992, p. 700)

Effective "teachers achieve despite the current system rather than because of it, whilst significant and increasing numbers of young people find school unfulfilling or reject it altogether" (Fielding, 2004a, p 198).

Again, we note that engagement is most important for students at risk from a host of dysfunctional conditions in society, the home, and the school (Connell & Wellborn, 1991; Mahoney & Cairns, 1997). Analysts all document that student engagement has an inverse relationship to student age (Brewster & Fager, 2000), that is, "school engagement tends to decrease over the course of adolescence" (Li et al., 2011, p. 329). As youngsters mature, peers are more and more likely to pull others into off-task behavior specifically and disengagement in general (Rudduck & Flutter, 2004): "By the time students reach middle school, lack of interest in schoolwork becomes increasingly apparent in more and more students, and by high school, as dropout rates attest, too many students are not sufficiently motivated to succeed in school" (Brewster & Fager, 2000, p. 4). Concomitantly, "engagement seems to have a 'rich-get-richer' quality which portends well for effective early interventions for students showing signs of school withdrawal" (Appleton et al., 2008, p. 374). Some students are able to overcome less-than-positive school culture in general and student–teacher relationships in particular. These students fight to stay engaged and generally realize the benefits of that engagement.

Antecedents

Not surprisingly, we find a robust connection between positive school cultures reflected through student–teacher relationships and school engagement (Moos & Moos, 1978). The overall storyline is that these powerful relations and strong academic norms promote active engagement, while the absence of these ingredients leads to disengagement. Fredricks and team (2004, p. 83) provide the anchoring statement here when they remind us that "engagement can result from a variety of antecedents in the context, both social and academic." "Schooling is an interpersonal as well as cognitive enterprise" (Ryan et al., 1994, p. 244). All of this works best when the ingredients of press and support unfold in an integrated manner (Levin, 2000; Murphy, 2013).

Starting with the academic press side of the narrative, the major point is that instructional activities mediate school engagement (Moos & Moos, 1978). We know that "how students view the way that teachers manage them has an influence on the extent to which they deploy off-task orientation" (Bru et al., 2002, p. 304). "Tailoring management strategies to individual students and avoiding individual favoritism" (p. 304) provide the opportunity to diminish actions that detract from student engagement (Freiberg et al., 2009). Likewise "children who report higher levels of perceived autonomy are reported by their teachers to be more engaged in class" (Connell & Wellborn, 1991, pp. 62–63). Connell and Wellborn (p. 60) go on to note "positive connections between positive perceived control and teacher rated student engagement" and proceed to the conclusion that "withdrawal of autonomy support and involvement erodes the motivational foundation for... engagement" (p. 68). That is, perceived autonomy (Levin, 2000; Wigfield et al., 1998) and "control beliefs are related to general levels of engagement" (Wentzel, 2002, p. 289). Students also inform us that more interesting and inviting schools are associated with greater engagement (Cook-Sather & Shultz, 2001). Newmann (1989, p. 35) reinforces the linkages between academic press and engagement when he explains that "engagement with learning and internalization of knowledge depend to a large degree on the opportunities students have to 'own' the work." What this entails, he goes on to explain, looks a great deal like the picture we saw in Chapters 5 and 6, students' perceptions of robust academic press.

> Rather than always toiling under predetermined routines dictated by school authorities, students must have some influence on the conception, execution, and evaluation of the work itself. At a minimum, this requires flexibility in the pace and procedures of learning, opportunities for students to ask questions and to study topics they consider important, and opportunities for students to construct and produce knowledge in their own words, rather than merely parroting the language of others. (Newmann, 1989, p. 35)

Maehr and Midgley (1996, p. 90) provide a similar narrative, telling us that

> if and as students saw their classrooms as emphasizing task goals[,] they were more likely to report that they used 'effective' learning strategies, preferred challenging tasks, and held more positive attitudes toward learning. Interesting also was the differential view of self vis-à-vis doing well in school. When the classroom was seen as task-oriented, students were more likely to stress effort as a cause of achievement.

Also "when students participate actively and when a variety of pedagogical methods are employed, students report a high level of interest and engagement" (Phelan et al., 1992, p. 700). We see a positive link as well between academic approach and engagement and between teacher challenge and engagement (Levin, 2000; Wallace, 1996b), "conveying high expectations verbally and through the use of challenging academic material" (Tyson, 2002, p. 1183).

> Tasks that are diverse, interesting, and challenging foster students' task-involved goals, as do tasks students think they have a reasonable chance to complete. When the authority in classrooms is structured such that students have opportunities to participate in decision-making and take responsibility for their own learning, students are more task involved. Recognition of students' effort (instead of only ability) and giving all students a chance to achieve recognition (rather than only the 'best' students) foster task-involved goals. As discussed earlier, task-involved goals are fostered when cooperative grouping is used and students have opportunities to work with a heterogeneous mix of classmates. When teachers evaluate students' progress and mastery rather than only their outcomes and provide students opportunities to improve, task involvement is more likely. Finally, time refers to how instruction is paced. Crucial elements for fostering task involvement are varying the amounts of time available for different students to complete their work and helping students learn to plan their own work schedule and organize how they progress through the work. (Wigfield et al., 1998, pp. 91–92)

Turning to the cultural support dimension, we uncover similar powerful effects on student engagement (Rudduck & Flutter, 2004). That is, "students in schools with more elements of communal organization show higher engagement and greater gains in engagement over time" (Fredricks et al., 2004, p. 73). Positive culture or positive school psychology (Bryk et al., 2010) for youngsters is shown to be a central catalyst in fostering student engagement, especially for students from lower SES families (Felner et al., 2007; Ma & Klinger, 2000; Rumberger, 2011). That is, the quality of student relationships with teachers is "significantly associated with active engagement in schools" (Goodenow & Grady, 1993, p. 23); "school culture that prioritizes relationships can significantly mediate academic engagement" (Rodriguez, 2008, p. 768). We see at the center of the story that the "engagement with a task ... is contingently related to personal and social relationships" (Wallace, 1996b, p. 53). When "the conditions of learning are experienced as congenial then students are more likely to commit themselves to learning" (Rudduck & Flutter, 2004, p. 133). "Relatedness is something that influences engagement" (Wigfield et al., 1998, p. 76).

Turning to the four norms of supportive culture, researchers confirm a strong positive linkage between care and engagement (Baker et al., 1997; Quint, 2006). They also substantiate an association between students' perceptions of teacher support and active investment and involvement in the classroom and school (Battistich et al., 1995; Conchas, 2001) with all three types of involvement we presented earlier—cognitive, emotional, and behavioral (Balfanz et al., 2007; Demaray & Malecki, 2002a, 2002b). Finally, an abundance of research draws empirical links between membership and engagement (Fredricks et al., 2004; Goodenow & Grady, 1993) as reflected in investment and participation (Ma, 2003; Osterman, 2000).

Delving into care, a number of elements that we discussed in Chapter 3 have important implications for engagement. In Johnson's (2009, p. 101) review, we learn that "teacher caring accounted for 47% of the variance in student engagement among high school juniors and seniors in a middle income suburban community." We would expect the number to be even larger in lower SES communities (Quiroz, 2001; Stanton-Salazar, 1997). Davis (2003, p. 211) confirms that "teachers' level of involvement with their students (both actual and perceived by the students) influenced quality of students' behavioral and emotional engagement in school." Research uncovers voice and agency linked to student engagement as well (Morgan & Streb, 2001; Smyth, 2006). "Students articulated how overlooking or negating students' needs and devaluing their voices ... produced disengagement from school and created apathy toward learning" (Rodriguez, 2008, p. 776). Being valued and being respected also are linked empirically to engagement (Kohl, 1991; McLean-Donaldson, 1994). Indeed for "many students respect precedes engagement" (Rodriguez, 2008, p. 767). "If pupils feel that they matter in a school and that they are respected they are more likely to commit themselves to the school's purposes" (Rudduck & Flutter,

2004, p. 133). That is, "students are more likely to engage in classroom activities if they feel supported and valued" (Wentzel, 1997, p. 417). For students from varied ethnicities and races, valuing is often conveyed in cultural appreciation (McLean-Donaldson, 1994; Tyson, 2002). For example, as is described in the McLean-Donaldson work (1994, p. 27),

> Students of color were very often resentful of unequal treatment and tended to internalize this mistreatment by withdrawing their interest in classes. . . . They also felt cheated and disrespected, because they were aware that their cultural groups made major contributions to the United States but were still ignored in the curricula.

Warmth is implicated in the engagement/disengagement narrative as well (Goldstein, 1999). So too are student assessments of fairness (or equal treatment) by teachers (Nichols, 2008). For example, Murdock and colleagues (2000, p. 329) inform us that "studies of high school dropouts document . . . perceived teacher disrespect/unfairness as central to students' decisions to leave school."

In parallel fashion, researchers document the robust role of teacher support, safety, and membership in enhancing engagement and preventing disengagement (Davis, 2003; Kosciw et al., 2012), what Ryan and team (1994, p. 237) refer to as "the real-world importance of students' underlying beliefs that teachers represent sources of interpersonal support." Powerfully, Appleton and team (2008, p. 374) conclude that "engaged students perceive more support from teachers and peers and that this perception leads to a beneficial cycle of increased levels of engagement and increased adult support." Open communication is one of the elements inside the domain of support that has been empirically linked to engagement (Birch & Ladd, 1997). So too are strategies that support students in the augmentation of social capital (Stanton-Salazar, 1997). Academic support is another piece of the narrative that prevents disengaged student actions (Bru et al., 2002). Wallace (1996b, p. 34) adds that "'engagement' is best sustained . . . in a supportive and interesting cultural environment," that is, "students feel supported when teachers take the time to create environments that are culturally relevant and meaningful places for learners." On the other hand, "attempts to 'monoculture'" (Nieto, 1994, p. 402) have been surfaced as a cause of student disengagement via dropping out (Wilson & Corbett, 2001). Continuing with our eyes on the negative aspects of support, analysts have determined that classrooms "low in teacher support tend to have higher rates of student absenteeism" (Moos & Moos, 1978, p. 265). Similarly, Quiroz (2001) and Stanton-Salazar (1997) report that antagonistic or apathetic actions by teachers can lead to "the institutionalization of detachment" (p. 7). Finally, researchers uncover connections between membership and student engagement (Davis, 2003). Or as Nichols (2006, pp. 256–257) reports, "A belief that one is part of the school culture has been linked to decreased at-risk behavior . . . and students who reported being more 'connected' to their school were less likely to drop out or be absent from school."

A nearly identical theme is evident with the three intermediate outcomes shown in Figure 7.1. Each of the three mediating variables can enrich or diminish student engagement. Sense of self in terms of "self-esteem and academic self-efficacy" (Saunders et al., 2004, p. 86) is associated with "intentions to complete the school year" (p. 86) for example. We also know that "students who value self-respect exhibit (statistically) significantly lower frequency on delinquent behavior" (Ma, 2003, p. 341). Pintrich and De Groot (1990, p. 37) also tell us that "self-respect plays a facilitative role in cognitive engagement." "Confident students will be more cognitively engaged in learning and thinking than students who doubt their capabilities to do well" (Pintrich, 2003, p. 671). Self-concept as reflected in measures of competence (Fredricks et al., 2004), "student appraisals of personal skillfulness" (Laffey, 1982, p. 62), and agency are powerfully linked with student engagement.

In a similar fashion, motivation is linked to engagement (Hattie, 2009; Opdenakker et al., 2012). "Students who are more motivated to learn the material (not just get good grades) . . . are more cognitively engaged in trying to learn and comprehend the material" (Pintrich & De Groot, 1990, p. 37). Pintrich and De Groot (1990, p. 37) argue that a focus on "intrinsic value for schoolwork . . . may lead to more cognitive engagement in the day-to-day work of the classroom." Appleton and team (2008) reach a similar conclusion on student identification.

Very powerful connections are also found in the research literature between social integration and student engagement (Gonzalez & Padilla, 1997; Newmann, 1992; Voelkl, 1997).

Turning to social integration, Gibson and team (2004, p. 129) tell us that research points ... to a strong and positive link between students' subjective sense of belonging in school and their participation.... Quite simply students function better and participate more in school settings and situations when they feel they belong.

McMahon and Wernsman (2009, p. 270) carry us a bit further, concluding that "students who feel greater school belonging are likely more motivated to attend school and to put forth greater effort because of external choice." More specifically still, Mahoney and Cairns's (1997) results indicate that social integration decreases early school dropout. This is especially the case for those students most at risk. "Students who report greater perceptions of belonging are less likely to be absent from school" as well (Nichols, 2006, p. 257). Social integration defined as greater opportunities to be involved in school decision-making provides an avenue to engage youngsters in the school community (Mitra & Gross, 2009).

Participation in extracurricular activities enjoys a special connection to student engagement in schools (Rudduck & Flutter, 2004). In an investigation using this measure of engagement, Mahoney and Cairns (1997) found that "dropouts participated in significantly fewer extracurricular activities at all grades [7–10] even several years prior to dropout.... As annual involvement increased, the dropout rates decreased" (p. 247). Thus, "it seems noteworthy that school dropout can be differentiated from nondropouts by virtue of their absence of involvement in extracurricular activities" (p. 250) and that "extracurricular involvement may be one component ... that can help shift the balance towards greater engagement in schools [by] strengthening the student-school connection" (pp. 248–249).

Peer relations as part of social integration have noticeable effects, for better or worse, on student engagement (Silverstein & Krate, 1975; Stinchcombe, 1964). In their work, Li and colleagues (2011, p. 337) concluded that "peer support is beneficial to youth emotional and behavioral engagement in schools, whereas problematic friends are negatively associated with emotional engagement."

On the downside, we learn that "many students do not feel accepted by their classmates or teachers. Gradually these students withdraw from school life and become disaffected from school" (Willms, 2003, p. 3). We also discover that in "contexts where students experience feelings of rejection or alienation, their participation declines" (Gibson et al., 2004, p. 129). Ma (2003, p. 340) informs us that research "indicates that sense of belonging is a direct cause of dropping out of high school." Such disengagement, disaffection, and/or alienation from school often has quite negative consequences, including rejection of the moral worth of the school (Stinchcombe, 1964); disruption in class and "exerting negative influence on other students" (Willms, 2003, p. 3); gang-connected problems (Ma, 2003); dropping out of school (Patterson, Beltyukova, Berman, & Francis, 2007); bullying (Chaplain 1996a, p. 107); and student resistance (Dillon, 1989), such as "maintaining a noisy and extrovert disdain for [school] work" (Rudduck & Flutter, 2004, p. 69).

Outcomes of Engagement

We have learned over the years that engagement is a direct proxy for social and academic school outcomes (Connell & Wellborn, 1991; Pintrich & De Groot, 1990), that is, "engagement is a predictor of academic performance" (Appleton et al., 2008, p. 374). On a broad front, engagement is always a necessity for acquiring knowledge and skills (Wallace, 1996a). The starting message is that to improve achievement, teachers need to first learn how to engage students (Levin, 2000). In their research, Connell and Wellborn (1991, p. 59) uncovered "direct relations between positive and negative aspects of perceived competence [and] student engagement support."

> A comparison of scores from the pupil self-concept of learner scale for the engaged and disengaged pupils showed that the scores of the disengaged pupils were significantly lower on every aspect of the scale. The disengaged pupils felt that they had greater difficulty in particular with task orientation and with more abstract problem solving tasks. They were more likely to experience difficulties with writing, coping with tests and doing homework. They were less likely to feel good about their school work. The disengaged pupils also indicated that they had a tendency to give up more easily in school work, to do things without thinking, to make mistakes because they didn't listen, and to give up if they didn't understand something. (Chaplain, 1996a, p. 106)

While researchers routinely have confirmed the conclusion that there is a strong relationship between participation and achievement, Appleton and colleagues (2008, p. 374) also find that there are "larger differences at higher levels of participation than at lower levels." Not surprisingly then, engagement is a powerful "predictor of children's long-term academic achievement and their eventual completion of school" (Furrer & Skinner, 2003, p. 149). For example, Saunders and associates (2004, p. 82) disclose that "when academic disengagement begins in elementary school, it is more difficult for young men to be well prepared for more challenging high school curriculums, putting them at risk for further failure and dropout." The summative message is that "classroom specific effort and engagement are related significantly to academic performance" (Wentzel, 1998, p. 203). That is, "engaged students tend to earn higher grades, perform better on tests, and drop out at lower rates, while lower levels of engagement place students at risk for negative outcomes" (Appleton et al., 2008, p. 383).

ACADEMIC AND SOCIAL LEARNING

Throughout this chapter in particular and the full volume in general, we have driven home three critical points. First, student–teacher relationships are the center of gravity for the effective schools universe. Second, these relations play out through a culture of care and support and an environment of academic press. Third, support and press power up a series of intermediate variables (i.e., sense of self, social integration, and motivation) that deepen student engagement, which, in turn, pushes social and academic outcomes upward. This script is both parsimonious and incredibly powerful. In this final section of the last chapter, we take on one more assignment, a review with the lens focused specifically on the outcome vector of the script just reviewed.

To start, we make clear that the academic outcomes fall into the last box in our model (see Figure 7.1). Many of the social learning outcomes measured by researchers, however, fall into the intermediate variables in the framework (e.g., self-efficacy). Research also makes the point that while the direction of the flow of influence in our model is dominant, reciprocity is evident as well; for example, motivation influences engagement, and engagement influences motivation. For example, Tyson (2002, p. 1184) informs us that his study "suggests that . . . achievement outcomes play a central role in the *development* of attitudes toward school," and Appleton and associates (2008, p. 376) find that "previous achievement bolsters future levels of identification." We also want to underscore the fact that researchers have assessed a variety of outcomes that extend beyond student academic and social learning, to benefits for teachers and the school (Rudduck, 2007). Included here is a benefit we introduced in Chapter 2, the fact that productive culture and academic press within the bond of positive teacher–student relationships can help teachers grow and to enrich the craft and success of their teaching. For example, "it is abundantly clear . . . that pupils can offer their teachers much thoughtful, constructive and helpful commentary on life and learning in their classrooms" (Arnot et al., 2004, p. 88). They bring their teachers understanding (Bragg, 2007; Fielding, 2004a, b), the grist for the formation of classrooms and schools as learning communities (Lodge, 2005; Rodriguez, 2008), including "the collective knowledge that emerges from a group sharing experiences and understanding the social influences that affect individual lives" (Wallerstein & Bernstein, 1988, p. 381).

Turning the lens back to students and moving beyond the confines of academic achievement and school social learning (e.g., student satisfaction, commitment to lifelong learning), we discover that press and support "make help seeking easier" (Rodriguez, 2008, p. 766). They often "open doors and provide the resources required for academic success" (Gibson et al., 2004, p. 131). Student well-being also may be enhanced by fostering a school environment of support (McNeely et al., 2002). Press and support can enhance the meaningfulness of schooling for youngsters (Hamilton, 1983) as well as promote a sense of specialness (Dillon, 1989). Action and climate in the type of classrooms we portray in this volume are associated with "more favorable reactions to school life" (Epstein, 1981b, p. 106). Students tend to feel "happier and more secure . . . in innovation oriented, structured affiliation oriented and supportive oriented classes" (Moos, 1978, p. 61). Students are "more satisfied and higher on well-being in less structured classes emphasizing teacher–student and student–student support" (Moos, 1979, p. 188). In his study, for example, Moos (1979, p. 190) found that "the classroom climate block explained . . . 20 to 25 percent of the predictable variance in students' sense of well-being and satisfaction with learning." In short, there is "strong support for the general hypothesis that the differences in classroom environments are systematically related to different student satisfactions" (Trickett & Moos, 1974, p. 7). Analysts also reveal that the effects of the full model include "a disposition to life-long learning" (Willms, 2003, p. 3). Press and support "give pupils the knowledge and skills necessary for taking an active role in a democratic society in later life" (Flutter & Rudduck, 2004, p. 18). Finally, researchers find "compelling evidence" that press and support inside healthy student–teacher relationships are related to longer term outcomes as well. Our two drivers are connected to health and well-being and "contribute to the quality of life of youths" (Willms, 2003, p. 86), now and in the future (Miron & Lauria, 1998). On the latter point, for example, we know that "through relationships with institutional agents, a segment of society gains the resources, privileges, and support necessary to advance and maintain their economic and political position in society" (Stanton-Salazar, 1997, p. 6). It is also hypothesized that students ensconced in relationships of press and support "will subsequently be engaged in their work environments [while] extreme disaffection from the school and truancy in particular are associated with marital problems, violence, adult criminality and incarceration" (Willms, 2003, p. 56). And while it is only lightly treated in the literature, there is some sense that all the outcomes associated with press and support grow the longer students are in such environments (Epstein, 1981a).

Returning specifically to a caring and supportive culture and an environment of academic press and their impacts, presented below is a summary of what we have reported so far. In the largest sense, we know that students crave meaningful relationships (Marquez-Zenkov, 2007). We know that these "relationships mediate learning" (Davis, 2003, p. 222). We understand that "relationships with teachers can have a profound effect on student learning and growth" (Kennedy, 2011, p. 9). "Teacher–child closeness" (Birch & Ladd, 1997, p. 61) and connection with teachers are related to academic and social outcomes (Davis, 2001). Pianta (1999, p. 12) taps this nicely when he tells us that "in both risk and nonrisk samples, a focus on enhancing child–teacher relationships can be expected to elevate competency levels and help attenuate the rates of failure currently present in public schools." Howard (2001, p. 134) adds the following on the downside of relationships: "Lack of personal teacher–student relationships as reflected in a lack of caring and overall teacher apathy were contributing factors to school failure." We know that "child–teacher relationships play an important role in developing skills in the areas of peer relations, emotional development, and self-regulation; in competencies such as problem solving and self-esteem" (Pianta, 1999, p. 67); in "effective growth" (Walberg & Anderson, 1968, p. 417); in engagement in school (Rodriguez, 2008); in students' "social and emotional functioning" (Roeser et al., 2000, p. 447); in academic effort (Howard, 2002; Johnson, 2009); and in achievement (Davis, 2003; Kennedy, 2011). We also have seen that "cognitive and social development are severely affected by extremely adverse environments" (Masten et al., 1990, 435).

We move the spotlight now to the environment of academic press and the culture of care and support that can take root in positive student–teacher relationships (Phelan et al., 1992). Here we are reminded by Cabello and Terrell (1994, p. 17) that "the social and pedagogical interaction between teachers and students" composes the heart of productive classrooms. These two core constructs explain how "cohesive classrooms are formed and framed" (Dillon, 1989, p. 255). On the press side, without revisiting already covered findings, we learn that the type of teacher norms and actions we unpacked in Chapters 5 and 6 push up the needle on student learning. For example, Moos (1979, p. 60) confirms that "students in control oriented classes were the least satisfied with the amount of material they were learning." We also know that "teacher expectations contribute uniquely to year-end achievement" (Brattesani et al., 1984, pp. 245–246), that "classes which students perceived as more difficult gained more ... than classes perceived as less difficult" (Trickett & Moos, 1974, p. 3). In another study, Moos (1979, p. 195) shows us that "primary grade students make the greatest gains in reading and mathematics in classes that are warm, task-oriented, and systematic and orderly." And in a third Moos study (Moos & Moos, 1978, p. 265) we find that "both students and teachers perceived classrooms with higher average final grades to be higher in involvement and lower in teacher control." Freiberg and team (2009, p. 63) add here, reporting that "involving students in a meaningful way in the management of their classrooms can benefit students' achievement." And Weinstein (1983, p. 300) informs us in his review that Haertel, Walberg, and Haertel found that "learning gains were positively associated with student-perceived cohesiveness ...

task difficulty, formality, goal direction, democracy, and the material environment."

Turning to supportive culture, "it is noteworthy that overall school culture . . . is associated with students' motivational orientation, which in turn was related to performance on standardized measures of achievement in major instructional domains" (Maehr & Midgley, 1996, p. 96). Or more succinctly, "children's perceptions of teacher support and caring have been related to a range of . . . student outcomes" (Pianta, 1999, p. 93). Or more succinctly still, "perceived quality of school climate is linked to academic performance" (Kuperminc et al., 1997. p. 76). It is the "psychological characteristics" that matter most (Maehr & Fyans, 1989, p. 243). Scholarly analyses have arrived at similar conclusions about the effect of school climate on math and reading grades (Wright & Cowen, 1982) and "different kinds of cognitive growth" (Walberg & Anderson, 1968, p. 417). Looking at the indicators developed in Chapters 3 and 4, we see evidence of their effects across a range of empirical studies and scholarly reviews. Respect, encouragement, and support in general are highlighted in these analyses (Booker, 2006; Rodriguez, 2008). So too is ownership (Wigfield et al., 1998) and voice (Arnot et al., 2004; Mitra & Gross, 2009). We discover also that "cultural and linguistic incorporation in the school curriculum is a significant predictor of academic success as measured by standardized tests of reading" (Zanger, 1993, p. 178). Warmth inside supportive relationships also is linked significantly to achievement (Booker, 2006). The takeaway message is that there is a "causal chain leading from school culture . . . to achievement" (Maehr & Fyans, 1989, p. 233).

References

Ackerman, R. H., & Maslin-Ostrowski, P. (2002). *The wounded leader: How real leadership emerges in times of crisis.* San Francisco, CA: Jossey-Bass.

Adams, R. S., & Biddle, B. J. (1971). Realities of teaching: An excerpt. In M. L. Silberman (Ed.), *The experience of schooling* (pp. 141–147). Chicago, IL: Holt McDougal.

Akos, P. (2002). Student perceptions of the transition from elementary to middle school. *Professional School Counseling, 5*(5), 339–345.

Alderson, P. (2000). Children as researchers: The effects of participation rights on research methodology. In P. Christensen & A. James (Eds.), *Research with children: Perspectives and practices* (pp. 241–275). London, England: Falmer Press.

Alderson, P. (2008). Children as researchers: The effects of participation rights on research methodology. In P. Christensen & A. James (Eds.), *Research with children: Perspectives and practices* (2nd ed.) (pp. 276–290). London, England: Falmer Press.

Alexander, K., & Entwisle, D. (1996). Schools and children at risk. In A. Booth & J. Dunn (Eds.), *Family–school links: How do they affect educational outcomes?* (pp. 67–88). Mahwah, NJ: Lawrence Erlbaum Associates.

Alexander, K., Entwisle, D., & Horsey, C. (1997). From first grade forward: Early foundations of high school dropout. *Sociology of Education, 70*(2), 87–107.

Alfaro, M., Letriz, L., Santos, M., Villanueva, M., & Freeman, R. (2001). Our world. In J. J. Shultz & A. Cook-Sather, A. (Eds.), *In our own words: Students' perspectives on school* (pp. 19–38). New York, NY: Rowman & Littlefield.

Allensworth, E. M., & Easton, J. Q. (2005). *The on-track indicator as a predictor of high school graduation.* Chicago, IL: Consortium on Chicago School Research at the University of Chicago.

Alvermann, D. E., Young, J. P., Weaver, D., Hinchman, K. A., Moore, D. W., Phelps, S. F., & Zalewski, P. (1996). Middle and high school students' perceptions of how they experience text-based discussions: A multicase study. *Reading Research Quarterly, 31*(3), 244–267.

Ancess, J. (2000). The reciprocal influence of teacher learning, teaching practice, school restructuring, and student learning outcomes. *Teachers College Record, 102*(3), 590–619.

Ancess, J. (2003). *Beating the odds: High schools as communities of commitment.* New York, NY: Teachers College Press.

Anderman, E. M., Maehr, M. L., & Midgley, C. (1999). Declining motivation after the transition to middle school: Schools can make a difference. *Journal of Research & Development in Education, 32*(3), 131–147.

Anderman, L. H. (2003). Academic and social perceptions as predictors of change in middle school students' sense of school belonging. *The Journal of Experimental Education, 72*(1), 5–22.

Antrop-Gonzalez, R. (2006). Toward the "school as sanctuary" concept in multicultural urban education: Implications for small high school reform. *Curriculum Inquiry, 36*(3), 273–301.

Antrop-Gonzalez, R., & De Jesus, A. (2006). Toward a theory of critical care in urban small school reform: Examining structures and pedagogies of caring in two Latino community-based schools. *International Journal of Qualitative Studies in Education, 19*(4), 409–433.

Appleton, J. J., Christenson, S. L., & Furlong, M. J. (2008). Student engagement with school: Critical conceptual and methodological issues of the construct. *Psychology in the Schools, 45*(5), 369–386.

Arhar, J., & Buck, G. (2000). Learning to look through the eyes of our students: Action research as a tool of inquiry. *Educational Action Research, 8*(2), 327–339.

Arnot, M., McIntyre, D., Pedder, D., & Reay, D. (2004). *Consultation in the classroom: Developing dialogue about teaching and learning.* Cambridge, England: Pearson Publishing.

Atweh, B., & Burton, L. (1995). Students as researchers: Rationale and critique. *British Educational Research Journal, 21*(5), 561–575.

Baker, J. A., Terry, T., Bridger, R., & Winsor, A. (1997). Schools as caring communities: A relational approach to school reform. *The School Psychology Review, 26*(4), 586–602.

Balfanz, R., Herzog, L., & MacIver, D. (2007). Preventing student disengagement and keeping students on the graduation path in urban middle-grades schools: Early identification and effective interventions. *Educational Psychologist, 42*(4), 223–235.

Bandura, A. (1993). Perceived self-efficacy in cognitive development and functioning. *Educational Psychologist, 28*(2), 117–148.

Barnett, K., & McCormick, J. (2004). Leadership and individual principal-teacher relationships in schools. *Educational Administration Quarterly, 40*(3), 406–434.

Battistich, V., & Hom, A. (1997). The relationship between students' sense of their school as a community and their involvement in problem behaviors. *American Journal of Public Health, 87*(12), 1997–2001.

Battistich, V., Solomon, D., Kim, D., Watson, M., & Schaps, E. (1995). Schools as communities, poverty levels of student populations, and students' attitudes, motives, and performance: A multilevel analysis. *American Educational Research Journal, 32*(3), 627–658.

Becker, B. E., & Luthar, S. S. (2002). Social-emotional factors affecting achievement outcomes among disadvantaged students: Closing the achievement gap. *Educational Psychologist, 37*(4), 197–214.

Beishuizen, J. J., Hof, E., Putten, C. M., Bouwmeester, S., & Asscher, J. J. (2001). Students' and teachers' cognitions about good teachers. *British Journal of Educational Psychology, 71*(2), 185–201.

Berndt, T. J., & Perry, T. B. (1986). Children's perceptions of friendships as supportive relationships. *Developmental Psychology, 22*(5), 640–648.

Birch, S. H., & Ladd, G. W. (1997). The teacher-child relationship and children's early school adjustment. *Journal of School Psychology, 35*(1), 61–79.

Birch, S. H., & Ladd, G. W. (1998). Children's interpersonal behaviors and the teacher–child relationship. *Developmental Psychology, 34*(5), 934–946.

Bloomberg, L., Ganey, A., Alba, V., Quintero, G., & Alvarez-Alcantara, L. (2003). Chicano-Latino youth leadership institute: An asset-based program for youth. *American Journal of Health Behavior, 27*(1), 45–54.

Boekaerts, M. (1993). Being concerned with well-being and with learning. *Educational Psychologist, 28*(2), 149–167.

Booker, K. C. (2006). School belonging and the African American adolescent: What do we know and where should we go? *The High School Journal, 89*(4), 1–7.

Bradley, B. S., Deighton, J., & Selby, J. (2004). The 'voices' project: Capacity-building in community development for youth at risk. *Journal of Health Psychology, 9*(2), 197–212.

Bragg, S. (2007). "It's not about systems, it's about relationships": Building a listening culture in a primary school. In D. Thiessen & A. Cook-Sather (Eds.), *International handbook of student experience in elementary and secondary school* (pp. 659–680). Dordrecht, The Netherlands: Springer.

Brattesani, K. A., Weinstein, R. S., & Marshall, H. H. (1984). Student perceptions of differential teacher treatment as moderators of teacher expectation effects. *Journal of Educational Psychology, 76*(2), 236–247.

Brewster, C., & Fager, J. (2000). *Increasing student engagement and motivation: From time-on-task to homework*. Portland, OR: Northwest Regional Educational Laboratory.

Bronfenbrenner, U. (1979). *The ecology of human development: Experiments by nature and design*. Cambridge, MA: Harvard University Press.

Bru, E., Stephens, P., & Torsheim, T. (2002). Students' perceptions of class management and reports of their own misbehavior. *Journal of School Psychology, 40*(4), 287–307.

Bruggencate, G., Luyten, H., Scheerens, J., & Sleegers, P. (2012). Modeling the influence of school leaders on student achievement: How can school leaders make a difference? *Educational Administration Quarterly, 48*(4), 699–732.

Bryk, A. S., Sebring, P. B., Allensworth, E., Luppescu, S., & Easton, J. (2010). *Organizing schools for improvement: Lessons from Chicago.* Chicago, IL: University of Chicago Press.

Burke, C., & Grosvenor, I. (2003). *The school I'd like: Children and young people's reflections on an education for the 21st century.* London, England: Routledge.

Cabello, B., & Terrell, R. (1994). Making students feel like family: How teachers create warm and caring classroom climates. *Journal of Classroom Interaction, 29*(1), 17–23.

Casey-Cannon, S., Hayward, C., & Gowen, K. (2001). Middle-school girls' reports of peer victimization: Concerns, consequences, and implications. *Professional School Counseling, 5*(2), 138–147.

Catalano, R. F., Loeber, R., & McKinney, K. C. (1999, October). School and community interventions to prevent serious and violent offending. *Juvenile Justice Bulletin.*

Chaplain, R. (1996a). Making a strategic withdrawal: Disengagement and self-worth protection in male pupils. In J. Rudduck, R. P. Chaplain, & G. Wallace (Eds.), *School improvement: What can pupils tell us?* (pp. 97–111). London, England: Routledge.

Chaplain, R. (1996b). Pupils under pressure: Coping with stress at school. In J. Rudduck, R. P. Chaplain, & G. Wallace (Eds.), *School improvement: What can pupils tell us?* (pp. 116–127). London, England: Routledge.

Cheney, D., Blum, C., & Walker, B. (2004). An analysis of leadership teams' perceptions of positive behavior support and the outcomes of typically developing and at-risk students in their schools. *Assessment for Effective Intervention, 30*(1), 7–24.

Christle, C. A., Jolivette, K., & Nelson, C. M. (2005). Breaking the school to prison pipeline: Identifying school risk and protective factors for youth delinquency. *Exceptionality, 13*(2), 69–88.

Clark, C. D. (1999). The autodriven interview: A photographic viewfinder into children's experience. *Visual Studies, 14*(1), 39–50.

Commeyras, M. (1995). What can we learn from students' questions? *Theory Into Practice, 34*(2), 101–106.

Conchas, G. (2001). Structuring failure and success: Understanding the variability in Latino school engagement. *Harvard Educational Review, 71*(3), 475–505.

Connell, J. P., & Wellborn, J. G. (1991) *Competence, autonomy, and relatedness: A motivational analysis of self-system processes*. In M. R. Gunnar & L. A. Sroufe (Eds.), *Minnesota symposia on child psychology* (vol. 23, pp. 43–77). Hillsdale, NJ: Lawrence Erlbaum.

Cook-Sather, A. (2002). Authorizing students' perspectives: Toward trust, dialogue, and change in education. *Educational Researcher*, *31*(4), 3–14.

Cook-Sather, A. (2006a). 'Change based on what students say': Preparing teachers for a paradoxical model of leadership. *International Journal of Leadership in Education*, *9*(4), 345–358.

Cook-Sather, A. (2006b). Sound, presence, and power: "Student voice" in educational research and reform. *Curriculum Inquiry*, *36*(4), 359–390.

Cook-Sather, A., & Shultz, J. (2001). Starting where the learner is: Listening to students. In J. Shultz & A. Cook-Sather (Eds.), *In our own words: Students' perspectives on school* (pp. 1–17). New York, NY: Rowman & Littlefield.

Cooper, J. E., Ponder, G., Merritt, S., & Matthews, C. (2005). High-performing high schools: Patterns of success. *NASSP Bulletin*, *89*(645), 2–23.

Cooper, R. (1996). Detracking reform in an urban California high school: Improving the schooling experiences of African American students. *Journal of Negro Education*, *(65)*2, 190–208.

Cooper, R. (1999). Urban school reform: Student responses to detracking in a racially mixed high school. *Journal of Education for Students Placed at Risk*, *4*(3), 259–275.

Corbett, H. D., & Wilson, B. (1995). Make a difference with, not for, students: A plea to researchers and reformers. *Educational Researcher*, *24*(5), 12–17.

Cotterell, J. L. (1992). The relation of attachments and supports to adolescent well-being and school adjustment. *Journal of Adolescent Research*, *7*(1), 28–42.

Cotton, K. (2000). *The schooling practices that matter most*. Alexandria, VA: Association for Supervision and Curriculum Development.

Creemers, B. P., & Reezigt, G. J. (1996). School level conditions affecting the effectiveness of instruction. *School Effectiveness and School Improvement*, *7*(3), 197–228.

Croninger, R., & Lee, V. (2001). Social capital and dropping out of high school: Benefits to at-risk students of teachers' support and guidance. *Teachers College Record*, *103*(4), 548–581.

Crosnoe, R. (2011). *Fitting in, standing out: Navigating the social challenges of high school to get an education*. Cambridge, England: Cambridge University Press.

Crosnoe, R., Johnson, M. K., & Elder, G. H. (2004). Intergenerational bonding in school: The behavioral and contextual correlates of student-teacher relationships. *Sociology of Education*, *77*(1), 60–81.

Goodlad, J. I. (1984). *A place called school: Prospects for the future.* New York, NY: McGraw-Hill.
Graham, G. (1995). Physical education through students' eyes and in students' voices: Introduction. *Journal of Teaching in Physical Education, 14*(4), 364–371.
Graham, S., Taylor, A. Z., & Hudley, C. (1998). Exploring achievement values among ethnic minority early adolescents. *Journal of Educational Psychology, 90*(4), 606–620.
Gray, J., Hopkins, D., Reynolds, D., Wilcox, B., Farrell, S., & Jesson, D. (1999). *Improving schools: Performance and potential.* Philadelphia, PA: Open University Press.
Guest, A., & Schneider, B. (2003). Adolescents' extracurricular participation in context: The mediating effects of schools. *Sociology of Education, 76*(2), 89–109.
Gurr, D., Drysdale, L., & Mulford, B. (2005). Successful principal leadership: Australian case studies. *Journal of Educational Administration, 43*(6), 539–551.
Hadfield, M., & Haw, K. (2001). 'Voice', young people, and action research. *Educational Action Research, 9*(3), 485–502.
Hallinan, M. T., & Kubitschek, W. N. (1999). Curriculum differentiation and high school achievement. *Social Psychology of Education, 3*(1), 41–62.
Hallinger, P., & Murphy, J. (1985, November). Assessing the instructional management behavior of principals. *Elementary School Journal, 86*(2), 217–247.
Hamilton, S. F. (1983). The social side of schooling: Ecological studies of classrooms and schools. *The Elementary School Journal, 83*(4), 313–334.
Harper, D. (2002). Talking about pictures: A case for photo elicitation. *Visual Studies, 17*(1), 13–26.
Harris, A. (2009). Distributed leadership and knowledge creation. In K. Leithwood, B. Mascall, & T. Strauss (Eds.), *Distributed leadership according to the evidence.* London, England: Routledge.
Hart, R. A. (1997). *Children's participation: The theory and practice of involving young citizens in community development and environmental care.* New York, NY: Earthscan.
Harper, W. W. (1989). Social relationships and their developmental significance. *American Psychologist, 44*(2), 120–126.
Harter, S. (1990). Issues in the assessment of the self-concept of children and adolescents. In A. M. La Greca (Ed.), *Through the eyes of the child: Obtaining self-reports from children and adolescents* (pp. 292–325). Needham Heights, MA: Allyn & Bacon.
Harter, S. (1996). Teacher and classmate influences on scholastic motivation, self-esteem, and level of voice of students. In J. Juvonen & K. R. Wentzel (Eds.), *Teacher and classmate influences on scholastic*

motivation, self-esteem, and level of voice in adolescents (pp. 11–44). New York, NY: Cambridge University Press.

Harter, S., Waters, P. L., & Whitesell, N. R. (1997). Lack of voice as a manifestation of false self-behavior among adolescents: The school setting as a stage upon which the drama of authenticity is enacted. *Educational Psychologist, 32*(3), 153–173.

Hartup, W. W. (1989). Social relationships and their developmental significance. *American Psychologist, 44*(2), 120–126.

Hattie, J. (2009). *Visible learning: A synthesis of over 800 meta-analyses relating to achievement*. New York NY: Routledge.

Hayes, C. B., Ryan, A., & Zseller, E. B. (1994). The middle school child's perceptions of caring teachers. *American Journal of Education, 103*(1), 1–19.

Heshusius, L. (1995). Listening to children: "What could we possibly have in common?" From concerns with self to participatory consciousness. *Theory Into Practice, 34*(2), 117–123.

Hoge, D. R., Smit, E. K., & Hanson, S. L. (1990). School experiences predicting changes in self-esteem of sixth- and seventh-grade students. *Journal of Educational Psychology, 82*(1), 117–127.

Holloway, S. L., & Valentine, G. (2004). Children's geographies and the new social studies of childhood. In S. L. Holloway & G. Valentine (Eds.), *Children's geographies: Playing, living, learning* (pp. 1–26). London, England: Routledge.

Howard, T. C. (2001). Telling their side of the story: African-American students' perceptions of culturally relevant teaching. *The Urban Review, 33*(2), 131–149.

Howard, T. C. (2002). Hearing footsteps in the dark: African American students' descriptions of effective teachers. *Journal of Education for Students Placed at Risk, 7*(4), 425–444.

Huberman, M., Parrish, T., Hannan, S., Arellanes, M., & Shambaugh, L. (2011). *Turnaround schools in California: Who are they and what strategies do they use?* San Francisco, CA: WestEd.

Irvine, J. J. (1990). *Black students and school failure: Policies, practices, and prescriptions*. New York, NY: Greenwood.

Jackson, P. W., & Wolfson, B. J. (1971). Varieties of constraint in a nursery school. *Young Children, 23*(6). 358–367.

Jackson, Y., & Warren, J. S. (2000). Appraisal, social support, and life events: Predicting outcome behavior in school-age children. *Child Development, 71*(5), 1441–1457.

Johnson J. F., Jr., & Asera, R. (1999). *Hope for urban education: A study of nine high-performing, high-poverty, urban elementary schools*. Washington, DC: U.S. Department of Education, Planning and Evaluation Services.

Muller, C., Katz, S. R., & Dance, L. J. (1999). Investing in teaching and learning dynamics of the teacher–student relationship from each actor's perspective. *Urban Education, 34*(3), 292–337.

Munoz, M., Ross, S., & McDonald, A. (2007). Comprehensive school reform in middle schools: The effects of different ways of knowing on student achievement in a large urban district. *Journal for Students Placed at Risk, 12*(2), 167–183.

Murdock, T. B., Anderman, L. H., & Hodge, S. A. (2000). Middle-grade predictors of students' motivation and behavior in high school. *Journal of Adolescent Research, 15*(3), 327–351.

Murdock, T. B., & Miller, A. (2003). Teachers as sources of middle school students' motivational identity: Variable-centered and person-centered analytic approaches. *The Elementary School Journal, 103*(4), 383–399.

Murphy, J. (1991). *Restructuring schools: Capturing and assessing the phenomena.* New York, NY: Teachers College Press.

Murphy, J. (1996). *The privatization of schooling: Problems and possibilities.* Newbury Park, CA: Corwin.

Murphy, J. (1999). New consumerism: The emergence of market-oriented governing structures for schools. In J. Murphy & K. S. Louis (Eds.), *The handbook of research on school administration* (pp. 405–419). San Francisco, CA: Jossey-Bass.

Murphy, J. (2002, April). Reculturing the profession of educational leadership: New blueprints. *Educational Administration Quarterly, 38*(3), 176–191.

Murphy, J. (2010). *The educator's handbook for understanding and closing achievement gaps.* Thousand Oaks, CA: Corwin.

Murphy, J. (2011). *Essential lessons for leaders.* Thousand Oaks, CA: Corwin.

Murphy, J. (2013). The architecture of school improvement. *Journal of Educational Administration, 51*(3), 252–263.

Murphy, J. (2016). *Creating instructional capacity.* Thousand Oaks, CA: Corwin.

Murphy, J., Elliott, S. N., Goldring, E., & Porter A. (2007, April). Leadership for learning: A research-based model and taxonomy of behaviors. *School Leadership & Management, 27*(2), 179–201.

Murphy, J., & Tobin, K. (2011). *Homelessness comes to school.* Thousand Oaks, CA: Corwin.

Murphy, J., & Torre, D. (2014). *Creating productive cultures in schools: For students, teachers, and parents.* Thousand Oaks, CA: Corwin.

Natriello, G., McDill, E. L., & Pallas, A. M. (1990). *Schooling disadvantaged children: Racing against catastrophe.* New York, NY: Teachers College Press.

Newmann, F. M. (1981). Reducing student alienation in high schools: Implications of theory. *Harvard Educational Review, 51*(4), 546–564.

Newmann, F. M. (1989). Student engagement and high school reform. *Educational Leadership, 46*(5), 34–36.

Newmann, F. M., Wehlage, G. G., & Lamburn, S. D. (1992). The significance and sources of student engagement. In F. M. Newmann (Ed.), *Student engagement and achievement in American secondary schools* (pp. 11–39). New York, NY: Teachers College Press.

Nichols, J. D., Ludwin, W. G., & Iadicola, P. (1999). A darker shade of gray: A year-end analysis of discipline and suspension data. *Equity & Excellence in Education, 32*(1), 43–54.

Nichols, S. L. (2006). Teachers' and students' beliefs about student belonging in one middle school. *The Elementary School Journal, 106*(3), 255–271.

Nieto, S. (1994). Lessons from students on creating a chance to dream. *Harvard Educational Review, 64*(4), 392–427.

Noddings, N. (1988). An ethic of caring and its implications for instructional arrangements. *American Journal of Education, 96*(2), 215–230.

Noguera, P. (1996). Responding to the crisis confronting California's black male youth: Providing support without furthering marginalization. *The Journal of Negro Education, 65*(2), 219–236.

Nolen, S. B., & Nicholls, J. G. (1993). Elementary school pupils' beliefs about practices for motivating pupils in mathematics. *British Journal of Educational Psychology, 63*(3), 414–430.

O'Connor, C. (1997). Dispositions toward (collective) struggle and educational resilience in the inner city: A case analysis of six African-American high school students. *American Educational Research Journal, 34*(4), 593–629.

Oakes, J., & Guiton, G. (1995). Matchmaking: The dynamics of high school tracking decisions. *American Educational Research Journal, 32*(1), 3–33.

Oelsner, J., Lippold, M. A., & Greenberg, M. T. (2011). Factors influencing the development of school bonding among middle school students. *The Journal of Early Adolescence, 31*(3), 463–487.

Ogbu, J. U. (1974). *The next generation: An ethnography of education in an urban neighborhood.* New York, NY: Academic Press.

Ogbu, J. U. (1985). Research currents: Cultural-ecological influences on minority school learning. *Language Arts, 62*(8), 860–869.

Oldfather, P. (1995). Songs "come back most to them": Students' experiences as researchers. *Theory Into Practice, 34*(2), 131–137.

Oldfather, P., Thomas, S., Eckert, L., Garcia, F., Grannis, N., Kilgore, J., & Tjioe, M. (1999). The nature and outcomes of students' longitudinal participatory research on literacy motivations and schooling. *Research in the Teaching of English, 34*(2). 281–320.

O'Loughlin, M. (1995). Daring the imagination: Unlocking voices of dissent and possibility in teaching. *Theory Into Practice, 34*(2), 107–116.

Rogers, D. L. (1994). Conceptions of caring in a fourth-grade classroom. In. A. R. Prillamen, D. J. Eaker, & D. M. Kendrick (Eds.), *A tapestry of caring* (pp. 33–47). Norwood, NJ: Ablex.

Rohrkemper, M. M. (1985). Individual differences in students' perceptions of routine classroom events. *Journal of Educational Psychology, 77*(1), 29–44.

Romanowski, M. H. (2003). Through the eyes of students: High school students' perspectives on character education. *American Secondary Education, 32*(1), 3–20.

Roth, J. L., & Brooks-Gunn, J. (2003). Youth development programs: Risk, prevention and policy. *Journal of Adolescent Health, 32*(3), 170–182.

Roth, J. L., Brooks-Gunn, J., Murray, L., & Foster, W. (1998). Promoting healthy adolescents: Synthesis of youth development program evaluations. *Journal of Research on Adolescence, 8*(4), 423–459.

Rothman, H. R., & Cosden, M. (1995). The relationship between self-perception of a learning disability and achievement, self-concept and social support. *Learning Disability Quarterly, 18*(3), 203–212.

Rudduck, J. (1996a). Going to "the big school": The turbulence of transition. In J. Rudduck, R. P. Chaplain, & G. Wallace (Eds.), *School improvement: What can pupils tell us?* (pp. 1–16). London, England: Routledge.

Rudduck, J. (1996b). Getting serious: The demands of coursework, revision, and examinations. J. Rudduck, R. P. Chaplain, & G. Wallace (Eds.), *School improvement: What can pupils tell us?* (pp. 129–141). London, England: Routledge.

Rudduck, J. (2007). Student voice, student engagement, and school reform. In D. Thiessen & A. Cook-Sather (Eds.), *International handbook of student experience in elementary and secondary school* (pp. 587–610). Dordrecht, The Netherlands: Springer.

Rudduck, J., & Fielding, M. (2006). Student voice and the perils of popularity. *Educational Review, 58*(2), 219–231.

Rudduck, J., & Flutter, J. (2004). *How to improve your school.* London, England: Continuum International.

Rudduck, J., Chaplain, R., & Wallace, G. (1996a). Pupil voices and school improvement. In J. Rudduck, R. P. Chaplain, & G. Wallace (Eds.), *School improvement: What can pupils tell us?* (pp. 17–27). London, England: Routledge.

Rudduck, J., Chaplain, R., & Wallace, G. (1996b). Reviewing the conditions of learning in school. In J. Rudduck, R. P. Chaplain, & G. Wallace (Eds.), *School improvement: What can pupils tell us?* (pp. 170–176). London, England: Routledge.

Rumberger, R. (2011). *Dropping out: Why students drop out of high school and what can be done about it.* Cambridge, MA: Harvard University Press.

Rumberger, R. W., & Palardy, G. J. (2005, September). Does segregation still matter? The impact of student composition on academic achievement in high school. *Teachers College Record, 107*(9), 1999–2043.

Russell, S. T., Seif, H., & Truong, N. L. (2001). School outcomes of sexual minority youth in the United States: Evidence from a national study. *Journal of Adolescence, 24*(1), 111–127.

Rutter, M., Maughan, B., Mortimore, P., & Ouston, J. (1979). *Fifteen thousand hours: Secondary schools and their effects on children.* Cambridge, MA: Harvard University Press.

Ryan, R. M., Stiller, J. D., & Lynch, J. H. (1994). Representations of relationships to teachers, parents, and friends as predictors of academic motivation and self-esteem. *The Journal of Early Adolescence, 14*(2), 226–249.

Sagor, R. (1996). Building resiliency in students. *Educational Leadership, 54*(1), 38–43.

Sanders, M. G., & Harvey, A. (2002). Beyond the school walls: A case study of principal leadership for school–community collaboration. *Teachers College Record, 104*(7), 1345–1368.

Sanon, F., Baxter, M., Fortune, L., & Opotow, S. (2001). Cutting class: Perspectives of urban high school students. In J. J. Shultz & A. Cook-Sather (Eds.), *In our own words: Students' perspectives on school* (pp. 73–92). New York, NY: Rowman & Littlefield.

Sarason, S. B. (1990). *The predictable failure of educational reform: Can we change course before it's too late?* The Jossey-Bass Education Series and the Jossey-Bass Social and Behavioral Science Series. ERIC. Retrieved from http://eric.ed.gov/?id=ED354587

Sather, S. E. (1999). Leading, lauding, and learning: Leadership in secondary schools serving diverse populations. *Journal of Negro Education, 69*, 511–528.

Saunders, J., Davis, L., Williams, T., & Williams, J. H. (2004). Gender differences in self-perceptions and academic outcomes: A study of African American high school students. *Journal of Youth and Adolescence, 33*(1), 81–90.

Scanlan, M., & Lopez, F. (2012). Vamos! How school leaders promote equity and excellence for bilingual students. *Educational Administration Quarterly, 48*(4), 583–625.

Sedlak, M. W., Wheeler, C. W., Pullin, D. C., & Cusick, P. A. (1986). *Selling students short: Classroom bargains and academic reform in the American high school.* New York, NY: Teachers College Press.

Seiler, G., & Elmesky, R. (2007, February). The role of communal practices in the generation of capital and emotional energy among urban African American students in science classrooms. *Teachers College Record, 100*(2), 391–419.

Shade, B. J., Kelly, C. A., & Oberg, M. (1997). *Creating culturally responsive classrooms.* Washington, DC: American Psychological Association.

Shannon, S. G., & Bylsma, P. (2002, November). *Addressing the achievement gap: A challenge for Washington state educators.* (ED 474 392) Olympia, WA: Washington Office of the State Superintendent of Public Instruction.

Shear, L., Means, B., Mitchell, K., House, A., Gorges, T., Joshi, A., Smerdon, B., & Shlonik, J. (2008). Contrasting paths to small-school reform: Results of a 5-year evaluation of the Bill & Melinda Gates Foundation's National High Schools Initiative. *Teachers College Record, 110*(9), 1986–2039.

Shouse, R. (1996). Academic press and sense of community: Conflict, congruence, and implications for student achievement. *Social Psychology of Education, 1*(1), 47–68.

Shultz, J. J., & Cook-Sather, A. (Eds.). (2001). *In our own words: Students' perspectives on school.* Oxford, England: Rowman & Littlefield.

Silins, H., & Mulford, B. (2010). Re-conceptualising school principalship that improves student outcomes. *Journal of Educational Leadership, Policy and Practice, 25*(2), 74–93.

Silva, E. (2001). "Squeaky wheels and flat tires": A case study of students as reform participants. *Forum (42)*2, 95–99.

Silverstein, B., & Krate, R. (1975). *Children of the dark ghetto: A developmental psychology.* Oxford, England: Praeger.

Sizer, T. R. (1984). *Horace's compromise: The dilemma of the American high school.* Boston, MA: Houghton Mifflin.

Skaalvik, E. M., & Hagtvet, K. A. (1990). Academic achievement and self-concept: An analysis of causal predominance in a developmental perspective. *Journal of Personality and Social Psychology, 58*(2), 292–307.

Slaughter-Defoe, D. T., & Carlson, K. G. (1996). Young African American and Latino children in high-poverty urban schools: How they perceive school climate. *Journal of Negro Education, 65*(1), 60–70.

Slavin, R. E., & Oickle, E. (1981, July). Effects of cooperative learning teams on student achievement and race relations: Treatment by race interactions. *Sociology of Education, 54*(3), 174–180.

Smerdon, B. A. (2002). Students' perceptions of membership in their high schools. *Sociology of Education, 75*(4), 287–305.

Smerdon, B. A., & Borman, K. M. (2009). Secondary school reform. In B. A. Smerdon & K. M. Borman (Eds.), *Saving America's high schools* (pp. 1–17). Washington, DC: The Urban Institute Press.

Smetana, J. G., & Bitz, B. (1996). Adolescents' conceptions of teachers' authority and their relations to rule violations in school. *Child Development, 67*(3), 1153–1172.

Smylie, M., Murphy, J., & Louis, K. S. (in press). Care: A cross occupational analysis. *American Journal of Education.*

Smyth, J. (2006). Educational leadership that fosters "student voice." *International Journal of Leadership in Education, 9*(4), 279–284.

Soohoo, S. (1993). Students as partners in research and restructuring schools. *The Educational Forum, 57*(4), 386–393.

Spires, H. A., Lee, J. K., Turner, K. A., & Johnson, J. (2008). Having our say: Middle grade student perspectives on school, technologies, and academic engagement. *Journal of Research on Technology in Education, 40*(4), 497–515.

St. Pierre, T. L., Mark, M. M., Kaltreider, D. L. & Aikin, K. J. (1997). Involving parents of high-risk youth in drug preventions: A three year longitudinal study in Boys & Girls Clubs. *Journal of Early Adolescence, 17*(1), 21–50.

Stajkovic, A. D., & Luthans, F. (1998). Self-efficacy and work-related performance. *Psychological Bulletin, 124*(2), 240–261.

Stanton-Salazar, R. D. (1997). A social capital framework for understanding the socialization of racial minority children and youths. *Harvard Educational Review, 67*(1), 1–41.

Steele, C. M. (1992, April). Race and the schooling of black Americans. *Atlantic Monthly, 269*(4), 68–78.

Steele, J. M., House, E. R., & Kerins, T. (1971). An instrument for assessing instructional climate through low-inference student judgments. *American Educational Research Journal, 8*(3), 447–466.

Stiggins, R., & Chappuis, J. (2006). Using student-involved classroom assessment to close achievement gaps. *Theory Into Practice, 44*(1), 11–18.

Stinchcombe, A. L. (1964). *Rebellion in a high school.* Chicago, IL: Quadrangle Books.

Storz, M. G. (2008). Educational inequity from the perspectives of those who live it: Urban middle school students' perspectives on the quality of their education. *The Urban Review, 40*(3), 247–267.

Strahan, D. (2003). Promoting a collaborative professional culture in three elementary schools that have beaten the odds. *The Elementary School Journal, 104*(2), 127–146.

Supovitz, J. (2002). Developing communities of instructional practice. *Teachers College Record, 104*(8), 1591–1626.

Supovitz, J. (2008). Instructional influence in American high schools. In M. M. Mangin, & S. R. Stoelinga (Eds.), *Effective teacher leadership: Using research to inform and reform* (pp. 144–162). New York NY: Teachers College Press.

Sweetland, S. R., & Hoy, W. K. (2000). School characteristics and educational outcomes: Toward an organizational model of student achievement in middle schools. *Educational Administration Quarterly, 36*(5), 703–729.

Taylor-Dunlop, K., & Norton, M. M. (1997). Out of the mouths of babes: Voices of at-risk adolescents. *The Clearing House: A Journal of Educational Strategies, Issues and Ideas, 70*(5), 274–278.

Thompson, C. L. & O'Quinn, S. D., III. (2001). *Eliminating the black-white achievement gap: A summary of research.* Chapel Hill: North Carolina Education Research Council.

Thompson, G. L. (2004). *Through ebony eyes: What teachers need to know but are afraid to ask about African-American students.* San Francisco, CA: Jossey-Bass.

Thomson, P., & Gunter, H. (2006). From 'consulting pupils' to 'pupils as researchers': A situated case narrative. *British Educational Research Journal, 32*(6), 839–856.

Thorkildsen, T. A. (1989). Justice in the classroom: The student's view. *Child Development, 60*(20), 323–334.

Trickett, E. J., & Moos, R. H. (1974). Personal correlates of contrasting environments: Student satisfactions in high school classrooms. *American Journal of Community Psychology, 2*(1), 1–12.

Trickett, E. J., & Quinlan, D. M. (1979). Three domains of classroom environment: Factor analysis of the classroom environment scale. *American Journal of Community Psychology, 7*(3), 279–291.

Trickett, E. J., & Todd, D. M. (1972). The high school culture: An ecological perspective. *Theory Into Practice, 11*(1), 28–37.

Tyson, K. (2002). Weighing In: Elementary-age students and the debate on attitudes toward school among black students. *Social Forces, 80*(4), 1157–1189.

Valentine, G. (1999). Being seen and heard? The ethical complexities of working with children and young people at home and at school. *Ethics, Place and Environment, 2*(2), 141–155.

Veaco, L., & Brandon, C. (1986). The preferred teacher: A content analysis of young adolescents' writings. *The Journal of Early Adolescence, 6*(3), 221–229.

Voelkl, K. E. (1997). Identification with school. *American Journal of Education, 105*(3), 294–318.

Walberg, H. J. (1976). Psychology of learning environments: Behavioral, structural, or perceptual? *Review of Research in Education, 4*(1), 142–178.

Walberg, H. J., & Anderson, G. J. (1968). Classroom climate and individual learning. *Journal of Educational Psychology, 59*(6), 414–419.

Wallace, G. (1996a). Engaging with learning. In J. Rudduck, R. P. Chaplain, & G. Wallace (Eds.), *School improvement: What can pupils tell us?* (pp. 52–65). London, England: Routledge.

Wallace, G. (1996b). Relating to teachers. In J. Rudduck, R. P. Chaplain, & G. Wallace (Eds.), *School improvement: What can pupils tell us?* (pp. 29–47). London, England: Routledge.

Wallerstein, N., & Bernstein, E. (1988). Empowerment education: Freire's ideas adapted to health education. *Health Education & Behavior, 15*(4), 379–394.

Warrington, M., & Younger, M. (1996). Homework: Dilemmas and difficulties. In J. Rudduck, R. P. Chaplain, & G. Wallace (Eds.), *School improvement: What can pupils tell us?* (pp. 83–96). London, England: Routledge.

Wehlage, G. G., Rutter, R. A., Smith, G. A., Lesko, N., & Fernandez, R. R. (1989). *Reducing the risk: Schools as communities of support*. New York, NY: Falmer.

Weil, M., & Murphy, J. (1982). Instructional processes. In H. E. Mitzel (Ed.), *The encyclopedia of educational research* (5th ed.) (vol. 2 pp. 890–917). New York, NY: Free Press.

Weinstein, R. S. (1983). Student perceptions of schooling. *The Elementary School Journal, 83*(4), 287–312.

Weinstein, R. S., Marshall, H. H., Sharp, L., & Botkin, M. (1987). Pygmalion and the student: Age and classroom differences in children's awareness of teacher expectations. *Child Development, 58*(4), 1079–1093.

Weis, L. (1990). *Working class without work: High school students in a deindustrializing economy*. New York, NY: Routledge.

Wentzel, K. R. (1997). Student motivation in middle school: The role of perceived pedagogical caring. *Journal of Educational Psychology, 89*(3), 411–419.

Wentzel, K. R. (1998). Social relationships and motivation in middle school: The role of parents, teachers, and peers. *Journal of Educational Psychology, 90*(2), 202–209.

Wentzel, K. R. (2002). Are effective teachers like good parents? Teaching styles and student adjustment in early adolescence. *Child Development, 73*(1), 287–301.

Wentzel, K. R., & Looney, L. (2007). Socialization in school settings. In J. E. Grusec & P. D. Hastings (Eds.), *Handbook of socialization: Theory and research* (pp. 82–403). New York, NY: Guilford Press.

Wenz-Gross, M., & Siperstein, G. N. (1998). Students with learning problems at risk in middle school: Stress, social support, and adjustment. *Exceptional Children, 65*(1), 91–100.

Wigfield, A., Eccles, J. S., & Rodriguez, D. (1998). The development of children's motivation in school contexts. *Review of Research in Education, 23*(1), 73–118.

Wilcox, K. (1982). Differential socialization in the classroom: Implications for equal opportunity. In G. Sprindler (Ed.), *Doing the ethnography of schooling* (pp. 268–309). Prospect Hills, IL: Waveland.

Willems, E. P. (1967). Sense of obligation to high school activities as related to school size and marginality of student. *Child Development, 38*(4), 1247–1260.

Willms, J. D. (2003). *A sense of belonging and participation: Results from PISA 2000*. Retrieved from http://www.oecd.org/edu/school/programmeforinternationalstudentassessmentpisa/33689437.pdf

Wilson, B. L., & Corbett, H. D. (2001). *Listening to urban kids: School reform and the teachers they want*. New York: SUNY Press.

Wilson, B., & Corbett, H. (1999). *No excuses: The eighth grade year in six Philadelphia middle schools*. Philadelphia, PA: Philadelphia Education Fund.

Wilson, T., Karimpour, R., & Rodkin, P. C. (2011). African American and European American students' peer groups during early adolescence: Structure, status, and academic achievement. *The Journal of Early Adolescence, 31*(1), 74–98.

Woloszyk, C. (1996). *Models for at risk youth*. Final Report. Kalamazoo, MI: Upjohn Institute for Employment Research.

Wright, S. (1982). Student perception of school environment and its relationship to mood, achievement, popularity, and adjustment. *American Journal of Community Psychology, 10*(6), 687–703.

Wright, S., & Cowen, E. L. (1982). Student perception of school environment and its relationship to mood, achievement, popularity, and adjustment. *American Journal of Community Psychology, 10*(6), 687–703.

Zamel, V. (1990). Through students' eyes: The experiences of three ESL writers. *Journal of Basic Writing, 9*(2), 83–98.

Zanger, V. V. (1991). Social and cultural dimensions of the education of language minority students. In A. N. Ambert (Ed.), *Bilingual education and English as a second language: A research handbook, 1988–1990* (pp. 3–53). New York, NY: Garland.

Zanger, V. V. (1993). Academic costs of social marginalization: An analysis of Latino students' perceptions at a Boston high school. In Rivera, R., & Nieto, S. (Eds.), *The education of Latino students in Massachusetts: Issues, research and policy implications* (pp. 170–190). Boston: University of Massachusetts Press.

Index

Ability-oriented work, 159–160
Absenteeism, 203, 215
Absenting behavior, 13, 173
Academic achievement
   learning environments, 161, 170
   motivation, 189, 198–199
   performance expectations, 122
   safety, 97
   sense of self, 185–187
   social integration, 174, 176–177
   student autonomy, 66
   student engagement, 216–218
Academic care, 130–133
Academic press
   importance, 6–7, 218–219
   influencing factors, 209–210
   intellectually challenging work, 136
   motivational impact, 193–195
   performance expectations, 63
   sense of self, 182
   social integration, 174, 180
   student-teacher relationships, 12, 166–167, 181, 217–220
   supportive learning communities, 168, 169 (figure), 170–171, 174, 187
   see also Motivation
Academic self-concept/self-efficacy, 179–181
Academic support, 76, 131–133
   see also Social support
Acceptance, 12–13, 173
Accountability, 140
Achievement expectations, 121–124, 131–133, 179, 195

Ackerman, R. H., 84
Active involvement, 204 (figure), 205
Adams, C., 11, 12, 16, 58, 59, 78, 92, 93, 109
Adams, R. S., 223
Adan, A. M., 15
   see also Felner, R. D.
Adler, T. F., 124
   see also Eccles-Parsons, J.
Adultist discipline, 30
Advocacy support, 80–81
Aesthetically-acceptable learning environments, 85–89
Affective factors, 6–7, 175
Affiliation, 12–13, 117, 169 (figure), 173, 218
Affinity, 13, 172
Agency, 108, 140–141
Age transition impacts, 20–21, 103, 170, 189–190, 208–209
Aikin, K. J., 91
   see also St. Pierre, T. L.
Akos, P., 14, 20, 21, 40, 84, 108
Alba, V., 64
   see also Bloomberg, L.
Alderson, P., 26, 31, 32, 34, 44, 49, 105
Alexander, K., 12, 62, 167, 173, 202
Alfaro, M., 85
Alienation, 13, 173, 176, 204 (figure), 206–209, 215–216
Allensworth, E. M., 11, 80, 84, 142
   see also Bryk, A. S.
Alvarez-Alcantara, L., 64
   see also Bloomberg, L.

249

Alvermann, D. E., 35, 126, 137, 138, 139, 140, 143, 152, 154, 155, 157, 168
Ambivalent attitudes, 204 (figure), 206
Ancess, J., 12, 13, 15, 16, 17, 63, 64, 67, 74, 75, 76, 77, 78, 80, 84, 93, 99, 105, 107, 109, 110, 167, 175, 206
see also Darling-Hammond, L.
Anderman, E. M., 145, 158, 161, 194, 195
Anderman, L. H., 19, 67, 70, 96, 139, 145, 158, 161, 170, 172, 173, 175, 184, 196, 197
see also Murdock, T. B.
Anderson, G. J., 67, 97, 106, 220, 221
Anderson, S., 106
see also Leithwood, K.
Antrop-Gonzalez, R., 13, 58, 61, 63, 64, 67, 74, 76, 77, 78, 84, 91, 92, 93, 105, 173
Apathetic attitudes, 204 (figure), 206
Appealing temperament, 119–120
Appleton, J. J., 6, 18, 185, 192, 197, 198, 201, 203, 209, 213, 214, 216, 217, 218
Appropriate behavior management, 89–97
Arbitrariness, 94–95
Arellanes, M., 63
see also Huberman, M.
Arhar, J., 48
Arnot, M., 8, 20, 27, 33, 39, 45, 59, 60, 66, 67, 68, 69, 71, 76, 77, 78, 85, 90, 91, 94, 108, 109, 110, 111, 125, 126, 127, 129, 131, 139, 140, 143, 144, 145, 147, 151, 155, 156, 157, 218, 221
Asera, R., 17, 63, 89, 93, 105, 114
Asscher, J. J., 29
see also Beishuizen, J. J.
Assessment practices, 130
Assistance, provision of, 78–80
Attachment, 12–14, 173
Atweh, B., 110, 111, 113, 156
Authentic adult responsiveness, 25–26, 73–83, 109

Authentic learning
see Meaningful learning
Authentic membership
see Membership
Authentic work, 146–152, 194
Authoritarianism, 58–59, 94–95
Autonomy, 14–15, 64–66, 109, 139–141, 194, 209–210
Availability, 56–57, 62, 75, 76–77
Ayala, J., 61

Baker, J. A., 13, 16, 84, 93, 95, 98, 105, 114, 175, 202, 212
Balfanz, R., 79, 80, 92, 201, 202, 212
Bandura, A., 6, 8, 136, 137, 158, 159, 161, 179, 183, 185, 186, 197
Barnett, K., 16
Bartkiewicz, M. J., 80
see also Kosciw, J. G.
Battistich, V., 12, 13, 14, 15, 16, 63, 98, 105, 109, 110, 113, 114, 173, 175, 181, 212
Baxter, M., 133
see also Sanon, F.
Becker, B. E., 7
Behavioral engagement, 202, 212, 215
Beishuizen, J. J., 29, 40, 117, 120
Bejinez, L. F., 53
see also Gibson, M. A.
Belongingness, 12–13, 82, 98–104, 169 (figure), 171–177, 184, 197–198, 212, 214–216
Beltyukova, S. A., 20, 216
see also Patterson, N. C.
Berebitsky, D., 76
Berman, K., 20, 216
see also Patterson, N. C.
Berndt, T. J., 39, 77
Bernstein, E., 65, 70, 108, 109, 167, 218
Best, K. M., 179
see also Masten, A. S.
Biddle, B. J., 223
Biographical narratives, 40
Birch, S. H., 10, 16, 17, 19, 20, 54, 56, 71, 74, 75, 82, 187, 193, 194, 213, 219

Bitz, B., 14, 19, 21, 84, 94, 96
Blair, M., 167
Blatt, S. J., 18
  see also Kuperminc, G. P.
Bloomberg, L., 64, 74, 105
Blum, C., 91
  see also Cheney, D.
Blumenfeld, P. C., 12
  see also Fredricks, J. A.
Blum, R. W., 65
  see also McNeely, C. A.
Boekaerts, M., 18, 83, 131, 184, 185
Boesen, M. J., 80
  see also Kosciw, J. G.
Bolton, N., 17
  see also Felner, R. D.
Bone, K., 29
Booker, K. C., 21, 60, 105, 175, 176, 177, 187, 193, 198, 199, 221
Boredom, 125–126, 136, 141–142, 153, 206–207
Borman, K. M., 85
Bosworth, K., 18, 53, 57, 166, 171
Botkin, M., 50
  see also Weinstein, R. S.
Bouwmeester, S., 29
  see also Beishuizen, J. J.
Bradley, B. S., 34, 110, 183
Bragg, S., 25, 30, 31, 34, 35, 41, 58, 69, 71, 108, 110, 112, 113, 139, 151, 155, 218
Brandon, C., 8, 9, 10, 20, 59, 61, 62, 66, 67, 68, 69, 93
Brand, S., 15, 17, 177
  see also DuBois, D. L.;
    Felner, R. D.
Brattesani, K. A., 123, 124, 220
Brewster, C., 61, 93, 121, 138, 140, 190, 193, 208, 209
Bridger, R., 13
  see also Baker, J. A.
Brock, P., 16
  see also Opdenakker, M.
Bronfenbrenner, U., 22, 207
Brooks-Gunn, J., 12, 63, 75, 78, 93, 98, 99, 108, 110, 114, 167, 172, 173
  see also Roth, J. L.

Bru, E., 57, 75, 91, 94, 97, 128, 131, 132, 166, 172, 194, 195, 209
Bruggencate, G., 142
Bryk, A. S., 11, 16, 92, 93, 211
Buck, G., 48
Burke, C., 25, 28, 29, 31, 57, 58, 60, 66, 68, 70, 78, 83, 85, 86, 87, 88–89, 94, 97, 120, 125, 126, 135, 140, 142, 143, 144, 145, 146, 150, 151, 172, 203
Burns, A., 17, 25
  see also Felner, R. D.; Fine, M.
Burton, L., 110, 111, 113, 157
Busy work, 141–142, 153
Bylsma, P., 7, 131

Cabello, B., 58, 61, 66, 69, 78, 79, 81, 94, 97, 137, 147, 150, 172, 220
Cairney, T., 89
  see also Dinham, S.
Cairns, R. B., 103, 106, 208, 215
Cao, H. T., 128
  see also Phelan, P.
Caring behaviors
  academic care, 130–133
  availability, 56–57, 62, 75, 76–77
  challenges, 55
  concern for well-being, 61–62
  effective teaching practices, 119–120
  fairness, 66–67
  importance, 53–56, 165–177, 169 (figure), 181–182, 187, 194–197, 217–221
  performance expectations, 62–64, 122–124
  respect, 67–70
  sensitive understanding, 59–60
  student autonomy, 64–66
  student engagement, 64, 71, 84, 93, 95, 212
  valuing, 70–71
  vulnerability, 58–59
  see also Social support
Carlson, K. G., 66, 69, 82, 122, 124
Carrera, J. W., 60, 70, 152, 178
Casey-Cannon, S., 40, 85

Catalano, R. F., 92, 95, 106
Challenging work,
    136–137, 210–211
Chaplain, R., 24, 26, 29, 43, 73, 74,
    75, 77, 87, 94, 122, 123, 125, 131,
    155, 159, 178, 182, 183, 184, 216
    see also Rudduck, J.
Chappuis, J., 106
Cheney, D., 91, 92, 93, 95
Child-centered research
    methodologies, 38–42
Child competency, 31–34
Child-mother relationships, 20, 169
Choice, student, 108–114, 140
Christenson, S. L., 6, 21, 121, 170
    see also Appleton, J. J.; Lehr, C. A.
Christle, C. A., 84, 85, 89, 92, 167
Cicchetti, D., 9
Clarity, 128–129
Clark, C. D., 25, 36, 37, 41
Classroom environment
    academic and socialization
        interactions, 6–12, 62–64
    contextual transitions, 21–22
    positive management systems, 89–97
    safety, 83–97
Class skipping, 203
Clear explanations, 128–129
Cognitive engagement, 198–199, 202,
    203, 212, 214
Cognitive processes, 201–202
Cohen-Dan, J., 173
Cohen, D. K., 131
Colston, T., 173
Comfortable learning
    environments, 85–89
Commeyras, M., 48, 140, 147, 153, 154
Commitment, 204 (figure), 205
Competency perceptions, 179,
    183–187
Competition, 159
Concern for well-being, 61–62
Conchas, G., 13, 17, 74, 107,
    110, 173, 212
Connectedness, 12–13, 98–100,
    169 (figure), 171–177, 184, 212,
    214–216
    see also Membership

Connell, J. P., 10, 21, 22, 109, 137,
    167, 169, 172, 184, 185, 199,
    203, 208, 209, 216
Consequences, 92–93
Constructed learning
    authentic work, 146–152
    basic concepts, 135–136
    cooperative work, 137–139,
        156–157
    empowering work, 139–141
    intellectually challenging work,
        136–137
    meaningful work, 141–146
    student-centered work, 152–157,
        210–211
    task-oriented work, 158–161,
        210–211
Constructive feedback, 130
Constructivist learning, 35, 153–154
Cook-Sather, A., 10, 24, 25, 26, 30, 31,
    32, 35, 36, 38, 42, 43, 46, 47, 49,
    71, 76, 100, 108, 109, 111, 112,
    154, 155, 207, 210
Cooperative discipline, 94
Cooperative work, 137–139,
    156–157, 194
Cooper, J. E., 8, 62, 77, 79, 80, 81, 85,
    105, 114, 121, 132
Cooper, R., 63, 64, 107, 194
Corbett, H. D., 16, 24, 25, 29, 39,
    44, 45, 46, 47, 50, 61, 62, 63,
    64, 85, 89, 93, 98, 100, 117, 120,
    121, 125, 126, 128, 129, 130,
    131, 132, 133, 137, 139, 143,
    145, 214
Corporal punishment, 95
Corso, M. J., 24, 25, 27, 29, 31, 196
Cosden, M., 15, 181
Cotterell, J. L., 75, 76, 81, 82,
    172, 177
Cotton, K., 62, 84, 92
Counterproductive values, 206
Cowen, E. L., 221
Craigie, D., 89
    see also Dinham, S.
Creemers, B. P., 84
Critical demandingness, 136–137
Croninger, R., 15, 61, 74, 75, 78, 167

Crosnoe, R., 9, 12, 14, 15, 16, 18, 19, 22, 24, 76, 79, 92, 93, 104, 114, 141, 167, 169, 174, 176, 181, 203, 205, 206
Crothers, L. M., 40, 42
Cruddas, L., 8, 60, 64, 67, 68, 77, 81, 105, 114, 125
Csikszentmihalyi, M., 14, 15, 22, 93, 114, 144, 181, 205
Culturally relevant instruction, 148–150, 213–214
Cultural norms, 85, 148, 172, 174, 203
  see also Caring behaviors; Membership; Safe learning environments; Social support
Cultural responsiveness, 127
Cultural variables, 18, 22, 84–85, 101, 104, 177–178
Cusick, P. A., 207

Dahl, K. L., 29, 44, 45, 60, 109, 152, 200
Dance, L. J., 11
  see also Muller, C.
Darling-Hammond, L., 12, 64
Data collection and analysis, 36–38
Datnow, A., 110, 199
Davidson, A. L., 128
  see also Phelan, P.
Davidson, H. H., 20, 82, 181, 182
David, T. G., 12, 33, 169
Davis, H. A., 6, 7, 8, 9, 10, 11, 12, 17, 18, 19, 20, 21, 58, 60, 64, 71, 74, 82, 83, 93, 94, 95, 117, 119, 120, 121, 126, 127, 130, 131, 137, 154, 166, 176, 178, 181, 184, 192, 193, 194, 195, 196, 200, 212, 213, 214, 219, 220
Davis, L., 123
  see also Saunders, J.
Decision-making skills
  see Student-centered work
Deficit-based educational practices, 148–149
De Groot, E. V., 121, 187, 194, 198, 199, 214, 216
Deighton, J., 34
  see also Bradley, B. S.

De Jesus, A., 61, 63, 64, 67, 74, 76, 84, 91, 92, 105
Delinquency, 176, 206
  see also Social integration
Demaray, M. K., 14, 16, 17, 74, 75, 76, 78, 167, 181, 212
Demographic variables, 18–19, 102, 170, 171, 173
Dennis, M. J. B., 40
Detachment, 13, 173
Differential treatment, 66–67, 121–124, 213
Differentiated instruction, 126–127
Dillon, D. R., 30, 60, 66, 79, 81, 120, 126, 141, 143, 144, 148, 151, 153, 157, 182, 216, 218, 220
Dinham, S., 84, 89, 114
Disaffiliation, 13, 15, 64, 173, 202, 204 (figure), 205–206
Discipline, 91–94
Disconnection, 13, 173, 175
Disengagement, 64, 67, 70, 200–209, 204 (figure)
  see also Engagement
Disidentification, 13, 173, 174
Disposition towards learning, 15–17, 96–97
Disrespect, 67–70, 95
Disruptive behaviors, 96, 125
Distributive justice, 66
Docking, J., 33, 45, 91, 145
Draw-and-write technique, 41
Dropouts, 83, 200, 209, 213, 215–216
Drysdale, L., 114
DuBois, D. L., 15, 177, 178
  see also Felner, R. D.
Dubow, E. F., 40, 45, 81, 82
Dysfunctional disciplinary systems, 94–95

Easton, J. Q., 11, 80, 84, 142
  see also Bryk, A. S.
Eccles, J. S., 14, 17, 19, 21, 24, 26, 36, 84, 108, 139, 182, 192, 195, 196
  see also Feldlaufer, H.; Midgley, C.; Roeser, R. W.; Wigfield, A.
Eccles-Parsons, J., 124, 179, 183, 184, 186, 192, 193

Eckert, L., 11
Eckert, P., 12, 13, 16, 17, 105, 106, 110, 114, 141, 173, 175, 205, 206
Economic status, 18, 19, 102–103, 170, 171, 173
Educational payoffs, 50
Effective discipline, 89–97
Effective educational practices, 119–120, 125–129
Eggert, L. L., 107
Elder, G. H., 9, 24
  see also Crosnoe, R.
Elliott, S. N., 80
Ellwood, C. M., 3, 23, 138, 139, 140, 153
Elmesky, R., 139
Emmons, C., 18
  see also Kuperminc, G. P.
Emotional engagement, 202, 212, 215
Emotional support, 76, 82
  see also Social support
Empowering work, 139–141
Empowerment, 99–100, 108–114, 122, 139–141
Encouragement support, 79
Engaged teaching
  characteristics, 119–121
  "getting to understanding", 128–133
  learning climate, 124–128
  performance expectations, 121–124
  see also Constructed learning
Engagement
  academic outcomes, 216–218
  basic concepts, 200–201
  boredom, 125–126, 136, 141–142, 153, 206–207
  caring environments, 64, 71, 84, 93, 95, 212
  components, 198–199, 201–203
  contextual factors, 117
  cooperative work, 139
  empowerment, 113
  fairness, 67
  importance, 199–200
  indicators, 203–204
  influencing factors, 209–210
  intellectually challenging work, 137
  levels of engagement continuum, 204 (figure), 204–209
  meaningful involvement, 104, 107, 209–211
  meaningful work, 141–142, 145
  motivation, 16, 187–189, 198–199, 214
  ownership, 108, 110
  research methodologies, 36–37
  respect, 70, 212–213
  responsive teaching, 125–127
  safety, 97
  sense of belonging, 99, 103–104, 212, 214–216
  sense of self, 180–181, 185, 214
  social integration, 174, 176–177, 214–216
  student autonomy, 66
  student-centered work, 152–157
  student–teacher relationships, 15, 56, 76–77, 83, 168, 200, 209–212
  supportive learning communities, 169 (figure), 169–171, 210–214, 217–221
  task-oriented work, 159
  see also Constructed learning; Engaged teaching; Motivation
Enjoyable activities, 144
Ensminger, M., 91
Enthusiastic teachers, 119–120
Entwisle, D., 12, 62, 167
  see also Alexander, K.
Epstein, J., 43, 99, 105, 140, 156, 166, 170, 194, 198, 218, 219
Equal treatment, 66–67, 121–124, 213
Estrangement, 13, 173
Ethnic identity, 18–19, 102, 103–104, 122, 170, 171, 173, 177–178
Evans, E. G., 15
  see also Felner, R. D.
Evertson, C. M., 97
Exciting activities, 144
Exclusion, 13, 27–30, 92, 95, 173
Extended relationships, 77–79
Extracurricular activities and involvement, 100, 101–104, 106–108, 215–216

Extrinsic motivation, 188–189
Eyes, student
  see Student perspectives

Fager, J., 61, 93, 121, 138, 140, 190, 193, 208, 209
Fairness, 66–67, 160, 213
Family involvement, 19–20, 92, 107
Farrar, E., 131
Farrell, E. W., 10, 13, 14, 15, 16, 17, 20, 58, 62, 114, 173, 181, 205, 206
Farrell, S., 86
  see also Gray, J.
Favoritism, 66–67, 121–124, 213
Fear, 94
Feedback, 25, 130
Feldlaufer, H., 14, 21, 130, 159, 182, 189, 190, 195
  see also Eccles, J. S.; Midgley, C.
Feldman, A., 12, 14, 15, 100, 101, 106, 107, 142, 171, 173, 181
Felner, R. D., 15, 17, 84, 104, 110, 131, 167, 177, 211
  see also DuBois, D. L.
Fernandez, R. R., 131
  see also Wehlage, G. G.
Ferreira, M. M., 18, 53, 57, 166, 171
Ferron, J. M., 85
  see also Mendez, L. M. R.
Fielding, M., 24, 26, 40, 55, 58, 104, 105, 109, 110, 111, 112, 113, 114, 208, 218
Fine, M., 25, 26, 34, 40, 42, 59, 60, 64, 84, 86, 87, 94, 112, 123, 124, 126, 132, 147, 173, 181, 184
Finn, J. D., 15, 85, 106, 182
First, J. M., 60, 70, 152, 178
Fisher, D. L., 45, 65, 117
Fitting in
  see Sense of belonging
Flutter, J., 3, 24, 25, 26, 27, 29, 30, 31, 32, 33, 35, 37, 40, 41, 42, 43, 45, 46, 47, 48, 49, 50, 61, 65, 66, 68, 69, 75, 86, 87, 98, 99, 100, 105, 110, 111, 113, 119, 120, 121, 122, 125, 126, 127, 130, 131, 132, 136, 137, 138, 139, 140, 141, 143, 144, 145, 147, 150, 151, 153, 155, 156, 157, 160, 166, 180, 182, 183, 185, 198, 199, 205, 206, 209, 211, 212, 215, 216, 219
Fordham, S., 79, 80, 81, 148
Forsyth, P., 12, 16, 58, 78, 109
Fortune, L., 133
  see also Sanon, F.
Foster, W., 78
  see also Roth, J. L.
Francis, A., 20, 216
  see also Patterson, N. C.
Fraser, B. J., 45, 65, 117
Fredricks, J. A., 12, 13, 15, 63, 77, 92, 130, 173, 174, 199, 201, 202, 209, 211, 212, 214
Freeman, R.
  see Alfaro, M.
Freiberg, H. J., 14, 84, 85, 91, 93, 94, 95, 96, 97, 101, 175, 209, 220
Freidenberg, E., 126
Fun, 144
Furlong, M. J., 6
  see also Appleton, J. J.
Furrer, C., 8, 36, 80, 82, 83, 185, 196, 200, 203, 217
Furst, N., 117
Futterman, R., 124
  see also Eccles-Parsons, J.
Fyans, L. J., Jr., 18, 19, 158, 161, 166, 169, 170, 187, 194, 195, 198, 221

Galletta, A., 61
Gamoran, A., 13, 174
Ganey, A., 64
  see also Bloomberg, L.
Garcia, F., 11, 39, 140
Garmezy, N., 65, 95, 113, 167, 179, 183
  see also Masten, A. S.
Gender differences, 19, 85, 102, 103, 122, 171, 173, 178
Gibson, M. A., 53, 57, 81, 89, 104, 106, 166, 171, 172, 173, 174, 175, 176, 177, 214, 216, 218

Goal orientation and adoption, 191–192, 196, 199
Goddard, H. W., 68, 176
Goddard, R. D., 62, 76, 168
Goff, B. G., 68, 176
Goff, S. B., 124
see also Eccles-Parsons, J.
Goldring, E., 80
Goldstein, L. S., 7, 57, 58, 68, 127, 166, 213
Gonzalez, R., 12, 15, 16, 70, 107, 167, 172, 173, 175, 176, 214
Goodenow, C., 12, 13, 15, 16, 17, 18, 74, 80, 83, 104, 127, 172, 174, 175, 176, 212
Goodlad, J. I., 21
Gorges, T.
see Shear, L.
Gowen, K., 40
see also Casey-Cannon, S.
Grady, K. E., 12, 13, 15, 16, 17, 18, 74, 80, 83, 104, 127, 172, 174, 175, 176, 212
Graham, G., 117
Graham, S., 19, 20, 21, 187, 190, 192
Grannis, N., 11
Gray, J., 86, 89
Greenberg, M. T., 21, 53
Greytak, E. A., 80
see also Kosciw, J. G.
Gross, S. J., 26, 29, 30, 35, 47, 48, 58, 59, 60, 70, 71, 94, 97, 108, 109, 112, 143, 166, 207, 215, 221
Grosvenor, I., 25, 28, 29, 31, 57, 58, 60, 66, 68, 70, 78, 83, 85, 86, 87, 88–89, 94, 97, 120, 125, 126, 135, 140, 142, 143, 144, 145, 146, 150, 151, 172, 203
Group work, 137–139, 156–157, 194
Guest, A., 14, 100, 101, 107, 108, 181
Guiton, G., 64, 123
Gunter, H., 105, 121, 129, 137
Gurr, D., 114

Hadfield, M., 25, 108
Haertel, G. D., 97, 220
Hagtvet, K. A., 180, 185, 186
Hallinan, M. T., 14, 175
Hallinger, P., 84
Hamilton, S. F., 7, 17, 44, 67, 70, 101, 102, 106, 122, 155, 156, 199, 218
Hannan, S., 63
see also Huberman, M.
Hanson, S. L., 20
see also Hoge, D. R.
Hard caring behaviors, 63
Harper, D., 41
Harper, W. W., 8
Harris, A., 105
Harter, S., 10, 19, 40, 100, 103, 113, 121, 153, 177, 178, 180, 181, 182, 184, 189
Hart, R. A., 37, 40, 41, 42
Hartup, W. W., 9, 12, 84
Harvey, A., 131
Hattie, J., 16, 62, 64, 67, 70, 106, 108, 143, 214
Haw, K., 25, 108
Hayes, C. B., 7, 18, 43, 56, 58, 60, 66, 67, 69, 71, 78, 83, 89, 92, 133, 142
Hayward, C., 40
see also Casey-Cannon, S.
Helping behaviors, 78–80
Herting, J. R., 107
see also Eggert, L. L.
Herzog, L., 79
see also Balfanz, R.
Heshusius, L., 58, 61, 62, 69, 74, 81, 82
Hidalgo, N., 53
see also Gibson, M. A.
Hinchman, K. A., 35
see also Alvermann, D. E.
Hodge, S. A., 67
see also Murdock, T. B.
Hof, E., 29
see also Beishuizen, J. J.
Hoge, D. R., 20, 43, 82, 104, 120, 180, 182, 183
Holloway, S. L., 30, 33, 34
Hom, A., 13, 14
Hopkins, D., 86
see also Gray, J.
Horizontal attachments, 9

Horsey, C., 12
  see also Alexander, K.
Hostile attitudes, 204 (figure), 206
House, A.
  see Shear, L.
House, E. R., 44
  see also Steele, J. M.
Howard, T. C., 23, 28, 29, 39, 45, 46, 47, 53, 55, 57, 58, 61, 62, 67, 71, 95, 119, 125, 130, 132, 133, 137, 144, 145, 148, 149, 150, 168, 219, 220
Hoy, W. K., 16
Huang, S., 84
  see also Freiberg, H. J.
Huberman, M., 63, 64
Hudley, C., 19
  see also Graham, S.
Human capital, 166–167, 174
Huzinec, C. A., 14

Iadicola, P., 85
  see also Nichols, J. D.
Identification, 12–13, 171–175
Identity, 14, 140
Inclusiveness, 12–13, 98–100, 106, 173, 212, 214–216
Independence, 140
Individualized instruction, 126–127
Inquiry-based learning
  see Student-centered work
Instructional improvement, 47–50
Instructional practices, 128–129
Integration, social, 12–13, 171–177
Intellectually challenging work, 136–137, 210–211
Internalized standards of performance, 15
Interpersonal relationships, 11–15, 20–22
  see also Membership; Supportive school culture
Interviewing skills and strategies, 37, 39–40
Intrinsic motivation, 189, 194–195
Involvement
  see Meaningful involvement
Irvine, J. J., 139

Irving, S. L., 45, 130
Isolation, 13, 173
Iver, D. M., 14
  see also Eccles, J. S.

Jaccard, J., 36
  see also Reid, M.
Jackson, P. W., 37
Jackson, Y., 14, 74, 76, 78, 108, 114, 181, 206
Jesson, D., 86
  see also Gray, J.
Johnson, J., 28
  see also Spires, H. A.
Johnson J. F., Jr., 17, 63, 89, 93, 105, 114
Johnson, L. S., 5, 26, 39, 48, 59, 80, 81, 82, 84, 98, 103, 108, 126, 130, 138, 146, 166, 172, 174, 176, 179, 181, 196, 200, 207, 208, 212, 220
Johnson, M. K., 9, 24
  see also Crosnoe, R.
Johnston, P. H., 70, 108, 131, 140, 142, 146, 154
Jolivette, K., 84
  see also Christle, C. A.
Joselowsky, F., 63, 78, 79, 84, 86, 89, 98, 104, 107, 108, 110, 113, 114, 199
Joshi, A.
  see Shear, L.
Journals, 40
Judson, Q., 173

Kaczala, C. M., 124
  see also Eccles-Parsons, J.
Kaltreider, D. L., 91
  see also St. Pierre, T. L.
Kalvin, C., 169
  see also Li, Y.
Karimpour, R., 138
  see also Wilson, T.
Katz, S. R., 11
  see also Muller, C.
Kelly, C. A., 58, 117
  see also Shade, B. J.
Kennedy, B. L., 11, 19, 58, 65, 67, 70, 79, 172, 199, 200, 201, 219, 220

Kerins, T., 44
  see also Steele, J. M.
Kershner, R., 121, 130, 133, 139, 141, 144, 147, 150, 171, 179, 191
Kilgore, J., 11, 39
  see also Garcia, F.
Kim, D.
  see Battistich, V.
Kleitman, S., 13, 14, 15, 16, 17, 104, 106, 107, 108, 171, 175, 181
Klinger, D., 211
Knoff, H. M., 85
  see also Mendez, L. M. R.
Knowledgeable teachers, 120
Kohl, H. R., 33, 206, 212
Kosciw, J. G., 80, 81, 83, 85, 171, 173, 178, 182, 213
Krate, R., 11, 18, 124, 170, 187, 208, 215
Kroeger, S., 33, 54, 79, 172
Kubitschek, W. N., 14, 175
Kuperminc, G. P., 18, 19, 21, 167, 170, 175, 221

Ladd, G. W., 10, 16, 17, 19, 20, 54, 56, 71, 74, 75, 82, 187, 193, 194, 213, 219
Laffey, J., 15, 17, 203, 214
Lamburn, S. D., 14, 90, 121
  see also Newmann, F. M.
Landesman, S., 36
  see also Reid, M.
Lang, G., 20, 82, 181, 182
Larkin, R. W., 10, 11, 16, 25, 125, 141, 142, 167, 170, 207
Larson, R., 14, 15, 22, 93, 114, 144, 181, 205
Latino identity, 177–178
Lauria, M., 70, 71, 78, 79, 120, 121, 124, 133, 141, 142, 155, 182, 219
LGBT children, 171, 173
  see also Sexual orientation
Leadbeater, B. J., 18
  see also Kuperminc, G. P.
Leadership opportunities, 105–106
Learned helplessness, 184
Learning climate, 117, 119–133

Learning dispositions, 15–17, 96–97
Learning-focused dialogue, 126–127
Learning outcomes, 50
Lee, J. K., 28
  see also Spires, H. A.
Lee, P. W., 42, 48, 123, 126, 127, 132, 137, 140, 142, 144, 145, 153, 173, 207
Lee, V., 15, 61, 74, 75, 78, 167
Lehr, C. A., 21, 121, 130, 170, 176
Leithwood, K., 106
Leonard, D., 173
Lerner, R. M., 169
  see also Li, Y.
Lesko, N., 131
  see also Wehlage, G. G.
Letriz, L.
  see Alfaro, M.
Levels of engagement continuum, 204 (figure), 204–209
Levin, B., 29, 30, 33, 35, 49, 111, 208, 209, 210, 211, 216
Levin, J. A., 110
Levinson, E. M., 40, 42
Lewis, A., 131
Life experiences, 146–147
Lincoln, Y. S., 25, 32, 35, 36, 45, 69, 111, 139
Lipman, P., 57, 59, 71, 132, 149
Lippold, M. A., 21, 53
Listening skills, 25–26, 69, 109, 111, 130
Liu, J., 169
  see also Li, Y.
Li, Y., 169, 201, 208, 215
Lloyd, C. A., 84
Lodge, C., 30, 31, 32, 33, 34, 105, 135, 137, 203, 218
Loeber, R., 78, 85, 92
  see also Catalano, R. F.
Looney, L., 16
Lopez, F., 12, 15, 70, 172
Louis, K. S., 74, 106
  see also Leithwood, K.; Smylie, M.
Low-achieving students, 208
Low expectations, 123, 195
  see also Performance expectations
Ludwin, W. G., 85
  see also Nichols, J. D.

Luppescu, S., 11
  see also Bryk, A. S.
Luthans, F., 183
Luthar, S. S., 7
Luyten, H., 142
Lynch, A. D., 169
  see also Li, Y.
Lynch, J. H., 12
  see also Ryan, R. M.
Lynch, M., 9

MacBeath, J., 105
MacIver, D., 79
  see also Balfanz, R.
Maehr, M. L., 18, 19, 22, 28, 43, 65, 84, 117, 136, 145, 153, 158, 160, 161, 165, 166, 168, 169, 170, 179, 182, 184, 185, 187, 188, 189, 190, 191, 192, 193, 194, 195, 196, 198, 206, 210, 221
  see also Anderman, E. M.
Maguin, E., 78, 85
Mahoney, J. L., 103, 106, 208, 215
Maladjustment, 206
Malecki, C. K., 14, 16, 17, 74, 75, 76, 78, 167, 181, 212
Mapping strategies, 41
Marginal participation, 111
Marginal students, 101, 102, 122–123, 148
Mark, M. M., 91
  see also St. Pierre, T. L.
Marks, H. M., 63, 74, 110, 199, 200
Marquez-Zenkov, K., 41, 122, 219
Marshall, H. H., 50, 123
  see also Brattesani, K. A.;
    Weinstein, R. S.
Marsh, H. W., 13, 14, 15, 16, 17, 104, 106, 107, 108, 171, 175, 181
Maslin-Ostrowski, P., 84
Masten, A. S., 179, 184, 220
Mastery goals, 158–161, 195
Matjasko, J., 12, 14, 15, 100, 101, 106, 107, 142, 171, 173, 181
Matthews, C., 8
  see also Cooper, J. E.
Maughan, B., 91
  see also Rutter, M.

Maulana, R., 16
  see also Opdenakker, M.
Mauthner, M., 33, 37, 38, 39, 40, 42
Ma, X., 12, 13, 14, 16, 40, 62, 104, 166, 173, 174, 184, 211, 212, 214, 216
McCormick, J., 16
McDill, E. L., 127
McDonald, A., 17
McIntyre, D., 8, 25, 26, 32, 33, 35, 137, 140, 146, 147, 150, 155, 156
  see also Arnot, M.
McKinney, K. C., 92
  see also Catalano, R. F.
McLaughlin, M., 59, 60, 109, 114, 131, 138, 152
McLean-Donaldson, K. B., 70, 157, 212, 213
McMahon, S., 156, 160, 161, 172, 173, 175, 178, 179, 184, 215
McMillan, D. W., 10, 59, 65, 66, 67, 85, 98, 114
McNeal, R. B., 20, 73, 86, 97, 102, 103, 106, 166, 174, 184
McNeely, C. A., 65, 100, 177, 218
McQuillan, P. J., 127
Meaningful connections
  see Membership; Social integration
Meaningful involvement, 94, 98, 104–108, 114, 152–157, 209–212, 215–216
Meaningful learning, 121–124, 152–157, 194–195
Meaningful responsiveness, 25–26
Meaningful work, 141–146, 151
Means, B.
  see Shear, L.
Meece, J. L., 124
  see also Eccles-Parsons, J.
Mehta, J. D., 237
Membership, 12–13, 82, 98–114, 169 (figure), 171–177, 184, 197–198, 212, 214–216
Mendez, L. M. R., 85, 90, 92, 93
Mergendoller, J. R., 6, 27, 28, 31, 37, 43, 44, 45, 57, 60, 62, 65, 68, 75, 90, 91, 92, 94, 119, 120, 125, 127, 128, 129, 130, 135, 137, 140, 141, 143

Patterson, J., 76, 93, 108, 109
Patterson, L. E., 19, 60, 61, 62, 71, 74, 79, 166
Patterson, N. C., 20, 54, 62, 63, 66, 78, 80, 109, 111, 112, 131, 133, 216
Pavri, S., 172, 174, 175, 197
Payne, Y. A., 26
   see also Fine, M.
Pedder, D., 8, 25, 137
   see also Arnot, M.; McIntyre, D.
Peer relationships, 20, 137–138, 140, 167, 169, 197, 215
Penna, A., 127, 191
Performance expectations, 62–64, 121–124, 131–133, 179, 195
Performance goals, 158–161
Perry, T. B., 39, 77
Personal investment
   see Motivation
Personalized relationships, 11–15, 56–57
   see also Caring behaviors; Membership; Supportive school culture
Personal logs, 40
Personal responsibility, 140–141, 182
Person-environmental interactions, 17–21, 102
Peterson, E. R., 45, 130
Peterson, K. D., 29, 33, 36, 43
Phelan, P., 128, 131, 176, 208, 211, 220
Phelps, S. F., 35
   see also Alvermann, D. E.
Phillips, R. S., 177
   see also DuBois, D. L.
Photography, 41
Pianta, R. C., 7, 8, 9, 10, 12, 14, 19, 20, 22, 24, 36, 39, 40, 54, 56, 60, 65, 74, 83, 166, 167, 168, 181, 219, 220, 221
Pintrich, P. R., 17, 121, 130, 158, 179, 184, 187, 188, 189, 191, 194, 197, 198, 199, 214, 216
Poems
   Drowned But Not Dead #1, 2
   A Good School #1, 52

A Good School #2, 116
High School #1, 164
Ponder, G., 8
   see also Cooper, J. E.
Poplin, M. S., 10, 35, 36, 42, 53, 55, 84, 85, 87, 88, 104, 137, 140, 142, 144, 145, 151, 153, 155
Porter A., 80
Positively grounded management systems, 89–97
Postive reinforcements, 92–93
Pounder, D. G., 14, 181
Powell, A. G., 131
Power struggles, 94–95
Preferential treatment, 66–67, 121–124, 213
Prevention strategies, 91–93
Prior knowledge factor, 146–147
Proactive teachers, 119–120
Problem-solving skills
   see Student-centered work
Procedural compliance, 204 (figure), 205
Projects, student, 42
Prosocial attitudes and behaviors, 14–16
Protection from harm, 85–86
   see also Safe learning environments
Provision of assistance, 78–80
Psychological engagement, 203
Psychological health, 14–15, 177
Pullin, D. C., 207
Punishment, 92, 95
Purposeful learning
   see Meaningful learning
Push factor, 132–133
   see also Performance expectations
Putten, C. M., 29
   see also Beishuizen, J. J.

Quaglia, R. J., 24, 25, 27, 29, 31, 196
Questionnaires, 40
Quinlan, D. M., 26, 33, 34, 59, 90
Quintero, G., 64
   see also Bloomberg, L.
Quint, J., 167, 212

Quiroz, P. A., 8, 43, 57, 61, 70, 75, 80, 81, 109, 111, 112, 121, 167, 176, 177, 178, 199, 205, 206, 212, 214

Racial identity, 18–19, 102, 103–104, 122, 170, 171, 173, 177–178
Rak, C. F., 19, 60, 61, 62, 71, 74, 79, 166
Raywid, M., 78, 81, 105
Real-world relevant instruction, 150–151
Reay, D., 8
  see also Arnot, M.
Reciprocal relationships, 11, 57, 138, 154, 171, 180
Reezigt, G. J., 84
Reid, M., 36, 37, 39
Reitzug, U. C., 76, 93, 108, 109
Relational environments
  see Caring behaviors
Relevant educational practices, 146–152
Required participation, 204 (figure), 205
Research methodologies and strategies
  academic and socialization importance, 217–221
  alternative strategies, 40–42
  ground rules, 36–38
  traditional methods, 38–40
Respect, 67–70, 93, 131, 212–213
Responsive teaching, 126–127
Reuman, D., 14
  see also Eccles, J. S.
Reynolds, D., 86
  see also Gray, J.
Riley, K., 33, 45, 91, 145
Robinson, V. M. J., 84, 92, 93
Rock, D., 15, 85, 106, 182
Rodkin, P. C., 138
  see also Wilson, T.
Rodriguez, D., 139
  see also Wigfield, A.
Rodriguez, L. F., 12, 15, 17, 22, 45, 54, 56, 57, 58, 59, 60, 62, 63, 64, 68, 69, 70, 74, 75, 76, 77, 109, 132, 142, 166, 196, 200, 212, 218, 220, 221

Rodriguez, P., 39
  see also Garcia, F.
Roeser, R. W., 17, 18, 19, 22, 57, 65, 82, 131, 140, 146, 147, 160, 171, 179, 183, 185, 186, 187, 195, 198, 199, 220
Rogers, D. L., 136, 142
Rohrkemper, M. M., 44, 49, 166
Role-playing activities, 42
Rolón, C., 53
  see also Gibson, M. A.
Romanowski, M. H., 23
Rose, D., 156
  see also McMahon, S.
Rosenshine, B., 117
Ross, S., 17
Roth, J. L., 12, 63, 75, 78, 79, 93, 98, 99, 107, 108, 110, 113, 114, 167, 172, 173
Rothman, H. R., 15, 181
Rowe, K. J., 84
Rudduck, J., 3, 24, 25, 26, 27, 28, 29, 30, 31, 32, 33, 34, 35, 37, 39, 40, 41, 42, 43, 45, 46, 47, 48, 49, 50, 56, 61, 64, 65, 66, 68, 69, 71, 75, 85, 86, 87, 98, 99, 100, 105, 108, 109, 110, 111, 113, 114, 119, 120, 121, 122, 125, 126, 127, 130, 131, 132, 136, 137, 138, 139, 140, 141, 143, 144, 145, 147, 150, 151, 153, 155, 156, 157, 160, 166, 179, 180, 182, 183, 184, 185, 197, 198, 199, 205, 206, 209, 211, 212, 215, 216, 218, 219
  see also McIntyre, D.
Rugged care, 63
Rumberger, R. W., 15, 80, 84, 106, 107, 182, 211
Russell, S. T., 19, 81
Rutter, M., 91, 92, 99
Rutter, R. A., 131
  see also Wehlage, G. G.
Ryan, A., 7, 142
  see also Hayes, C. B.
Ryan, R. M., 12, 14, 19, 20, 71, 166, 181, 195, 197, 198, 203, 209, 213

Safe learning environments, 83–97
Safety nets, 80
Sagor, R., 44, 71, 158, 161
Salloum, S. J., 76
Sameroff, A. J., 17
  see also Roeser, R. W.
Sanders, M. G., 130
Sanon, F., 133, 141, 142, 144, 145, 155, 156
Santos, M.
  see Alfaro, M.
Sarason, S. B., 142
Satcher, J., 40
Sather, S. E., 105, 114
Saunders, J., 123, 177, 179, 183, 185, 186, 214, 217
Scaffolding practices, 127
Scanlan, M., 12, 15, 70, 172
Schaps, E., 12
  see also Battistich, V.
Scheerens, J., 142
Schneider, B., 14, 101, 107, 108, 181
School improvements, 47–50
School membership
  see Membership
Sebring, P. B., 11
  see also Bryk, A. S.
Security
  see Safe learning environments
Sedlak, M. W., 207
Seif, H., 19
  see also Russell, S. T.
Seiler, G., 139
Seitsinger, A., 17
  see also Felner, R. D.
Selby, J., 34
  see also Bradley, B. S.
Self-concept, 14–15, 175, 177–179, 181–187, 214
Self-confidence, 16–17, 139, 179, 186, 214
Self-determination, 109, 140
Self-discipline, 94, 96, 138
Self-efficacy, 15, 124, 161, 175, 178–187, 197, 214
Self-esteem, 14–15, 82, 139, 175, 177, 180–182, 185–186, 214

Self-expression, 64–66
Self-regulated learning, 152–157
Self-respect, 214
Sense of attachment, 12–14, 173
Sense of belonging, 12–13, 82, 98–104, 169 (figure), 171–177, 184, 197–198, 212, 214–216
Sense of self, 175, 177–187, 191, 197, 214
Sensitive understanding, 59–60
Sentence completions, 40
Separation, 13, 173
Serriere, S. C., 81
Sexual orientation, 19, 103, 173, 178
Shade, B. J., 58, 70, 71, 85, 86, 89, 92, 94, 95, 96, 97, 98, 117, 123, 124, 137, 138, 140, 145, 146, 148, 149, 150, 151, 152, 154, 155, 156, 157, 179, 201
Shambaugh, L., 63
  see also Huberman, M.
Shame, 85
  see also Safe learning environments
Shannon, S. G., 7, 131
Shared responsibility, 94
Sharp, L., 50
  see also Weinstein, R. S.
Shear, L., 64
Shlonik, J.
  see Shear, L.
Shouse, R., 63
Shultz, J. J., 25, 26, 30, 35, 43, 71, 76, 155, 207, 210
Silins, H., 15, 17, 104, 108, 182
Silva, E., 26, 171
Silverstein, B., 11, 18, 124, 170, 187, 208, 215
Sinclair, M. F., 21, 121, 170
  see also Lehr, C. A.
Siperstein, G. N., 19, 21, 83, 133
Sizer, T. R., 21
Skaalvik, E. M., 180, 185, 186
Skinner, E., 8, 36, 81, 82, 83, 185, 196, 200, 203, 217
Slaughter-Defoe, D. T., 66, 69, 82, 122, 124
Slavin, R. E., 139

Index

Sleegers, P., 142
Slusarcick, A., 91
Smerdon, B. A., 60, 73, 82, 85, 98, 99, 100, 101, 102, 103, 104, 137, 140, 151, 166, 172, 183, 184, 199
    see also Shear, L.
Smetana, J. G., 14, 19, 21, 84, 94, 96
Smit, E. K., 20
    see also Hoge, D. R.
Smith, G. A., 131
    see also Wehlage, G. G.
Smylie, M., 56
Smyth, J., 28, 29, 65, 126, 151, 212
Social bonding, 54, 169 (figure), 171–177
Social capital, 166–167, 174, 213
Social integration, 169 (figure), 171–177, 183–184, 197–198, 214–216
Social support
    student engagement, 210–214
    student-teacher relationships, 73–83, 131–133, 181–182, 187, 194–197, 217–221
    supportive learning communities, 165–177, 169 (figure)
    see also Caring behaviors
Socioeconomic status (SES), 18, 19, 102–103, 170, 171, 173
Solomon, D., 12
    see also Battistich, V.
Soohoo, S., 24, 40, 41, 42, 43
Spires, H. A., 28, 40, 45, 87, 88, 141, 144, 145, 146, 150, 151
Stajkovic, A. D., 183
Stanton-Salazar, R. D., 18, 19, 71, 75, 80, 81, 82, 130, 168, 170, 212, 213, 214, 219
Steele, C. M., 62
Steele, J. M., 43, 44, 136, 140, 165, 206, 207
Steinberg, M., 40, 65, 74, 83, 125
Stein, T. A., 84
    see also Freiberg, H. J.
Stephens, P., 57
    see also Bru, E.
Stiggins, R., 106

Stiller, J. D., 12
    see also Ryan, R. M.
Stinchcombe, A. L., 169, 170, 215, 216
Stinson, S., 173
Stories, 40
Storyboards, 41
Storz, M. G., 33, 39, 40, 43, 46, 54, 56, 78, 90, 135
St. Pierre, T. L., 91, 92
Strahan, D., 64
Streb, M., 109, 182, 212
Structured involvement activities, 106–107
Struggling learners, 48, 208
Student agency, 108, 140–141
Student-centered work, 152–157, 210–211
Student interest, 191, 196, 199
Student perspectives
    analytical perspectives, 26–27
    basic concepts, 24–25
    benefits, 33
    call for action, 24
    caring teachers, 53–71
    contemporary patterns, 30–35
    contextual factors, 17–21, 26, 102, 170
    exclusionary practices, 13, 27–30, 92, 95
    historical patterns, 27–30
    importance, 3, 33–35, 42–50, 165–177, 169 (figure)
    learning climate, 117, 119–133
    legitimization, 30–35, 108–114
    meaningful involvement, 94, 98, 104–108, 114, 152–157, 209–212, 215–216
    meaningful responsiveness, 25–26
    membership, 12–13, 82, 98–114, 169 (figure), 171–177, 184, 197–198, 212, 214–216
    motivation, 169 (figure), 187–199
    ownership, 99–100, 108–114, 122, 139–141, 153
    research methodologies and strategies, 36–38

safety, 83–97
sense of self, 175, 177–187, 191, 197, 214
social integration, 169 (figure), 171–177, 183–184, 197–198, 214–216
see also Engagement; Social support; Supportive school culture
Student-teacher relationships
  academic and socialization importance, 6–12, 76–83, 165–177, 169 (figure), 181–182, 187, 194–197
  academic care, 130–133
  belief and value systems, 9
  benefits, 11–17, 217–221
  contextual influences, 17–21, 26, 102, 170
  engagement, 15, 56, 76–77, 83, 168, 200, 209–212
  learning disposition, 15–17
  meaningful involvement, 98, 104–108
  motivation, 169 (figure), 187–199
  performance expectations, 121–124, 131–133, 179, 195
  positive management systems, 89–97
  psychological health, 14–15
  sense of attachment, 12–14
  sense of self, 175, 177–187, 191, 197, 214
  social integration, 169 (figure), 171–177, 183–184, 197–198, 214–216
  social support, 73–83, 131–133, 165–172, 169 (figure)
  student perspective impacts, 49–50, 165–177, 169 (figure)
  transition periods, 20–22
  trust development, 11, 71
  see also Caring behaviors; Social support
Supovitz, J., 167
Supportive school culture
  importance, 6–7
  performance expectations, 63
  student engagement, 210–214
  student-teacher relationships, 6–7, 73–83, 131–133, 181–182, 187, 194–197, 217–221
  supportive learning communities, 165–177, 169 (figure)
  see also Caring behaviors
Sweetland, S. R., 16

Talbert, J. E., 109, 114
Tallerico, M., 127, 191
Tardiness, 203
Task-oriented work, 158–161, 194, 210–211
Taylor, A. Z., 19
  see also Graham, S.
Taylor-Dunlop, K., 26, 55, 57, 68, 69, 75, 77, 94, 145, 200, 201
Teacher-student relationships
  see Caring behaviors; Social support; Student-teacher relationships; Supportive school culture
Templeton, S. M., 14
Terrell, R., 58, 61, 66, 69, 78, 79, 81, 94, 97, 137, 147, 150, 172, 220
Terry, T., 13
  see also Baker, J. A.
Thomas, S., 11, 39
  see also Garcia, F.
Thompson, C. L., 7
Thompson, E. A., 107
  see also Eggert, L. L.
Thompson, G. L., 90, 92, 93, 95, 120, 124, 130, 133, 139, 141, 143, 145, 146, 178
Thomson, P., 105, 121, 129, 137
Thorkildsen, T. A., 39, 45, 66
Tjioe, M., 11
Tobin, K., 74, 104
Todd, D. M., 17, 18
Torre, D., 11, 25, 35, 54, 60, 64, 65, 66, 74, 84, 130, 176, 194, 200
Torre, M. E., 25
  see also Fine, M.
Torsheim, T., 57
  see also Bru, E.
Track placement, 102

Transition periods, 20–22
Treder, R., 36
  see also Reid, M.
Trickett, E. J., 6, 17, 18, 26, 33, 34, 40, 59, 83, 90, 96, 165, 181, 219, 220
Truancy, 203
Truong, N. L., 19
  see also Russell, S. T.
Trust development, 11, 71
Turner, K. A., 28
  see also Spires, H. A.
Tyson, K., 150, 207, 211, 213, 217

Ullman, D. G., 40, 45, 81, 82
Unequal treatment/unfairness, 66–67, 213
Unhealthy relationships, 15
Urdan, T. C., 198

Valentine, G., 30, 32, 33, 34
Valuing behaviors
  age transition impacts, 21
  community respect, 91, 93, 99
  cooperative work, 137–138
  engaged teaching, 121–122
  extracurricular activities and involvement, 107
  importance, 12–14
  internalized values, 198
  learning disposition, 16
  meaningful work, 143–144, 151
  motivational impact, 187–189, 192–193, 199
  safe learning environments, 87
  sense of self, 214
  social integration, 172–175
  social support, 83, 196–197
  student engagement, 205–206, 212–213
  student perspectives, 36, 44–46, 49, 152
  student-teacher relationships, 70–71, 131
  supportive learning communities, 196–197
Veaco, L., 8, 9, 10, 20, 59, 61, 62, 66, 67, 68, 69, 93

Vertical attachments, 9, 84
Victimization, 85
  see also Safe learning environments
Villanueva, M.
  see Alfaro, M.
Voelkl, K. E., 12, 13, 14, 98, 101, 171, 173, 174, 175, 202, 205, 214
Voice, student
  see Student perspectives
Vulnerability, 58–59, 86

Wahlquist, C., 29
Wahlstrom, K., 106
  see also Leithwood, K.
Walberg, H. J., 44, 50, 67, 97, 106, 198, 220, 221
Walker, B., 91
  see also Cheney, D.
Wallace, G., 24, 26, 46, 117, 127, 133, 136, 139, 143, 145, 146, 155, 159, 160, 189, 190, 201, 211, 212, 213, 216
  see also Rudduck, J.
Wallerstein, N., 65, 70, 108, 109, 167, 218
Wang, M. C., 97
Warren, J. S., 14, 74, 76, 78, 108, 114, 181, 206
Warrington, M., 121
Waters, P. L., 10
  see also Harter, S.
Watson, M., 12
  see also Battistich, V.
Weade, G., 97
Weaver, D., 35
  see also Alvermann, D. E.
Weeres, J. G., 10, 35, 36, 42, 85, 87, 88, 104, 137, 140, 142, 144, 145, 151, 153, 155
Wehlage, G. G., 13, 90, 121, 131
  see also Newmann, F. M.
Weil, M., 95
Weinstein, R. S., 3, 30, 31, 44, 45, 48, 50, 61, 66, 67, 108, 121, 122, 123, 130, 170, 181, 182, 220
  see also Brattesani, K. A.
Weis, L., 11, 114, 141, 205, 206

Wellborn, J. G., 10, 21, 22, 109, 137, 167, 169, 172, 184, 185, 199, 203, 208, 209, 216
Wentzel, K. R., 16, 18, 44, 53, 65, 66, 70, 71, 82, 83, 90, 120, 168, 181, 184, 188, 191, 192, 193, 195, 196, 199, 210, 213, 217
Wenz-Gross, M., 19, 21, 83, 133
Wernsman, J., 156, 172, 173, 175, 178, 179, 184, 215
see also McMahon, S.
Wheeler, C. W., 207
Whitesell, N. R., 10
see also Harter, S.
Wigfield, A., 14, 117, 120, 130, 139, 140, 142, 151, 159, 161, 173, 176, 182, 187, 188, 194, 196, 197, 198, 210, 211, 212, 221
see also Eccles, J. S.
Wilcox, B., 86
see also Gray, J.
Wilcox, K., 12
Willems, E. P., 101, 102, 114, 191
Williams, J. H., 123
see also Saunders, J.
Williams, T., 123
see also Saunders, J.
Willms, J. D., 22, 66, 83, 90, 97, 169, 170, 172, 173, 174, 203, 215, 216, 219

Wilson, B. L., 16, 24, 25, 29, 39, 44, 45, 46, 47, 50, 61, 62, 63, 64, 85, 89, 93, 98, 100, 117, 120, 121, 125, 126, 128, 129, 130, 131, 132, 133, 137, 139, 143, 145, 214
Wilson, S., 89
see also Dinham, S.
Wilson, T., 138, 139, 175, 206
Winsor, A., 13
see also Baker, J. A.
Withdrawal, 13, 173, 204 (figure), 205–206
Wolfson, B. J., 37
Woloszyk, C., 78, 81, 105
Wright, S., 14, 221
Writing strategies, 40–41

Younger, M., 121
Young, J. P., 35
see also Alvermann, D. E.

Zalewski, P., 35
see also Alvermann, D. E.
Zamel, V., 24, 43, 155
Zanger, V. V., 8, 67, 68, 70, 71, 81, 122, 138, 144, 148, 150, 151, 206, 221
Zseller, E. B., 7, 142
see also Hayes, C. B.

CORWIN
A SAGE Publishing Company

Helping educators make the greatest impact

CORWIN HAS ONE MISSION: to enhance education through intentional professional learning.

We build long-term relationships with our authors, educators, clients, and associations who partner with us to develop and continuously improve the best evidence-based practices that establish and support lifelong learning.

Solutions you want. Experts you trust. Results you need.

AUTHOR CONSULTING

Author Consulting

On-site professional learning with sustainable results! Let us help you design a professional learning plan to meet the unique needs of your school or district. www.corwin.com/pd

INSTITUTES

Institutes

Corwin Institutes provide collaborative learning experiences that equip your team with tools and action plans ready for immediate implementation. www.corwin.com/institutes

eCOURSES

eCourses

Practical, flexible online professional learning designed to let you go at your own pace. www.corwin.com/ecourses

READ2EARN

Read2Earn

Did you know you can earn graduate credit for reading this book? Find out how: www.corwin.com/read2earn

Contact an account manager at (800) 831-6640 or visit **www.corwin.com** for more information.

CORWIN